PRAISE F
WASTELAND TO PURELAND:
REFLECTIONS ON THE PATH TO AWAKENING

Wasteland to Pureland is a crystal clear guide to the many pitfalls, nuances, and puzzlements that can arise on the path to enlightenment. Authors Duncan and Pawasarat write from experience, offering the reader calm authenticity and heartfelt encouragement. Highly recommended for both fledgling and experienced travelers.

—**Dean Radin, Ph.D.**, *Chief Scientist, Institute of Noetic Sciences*

Catherine and Doug skillfully apply insights from their years of spiritual practice to the critical issues of modern life. Their book challenges us to explore what is truly needed to live a fulfilling life and to make a contribution that is larger than ourselves.

—**Susan Skjei, Ph.D.**, *Director, Authentic Leadership Center, Naropa University*

Wasteland to Pureland provides a priceless map to guide you to your Best Life through a practical, accessible and deeply enjoyable program of spiritual growth. Longtime Buddhist teachers Doug Duncan and Catherine Pawasarat have described a path that anyone can follow through the process of engaging spirituality with your life, your family and your work. Their path leads from your office to the stars and back, providing a limitless environment in which to fully engage with your life and your world. I can imagine returning to this book again and again.

—**Bryan Welch**, *writer, consultant, entrepreneur, longtime publisher of Mother Earth News, Utne Reader and many other magazines about mindfulness and sustainability.*

This wonderful book is a timely and welcome beacon of light and hope in a world increasingly consumed by chaos and darkness. Profound, yet filled with practical and grounded wisdom, *Wasteland to Pureland* is not merely a book, it is itself a journey that if followed, offers a clear path to liberation and awakening. This is a must-read guidebook for all spiritual seekers.

—**Deborah Price**, *Founder/CEO of the Money Coaching Institute and author* of Money Magic: Unleashing your Potential for Wealth and Prosperity *and* The Heart of Money: A Couple's Guide to Creating Financial Intimacy.

Continuing on the path of the great wisdom traditions, Doug Duncan and Catherine Pawasarat provide us with an invaluable contribution—relevant teachings placed within the contemporary crisis of our time. In these writings, we are given a map to negotiate the spiritual and the material, the inner and outer landscapes of our collective soul co-evolving here on this planet. As we arrive in this illuminated state called "the Great Healing," we discover that we can invoke awe, wisdom, and wonder to solve even the deepest challenges of our wounded world.

—**Lauralee Alben**, *Founder and CEO, Sea Change Design Institute*

Doug and Catherine have always touched me with the depth of their presence, wisdom, humility, and humor. All of them comes through as a clear transmission of deeper states in this book, and their descriptions of how to recognize, journey toward and enter into those deeper states are invaluable. This is not a book only for the mind, or for the body, or for the spirit, but all of them at once. In the world of spiritual literature, esoteric teachings can become dry and removed. Nope—this book is juicy!

—**Mark Silver, M.Div.**, *Master Teacher in the Shaddhulliyya Sufi Tariqa and founder of Heart of Business*

If we include the health of the planet and communities in our notions of self and value, as this book resoundingly does, a culture of generosity emerges naturally. This fresh and visionary book offers maps for true economic freedom—where wealth is generative, interdependent and sustainable.

—*Joel Solomon*, *Chair & Co-Founder, Renewal Funds, author of* The Clean Money Revolution

Wasteland to Pureland is a journey. The authors have walked the path of spiritual awareness and share insights gathered along the way. This book is an in-depth exploration of the journey. Well written, it guides the reader in the exploration of enduring spiritual truths and the quest towards wholeness.

—*Bob Stilger, Ph.D., Co-President, NewStories, and author of* AfterNow: When We Cannot See the Future, Where Do We Begin?

EXPERIENCE MORE OF THE *PURELAND*

For a comprehensive package of free resources designed to give you more of a taste of the Pureland, please visit our website.

Here you'll also find our retreats, online courses, a minicourse, blogs, videos, exercises and other supports to your ongoing spiritual unfoldment.

To ensure you get the most out of the journey from the *Wasteland to Pureland*, access bonuses at this link:

www.planetdharma.com/pureland-paperback

The spiritual path is, among other things, about using bliss and insight to decrease suffering and ignorance. That's why a healthy spiritual path feels so rich, wonder-filled and generally happy. The Great Happiness arises when bliss and insight come together to manifest through everything we do and are.

...

Training helps us see how much of our ego gratification is hidden in unconscious habits of manipulation and control. We also begin to perceive how it's these very habits that are interfering with our desire and ability to experience spiritual transcendence.

...

When we transcend the ego's limits we find ourselves reunited with totality or oneness of awakening. That experience is spacious, clear, radiant, and incredibly blissful. From there we put our egos back on and go work out the solutions to the problems egos tend to cause.

...

While neuroscience is making astounding beneficial discoveries about the nature of the brain and how it functions, the experiential study of the mind is a distinct pursuit of its own, and of consummate benefit. All kinds of mental/physical states can arise that are difficult to conjure up without meditation. The inner world is as rich and as diverse as our outer world.

...

If happiness is a result, it begs the question: result of what? If objects don't make us reliably happy, what does? The ego may be temporarily satisfied, but never satiated. Moreover, happiness is a result of living a good life that we love and feel fulfilled by, not an object to get to help us feel fulfilled.

...

A spiritually awakening being is one who abides in the clear sky realization, even as they live, relate and work in the world with clouds.

...

When the Buddha said that "all formations are struggling," it was a call to freedom. The purpose of the Hero's Journey is to resolve this dilemma. Most of us try to drown out this fact of struggling by ignoring it or distracting ourselves from it with bread and circuses. Some of us can't or won't do this: this is when the call to awakening is heard. In fact, for those of us who can't escape the suffering of our lives by burying it under possessions, relationships, families, career, entertainment or drugs, the spiritual life is not just the best option, it's the only option.

...

Spiritual awakening involves abiding in a unitive state that allows us to act with loving-kindness and compassion.

...

Even though the universe can appear chaotic, it is in fact highly ordered, and spiritual awakening is no different. The work of the human being is to perceive and understand patterns, and that is what the discipline of the spiritual quest is about.

...

Perhaps the greatest anxiety the modern being faces is loneliness. The self always is alone by definition. Awakening conquers loneliness by stepping over the self into a state of totality, and from here one returns to the world and acts.

...

Hopes, fears and everything in between arise in meditation and as one watches them come and go and repeat, and repeat again, one sees their coming and going as impermanence. In a sense, they have nothing to do with you. They are seen as movie scripts with movie characters and one starts to relate to them less personally. This letting go opens the door to radiant spaciousness, the good emptiness, whereas before emptiness was seen as the bad kind, meaninglessness. Only in retreat can we learn to cultivate the calm and quiet necessary to hear the depths of our mind as it connects to the Universal Mind.

...

It seems fairly clear that most of us busy, modern people aren't really geared towards being still and contemplating. This is particularly true in the West, where we don't have a millennium or more of history with sitting meditation. But we have good news for people who feel challenged around having a regular meditation practice: there are alternatives! We propose that the path of spiritual awakening for modern beings may well be through action.

...

Spiritual awakening is the only sustainable mindstate. In other words, coming from a place of ego or self-centeredness is tiring and actually unpleasant—and ultimately, unprofitable—both for ourselves and others. Unawakening or unwholesome mindstates could be considered pollution of the mind's natural, radiant, awakening state. Since unwholesome mindstates manifest through our actions, the latter become defiled as well. Conversely, an awakening mindstate naturally leads to sustainable actions in the world, taking into account the karma of our decisions regarding the environment, people, and finances ... and anything else. With this in mind, we naturally make the best choices we are aware of, to support the best possible results for everyone and everything that's involved.

...

What is awakening? Simply put, awake is the opposite of asleep. Our habitual pursuit of comfort puts us to sleep. It does take effort to wake up. But once we are spiritually awake, life becomes so much better and so much easier. It is the most sustainable, ethical, efficient, fruitful and joyous state available to human beings. It takes far less effort than all the other pursuits of the self-referencing ego identity, because we are no longer attached to the struggle and concomitant pain of chasing them.

WASTELAND TO PURELAND

REFLECTIONS ON
THE PATH TO AWAKENING

DOUG DUNCAN
AND
CATHERINE PAWASARAT

TABLE OF CONTENTS

PART 1: THE PEARL WITHOUT PRICE
Why Awaken?

TABLE OF CONTENTS

PART 2: RIDING THE DRAGON
Spiritual Awakening in Modern Daily Life

PART 3: CRAZY WISDOM
Taking a Walk on the Wild Side

Dedication

We dedicate this book to all those sentient beings
seeking greater wisdom and understanding,
to our teachers who open our minds to new lands,
and especially to the late Namgyal Rinpoche.

INTRODUCTION

"The greatest obstacle to knowledge is not ignorance; it is the illusion of knowledge."

—Daniel J. Boorstin

Most of our problems, personal and collective, stem from a spiritual misalignment, a false refuge, under the spell of which we try to find safety, satisfaction, and happiness where it cannot be found. This is what we call the Wasteland dilemma. This false refuge colors our choices, opinions, and values, making for muddy-hued versions of what they could be. This book is not an argument for a return to staid and outmoded social mores or primitive belief systems. Instead, it is a call to embrace the best of ourselves and others. This is the search for the Pureland.

What is the wasteland? As Joseph Campbell explained, "It is a land where everybody is living an inauthentic life, doing as other people do, doing as you're told, with no courage for your own life. That is the wasteland. And that is what T.S. Eliot meant in his poem 'The Waste Land.'"[1]

---

[1] Joseph Campbell, Bill Moyers, *The Power of Myth* (New York: Anchor Books, 1988), 244.

In essence, the wasteland is a result of clinging and ignorance. Clinging to sensorial, emotional or mental objects can only lead to dissatisfaction, a wasteland, because they are impermanent, subject to change, and fundamentally out of our control.

From a Mahayana Buddhist perspective, a Pureland is the celestial realm or pure abode of a Buddha or bodhisattva, that is, of a being dwelling in bliss and clarity, free from being *subject* to the cares of this world. The metaphor of a Pureland implies that there is a state of consciousness that supersedes or transcends the struggles of life, a state based in non-clinging that's free from hatred and numbing desire. Buddhist teachings aver that this state is available to us always if we should choose it, but making such choices takes much diligent searching and sometimes strenuous effort. In Western terms, the Pureland quest is for the Holy Grail.

Our teacher the Venerable Namgyal Rinpoche once said, "Complete living is the most beautiful for the least effort."[2] The "most beautiful" part refers to the best state available to us and has been called spiritual awakening, Christ consciousness, cosmic consciousness, and so on. This is a true or right refuge, one that protects and supports the best in each of us.

It is also a "complete life" in the sense that a life without the awakened state often does not feel complete, while the life of an awakening being does, regardless of life's difficulties. This is why so many of us feel unfulfilled: we're missing the awakened state. One major bonus of this "most beautiful" state of being is that it involves far less effort than a status quo life, rooted as the latter is in conditioned—and typically unconscious—patterns.

Human beings are the inheritors of a powerful birthright: an incredible ability to perceive, reflect, and problem solve, to explore and discover, not only our exterior world but also within ourselves, our own minds. We can empathize with others and work together to develop skills and methods that enrich our lives and that of the planetary collective. We now know that mirror

---

[2] The Venerable Namgyal Rinpoche, *Right Livelihood* (Kinmount, ON: Bodhi Publishing, 2008), 1.

neurons fire in sympathy when watching other people's actions; for instance, we wince when we see someone have an accident. These mirror neurons operate like a direct link between minds and bodies, providing us with a tremendous ability to learn from one another; to share feelings, knowledge, and experience; and work as a team. The extent of our abilities makes us, by some definitions at least, the smartest creature on the planet.

Our intelligence allows us to explore the stars. It also allows us to heal the planet; once we as a collective are willing, we'll be able to resolve planetary resource depletion and human instigated pollution and solve our societal problems. We are capable of seeing the consequences of our actions and respond accordingly. This raises the question: Then why don't we? In sum, because we are not raised or trained according to principles and behavior that are conducive to a Pureland. This is our karma, and another word for karma is habit. Insecurities around survival make all animals greedy, but only humans institutionalize greed as a raison d'être.

And we humans have the power to change.

Behind our search for improved science and technology is a very human quest for meaning and purpose, fired by empathy and ingenuity. The scientific search is rooted in the material realm—a search outside of us—while the search for meaning is in the non-material realm, essentially an inner quest. One without the other makes for imbalance. Together they form an incredibly potent resource.

If we look around at the current state of the world, in spite of the recent surge of interest in spiritual matters, it's apparent that the outer quest has been predominating over the inner. Some of the markers include overpopulation, unsustainable resource consumption, environmental degradation, and the growing gap between the rich and the poor. It's the premise of this book that the depth work of awakening—the word used here to describe the development of consciousness—is not what it could be or in fact should be. Our over-focus on materialism and its agent, consumerism, has discolored the spiritual search, leading to a tendency toward the superficial.

For instance, we love Hatha yoga as a healthy, valuable, and wholesome activity that improves our lives. It's helpful to remember that its original purpose was spiritual exercises leading to transcending the illusion of a fixed and permanent self. It's not about being fit or being spiritual.

We can see here why we're not healing the planet and its concomitant problems: it's not our principle agenda. But it could be. That's what we, the authors, live and work for, and it's the subject of this book.

The Descent Into Darkness

If we let them, our insecurities and old patterns of conditioning manifesting as unhealthy habits will hold us back as a default. T.S. Eliot called this unease "The Waste Land:"

> *I have heard the key*
> *Turn in the door once and turn once only*
> *We think of the key, each in his prison*
> *Thinking of the key, each confirms a prison*[3]

The societal decay that Eliot described in the 1920s manifests today in many ways, including feelings of ambivalence or even apathy regarding humanity's pursuit of wisdom. This decay has affected the current generation with a sense of malaise that includes feelings of "it can't be fixed" and "there's no point in trying." Fortunately, we also hear contemporary calls for relevancy, integrity, and transparency. These serve us best when they're rooted in kindness and compassion, rather than a kind of fundamentalist moral certitude. Our investigation of truth must be resolute and ongoing; cursory examinations keep us asleep and in the same place as before we started.

Fast-forward one hundred years from Eliot's "The Waste Land," and we find ourselves suffering from dissociation, rooted in an

---

[3] T.S. Eliot, "The Waste Land," lines 412-414.

inane search for an ill-defined concept called "happiness." We try to purchase or otherwise acquire this conceptual state of being called happiness by chasing illusions sold to us by very skilled if amoral advertising firms. Can amoral advertising lead us to moral or wholesome behavior? No wonder we feel uncomfortable!

And there's a solution, a real one. This is the state of being called spiritual awakening, which we describe throughout this book. The ego is rooted in and defined by separation, which causes unease and confusion. This confusion manifests as greed, aversion, or more confusion. When we transcend the ego's limits, we find ourselves reunited with totality or oneness of awakening. That experience is spacious, clear, radiant, and incredibly blissful. From there we "put our egos back on" and work out the solutions to the problems egos tend to cause.

As in the legend of the Holy Grail, healing comes when we can sacrifice our social image or persona, to pursue our deepest impulses. The Holy Grail was the cup that Jesus drank from at the Last Supper and was later used to collect his blood at the crucifixion. It has come down to us through the legends of King Arthur,[4] and the search for meaning that makes us whole and pure of heart. This Western manifestation of the Eastern quest for awakening demonstrates the universality of our longing, this very human urge for ever-greater wisdom and compassion.

Joseph Campbell pointed to our obsession with our social image as a critical problem. He posed that today's mythology—marked by rampant consumerism, the implication that fame equals success, or that information is the same as wisdom—will alienate people, and youth in particular, from the world. Rather than attuning them more profoundly to the world in which they are going to live, modern mythology roots them in paranoia and isolationism.[5] The result is a miseducated individual, as Campbell claims, and "When it is badly resolved, it is what is known in mythological terms, as a Waste Land situation."[6]

---

[4] Particularly, those of Sir Galahad.
[5] Joseph Campbell, *Myths To Live By* (New York: Bantam Books, 1972), 220.
[6] Ibid, 220-221.

This is the mythological context of the wasteland, according to Campbell: "The world does not talk to him; he does not talk to the world. When that is the case, there is a cut-off, the individual is thrown back on himself, and he is in prime shape for that psychotic break-away that will turn him into either an essential schizophrenic in a padded cell, or a paranoid screaming slogans at large, in a bughouse without walls."[7]

This is the proverbial descent into darkness. But there is also a return, based on a sincere undertaking of the inward journey to light and love: the Hero's Journey, from dark to light is, in essence, identical to the path of awakening. Every mystic walks this road. In fact, if you walk this road, you are a mystic. When this journey to realization or spiritual awakening is walked successfully, the natural result is a sense of awe and gratitude.

There have always been paths to freedom typified by awakening and the Hero's Journey. These paths await the seeker, but their search must be true and courageous, not just hip or cool. To culminate successfully, the search must be based on a real and driving need. There is a sense of living fully in the moment, within our time; it's not a clinging to some distant religion or practice of the past, but a living mythology that feels wholly up to date and in step with our ever-evolving culture. Campbell describes how this journey "guides him or her stage by stage, in health, strength and harmony of spirit through the whole of a useful life."[8]

RELIGION AND AWAKENING

The search for awakening uses many languages and paradigms but is not to be confused with religion. The primary purpose of religion is twofold. One is to present the idea of a higher good, often referred to as God (Allah, Goddess, or the equivalent) or part of God's domain. This helps us to see our life as something

---

[7] Ibid, 221.
[8] Ibid, p. 213.

more than just survival. The second purpose is to establish a social order—usually referred to as morality or ethics—so that people can live and work together, more or less harmoniously.

Originally the word religion came from *re + ligare*, meaning "to relink" in Latin. *Ligare* is also the root for the word ligament. Religion links us back to our roots, the source of our being; it links us to our neighbors and communities and promises a pleasing future.

Spiritual awakening pays due respect to this critical level of organization. But its fundamental aim is grander: our eyes are on transcendence.

Transcendence or awakening doesn't imply ignoring or devaluing the social order. But it does indicate a larger view, one that may include religious order, but also recognizes its limitations, to which this broader view is not beholden. This has been the principal path of every saint in every wisdom tradition throughout human history.

Awakening goes by various names and guises. It's been referred to as the search for the Holy Grail, the Hero's Journey, shamanic journeys, and so on. This experience is the focus of this book. Our history of beings who have successfully walked this path includes people like the Buddha, Laozi, Christ, and so on, as well as many others whose realization is or was as great, but whose names we may never know.

EMERGENCE INTO LIGHT: THE ROUGH GUIDE

Transcendence, or spiritual awakening, entails a shift of view. Our view changes because when we re-orient ourselves in a practice of kindness and compassion, wisdom is the result. This adaptation of our view also requires some remodeling of our identities. For those who hear the call to do this, the path awaits. The critical element in the experience or event of awakening is a realization of not-self (some say God). We're linked to something far, far greater than just "me." While it does not negate the self, it does step over it. It does not need a belief of any kind, as it is a visceral knowing. We feel at one with everything, and most importantly this is not a passing experience: it lasts. The resulting behavior of one who has been there is rooted in loving-kindness and compassion. It's been said that where bishops argue, saints laugh.

Even though the universe can appear chaotic, it is in fact highly ordered, and spiritual awakening is no different. The work of the human being is to perceive and understand patterns, and that is what the discipline of the spiritual quest is about. However, patterns are not always easily seen and often require specialized equipment. In the material world, we have devices like microscopes and telescopes and disciplines like chemistry and physics to help us perceive underlying patterns. In the so-called spiritual realm, we have our minds' vast ability to observe itself as our principal instrument.

Ultimately, the spiritual realm and the material realm are the same. Remember, after all, that early scientists were also mystics: alchemy and chemistry were part of a single discipline, as were astronomy and astrology. We often make the mistake of using the same yardstick to measure the visible and invisible: while astronomy and chemistry are measures of the material world, astrology and alchemy are largely metaphorical and apply to our understanding of ourselves. The same rules do not apply. Nevertheless, whether scientific or spiritual, pattern recognition involves measuring.

To help think through this problematic idea of measuring, I (Doug) invented this kōan:[9] What measure measures the measurer's measure?

How do we measure? What do we measure? Who is measuring? It may be helpful to remember that there are no mistakes in nature, only experiments. And experiments involve measurements. This is especially useful to recall while we examine the journey to awakening.

---

[9] Originating with Zen or Cha'an Buddhism, a kōan is a question unanswerable by analytical thinking alone. Fundamentally, this is known in Buddhism as insight.

One kind of measurement is mental health. Some have suggested that there is no mental illness per se; rather there are spiritual crises.[10] From this point of view, acute spiritual unease can manifest as what we label mental illness, even triggering latent genetic patterns (biogenetic issues, the karma of our family or tribe) and affecting the chemistry of the brain. From this point of view, mental illnesses are one kind of wasteland-based crises, calling the individual to find the Great Healing known as awakening. These wasteland-based crises call the being to seek the "pearl without price,"[11] awakening.

The Buddha called this wasteland dilemma *dukkha*. Dukkha is a word in the Pali language (which the Buddha spoke) that can be translated as suffering, struggle, trauma, or even agendas! However we interpret it, *dukkha* shows up in our lives inevitably and repeatedly. When the Buddha said that "all formations are struggling," it was a call to freedom. The purpose of the Hero's Journey is to resolve this dilemma.

Most of us try to drown out this fact of struggling by ignoring it or distracting ourselves from it with bread and circuses.[12] Some of us can't or won't do this: this is when the call to awakening is heard. In fact, for those of us who can't escape the suffering of our lives by burying it under possessions, relationships, families, career, entertainment, or drugs, the spiritual life is not just the best option; it's the *only* option.

We are all touched by trauma of some sort, somewhere in our lives. Some learn to live with it through therapy, others through

---

[10] See, for example, the groundbreaking work of Stanislav Grof and Christina Grof in *Spiritual Emergency: When Personal Transformation Becomes a Crisis.* (New York: St. Martin's Press, 1989).

[11] Matthew 13:45–46 (NKJV).

[12] "Activities or official plans that are intended to keep people happy and to stop them from noticing or complaining about problems," *Cambridge Dictionary*, accessed Oct. 20, 2017, http://dictionary.cambridge.org/dictionary/english/bread-and-circuses. From the 1st-century Roman satirist Juvenal's description of the relationship exchange between the Roman government and general populace.

distractions like entertainment or shopping, and others through medication. Although research shows that medication often makes things far worse over time, drugs are increasingly prescribed as a short-term solution.[13,14]

Neurosis is a relatively mild mental illness involving symptoms of stress, such as depression, anxiety, obsessive behavior, and hypochondria. It is not marked by a radical loss of touch with reality. Neuroses are a fact of life, and most of us learn to live with them.

Recognizing this more than fifteen hundred years ago, fifth-century Indian Theravadin Buddhist commentator and scholar Buddhaghosa reported, "All *puthujjana* are mad."[15] *Putthujjana* is the Pali word for "ordinary (unenlightened) person." *Putthujjana* also means "lump of sticky dough," basically uncooked bread, something that is not yet finished or ready. This implies firstly that awakened beings—at least fully awakened beings—aren't neurotic, and secondly, that being slightly neurotic at best is true for the rest of us. If we look around at the state of the world today, doesn't it seem like, as a species, we are still somewhat half-baked? The role of the path to spiritual awakening is to help us become fully cooked.

We argue that spiritual awakening is the most reliable and valid resolution of trauma and neuroses because it entails transcending the ego that holds the trauma. However, not all complete the journey, and some get stuck in the middle, as it were. Those that complete the path return to the world reborn. This does not mean

---

[13] Robert Whitaker, *Anatomy of an Epidemic: Magic Bullets, Psychiatric Drugs, and the Astonishing Rise of Mental Illness in America* (New York: Broadway Books, 2011).

[14] Sara G. Miller, "1 in 6 Americans Takes a Psychiatric Drug: Antidepressants were most common, followed by anxiety relievers and antipsychotics," *Scientific American,* Dec. 13, 2016, https://www.scientificamerican.com/article/1-in-6-americans-takes-a-psychiatric-drug/.

[15] Buddhaghosa, *Visuddhimagga* (Kandy, Sri Lanka: Buddhist Publication Society, 2010) http://www.accesstoinsight.org/lib/authors/nanamoli/PathofPurification2011.pdf, p 595.

mere lip service to a belief or an idea but an actual transformative change in the view—the measurement—of one's sense of self.

One of many ways we could get stuck, for example, would be to suffer from schizophrenia. Joseph Campbell pointed out that the process some people with schizophrenia experience perfectly matches that of the mythological Hero's Journey:

> For the person with schizophrenia the usual pattern is first, a break away or departure from the local social order and context; next, a long deep retreat inward and backward, as it were, in time, and inward, deep into the psyche; a chaotic series of encounters there, darkly terrifying experiences, and presently (if the victim is fortunate) encounters of a centering kind, fulfilling, harmonizing, giving new courage; and then finally, in such fortunate cases, a return journey of rebirth to life. And that is the universal formula also of the mythological Hero's Journey, which I, in my own published work, have described as: 1) separation, 2) initiation, and 3) return.[16]

While spiritual crises can be distressing, the best advice is to let the seeker go. We shouldn't try to abort this journey; instead we can help the searcher along! In essence, it is a shamanistic apprenticeship. This is the same journey taken by Christ, Buddha, and Igjugarjuk, an Inuit shaman.

Igjugarjuk explained, "The only true wisdom lives far from mankind, out in the great loneliness, and can only be reached through suffering. Privation and suffering alone open the mind of a man to all that is hidden to others."[17]

Then there is the return journey. It is by virtue of his or her contact with consensual reality that the seeker returns to rational or normal consciousness. The seeker, now a hero, returns with the gift of her experience, which helps wake the populace from their (mostly) unconscious sleep in the wasteland. The hero uses and

---

[16] Joseph Campbell, *Myths to Live By* (New York: Bantam Books, 1972), 208-9.

[17] Ibid., p 209.

integrates his experience with dream-like symbology to stimulate the society and its forms toward new discoveries.

THE WASTELAND DILEMMA

Before we turn to an examination of the journey to wisdom, a word on the reason for this book. All of us have this critical problem, the wasteland dilemma.

Unique among animals, humans have an extended childhood. We are not ready to meet the world independently soon after we are born in the way that a deer or a turtle is. We need about twelve years to prepare to meet the world independently, and often even more. How we respond and act are inherited patterns of behavior that tie our biology with our sociology. We'll explain.

Every person is an organization of culturally conditioned behavior patterns. The person or the brain, educated by family and biology, may interfere with, misinterpret or short-circuit the messages. When that happens, the signs no longer function as they should. The inherited mythology of the tribe (family, community, society, etc.) gets fractured, and its guiding value is lost or misinterpreted. At worst, the signs being responded to are not even in the collective environment, but strange imaginations that can further isolate and alienate the individual. A modern example is the sense of real community that can get lost as we transition from personal interactions to online and digital avatars. While the latter are intended to help us connect, they can leave us feeling more alone.

Such a person could become alienated and somewhat paranoid and might retreat to lost or even dangerous backwaters of society. So, it's critical for healthy individuals and healthy society to imprint children with what will attune them to, not alienate them from, the world in which they'll live. We have many examples in society of this alienation, from doomsday cults that lead their followers to suicide to gun-toting teenagers who think shooting people will alleviate their suffering to political or social extremists who think the enemy is "over there."

As awakening beings, we need to co-create contemporary mythology that triggers healthy behavior patterns that attune us to a vibrant and vital environment and society, not some outdated cliché or fad. The wasteland situation arises when and where we can't relate to the world. And, more tragically, when we don't care.

So, let's be clear: the wasteland is life oriented around self-image and acquisition with little real concern for the environment or other people's welfare. It is a kind of selfishness that measures success in terms of consumption and power. If we are all buried in the current ethic, if this is considered normal, how do we transcend it, or even want to? The average person is so immersed in these waters that they cannot see it. Eliot described it thus: *We think of the key, each in his prison / Thinking of the key, each confirms a prison.*

DESTINATION: PURELAND

Whether we call it spiritual awakening, the Hero's Journey, or something else, the fundamental message is: "Wake up! The universe is love. Go forth and explore and share. You are free." The hero, the seeker of liberation, awakening, follows a path that is fairly common to that of others of her kind. This seeker moves toward the Pureland. Buddhism defines a Pureland as a realm of Buddhas, or a Buddha-field. It's a metaphor for a wise, blissful state of being that rests in loving-kindness and compassion. It is built on practices such as generosity (*dāna* in Sanskrit), patience, applied energy, focused attention, responsible conduct, and wisdom.

These practices or virtues create, establish and support wholesome states of mind and, consequently, wholesome actions and interactions. But while a state of mind is in a sense a state of grace, how we manifest in the world depends on how we apply this state to our actions. This application to action is a path of practice known as *karma yoga,* developed in hermitages and monasteries over millennia.[18]

These days not many people want the lifestyle of a hermit or a monk; nonetheless "the world is my cloister,"[19] so we are developing paths and practices to adapt, modernize and renew the relevance and applicability of spiritual practice. We call this the Planetary Vehicle. It can include relationships, careers, and families, but the idea is that as a path it matches the dedication and commitment that has been traditionally found in more formal environments such as the hermitage or convent.

How all this plays out in the world is the subject of the reflections in this book. Each reflection is designed to stand on its own, so the reader is welcome to move through the reflections as your interest guides you.

In the first part of the book, *The Pearl Without Price,* we provide some context for the journey of spiritual awakening. Everyone has heard of some version of this transcendent, unitive experience. While it can seem like something that happens to historical figures, some of whom may seem too perfect to be real people, awakening beings are ordinary humans like us. Being human is an ongoing quest for greater freedom and greater connection at the same time. Part One shares how, for anyone who wants to live a good and happy life, who cares about their loved ones and communities, who dreams of a healthier and more harmonious planet, spiritual awakening in this lifetime is an accessible, compelling and very sane aspiration, particularly in these times of uncertain change.

In Part Two, *Riding The Dragon,* we address some of the common challenges we've seen many contemporary spiritual practitioners face. Spiritual awakening takes effort. And time.

---

[18] As described, for example, in the *Yoga Sutras of Patanjali,* compiled before 400 C.E., or in the *Bhagavad Gita,* composed between the 5th and 2nd centuries B.C.E. See our Reflections 5 and 6 for more on our contemporary interpretations of this path.

[19] "The world is my cloister, my body is my cell, and my soul is the hermit within!" —St. Francis of Assisi (1181-1226).

And while not everyone wants to be a nun or monk, enough lay practitioners are awakening that the lay path has become an attractive and viable one. Since we have other interests and commitments in our lives, such as career and relationships, we need to understand how our spiritual practice can enrich these and make them more successful. We've had some time to conjoin spiritual practice with the demands of our modern lives, and we'd like to help ease the learning curve for others.

There are diverse paths within any wisdom tradition: some are by the book, whereas some are specifically off road. While the latter may be unsettling and controversial, that doesn't mean they are necessarily inappropriate or scandalous. In Part Three, *Crazy Wisdom,* we explain how it takes courage and an open mind to explore the frontiers of awakening. Meditation trains us to pay attention in any and every situation, making a broader range of experience available to seekers of every type. What's more, this greater range of understanding creates something we all desire: greater degrees of freedom.

For the mystic, the person on a vision quest, the spiritual seeker, our journey may start off as a kind of psychic breakdown. But a healthy society or community has rites of passage that contain and enhance our training and guide our efforts. Together, with qualified teachers and teachings relevant to our times, our spiritual journey is supported throughout its peaks and nadirs. Through this process, with our vision intact and the methods clear, everyone and everything on the planet benefits.

Let us repeat that a key element here is *training.* Classic texts call the Buddha a *trainer,*[20] not a god, savior, nor even a religious figure.[21] *Wasteland to Pureland* describes some of the training we've found useful along a sincere path toward spiritual awakening.

---

[20] In the prayer "Salutation to the Buddha" (see below), the Pali word—vinnuhi'ti—is translated as "tamer." In the English-Pali dictionary "tamer" is translated back to veneti and Vinita ". . . to lead, instruct, train, educate."

[21] Narada Thera and Bhikkhu Kassapa, *The Mirror of the Dhamma,* "Salutation to the Buddha" (Kandy, Sri Lanka: Buddhist Publication Society, 1963), 5.

INTRODUCTION

As we begin to traverse the path to awakening let's start by stating our intention to support all beings to enjoy enriching, generous lives of discovery and exploration. Let's attempt to create a world of material support, environmental sustainability, social harmony, and spiritual states of epiphany and wonder. We remember all those who have gone before who have worked and played and struggled to make the world a more aware and amazing place, often with little reward or fanfare. We appreciate all those walking beside us who support, cajole, and nourish us in our quest to be more aware and a more significant source of light. And we express our gratitude to the frequency holders who keep the home fires burning, maintain the status quo, and may not read this book—we couldn't be doing this without you![22]

Doug Duncan and Catherine Pawasarat
Clear Sky Meditation and Study Center
August 2018

---

[22] In *A New Earth*, Eckhart Tolle defines frequency holders as people who "lead an outwardly unremarkable, seemingly more passive and relatively uneventful existence . . . They have no desire to get strongly involved in or change the world . . . There is no place for them, it seems, in our contemporary civilization. On the arising new earth, however, their role is just as vital as that of the creators, the doers, the reformers. Their function is to anchor the frequency of the new consciousness on this planet."

PART 1

THE PEARL
WITHOUT PRICE

Why Awaken?

REFLECTION 1

THE VISION

The Most Beautiful Result for the Least Effort

Every creature reaches for the stars in its own way. Another way to say this is that every creature looks for the best advantage. While the dog tries to get up on the sofa, humans try to stream movies for free. On a grander scale, dogs have learned to protect people in exchange for belonging and care, while humans have long searched for purpose through God, in whatever guise we as individuals or as a culture define that.

God, the goddess or a higher power resides in a unitive state, and the purpose of this unitive state is to be known. Ironically, the unity needs separation to be seen. In the unitive state, there is no recognized self or other: it is spacious emptiness. But sooner or later something happens. Something arises or emerges from this infinitely blissful state of being, and, simultaneously, a separation occurs: the self notes the previous unity but is now out of it. This is how the unitive state can be recognized once the consciousness has left it. It's a bit like needing a mirror to see your own face. A more mundane example is a pie. The pieces we cut inform us of the whole.

Humans were created to know God, the unitive state. As far as we know, only through us is this knowing fulfilled. And

3

ironically, it is through separation that we can come to this realization, and of our purpose.

Another word for purpose is vision. To thrive, we all need a sense of something wonderful and powerful that is not yet seen but nevertheless is felt or intuited. It's this aspiration or vision that links us to whatever we call it: God, spiritual awakening or transcendent liberation. And it is this seeking through a vision that creates our sense of God.

It's the vision that makes life worth living, and the struggle of separation is what leads us to become more aware. Whatever we call "God" provides us with a mirror to see ourselves. Shintō[23] literally enshrines this metaphor: at the very heart of their innermost shrines, there is nothing but a mirror. The journey to *awakening* is a struggle of search and remembrance, but principally an exercise in deepening self-awareness driven by curiosity sparked by "otherness:" when we look in the mirror of divinity, what "other" do we see?

All of life is unity, a summation of billions of years of reaching out and exploring. Humankind is an aspect of this exploration. We embody the most complex form of consciousness on earth, and the greater the complexity, the greater the freedom. Every creature wants to live, but humans *know* they want to live. For instance, plants reach for the light—their own form of God—as does humankind. But plants are unconscious (not self-aware) of reaching for the light, whereas humans can become conscious of this reach. Every creature is curious, but a self-aware being can focus this curiosity. That focus creates complexity with the potential for greater degrees of freedom.

UNITY IN SEPARATION, LIGHT IN DARKNESS

The features of light are clarity and luminescence, which are metaphors for enlightenment. Enlightenment is consciousness

---

[23] Japan's indigenous, animistic belief system. The word "Shintō" translates to "the way of the gods" or spirits.

unified with life itself plus that which is aware of this unity as an ongoing experience. It is also empty space, which appears to have an absence of life. That is to say the universe, empty space, is consciousness itself. And as far as corroborating evidence indicates so far, we are its most self-conscious of creatures.

Our human purpose is to make ourselves more conscious of the light, of the unitive experience that we call God or spiritual awakening. Awakening is seen through compassionate appearances because we need to see self in other and other in self to be more conscious. To have compassion there needs to be a "me" and a "you." As mentioned, the unitive experience emerges through separation. In deepest meditation, there is a profoundly peaceful and healing sense of unity, but no awareness of this unity; we have to emerge from or separate from the unity to know that we had the experience.

To complete the journey back to unity, we need to look beyond the senses that are central to our animal nature. Experiences that go beyond the senses will inform our search; they are a form of consciousness that makes us more aware of the nature of the light of transcendence. For example, Theravadin Buddhism's arupa jhanas (formless meditative absorptions) are meditations on boundless space, boundless consciousness, nothingness, and neither perception nor non-perception.[24] But perhaps more simply, think of an epiphany you have had that rested you in an altered state. While the senses may have triggered the state, the experience itself was somehow "other," or beyond the senses. One day, while sitting on a dock at the beach resting peacefully in the moment, everything seemed brighter, more alive, the senses seemed more vibrant or clearer. Then the mind changed modes; it's hard to explain in words, but we could say the mind expanded from the sensual nature of the scene and entered into an altered state of absorption. The sense experience was still there but became more background to the mind's bliss and clarity aspects.

---

[24] Bhadantacariya Buddhaghosa, *The Path of Purification* (Boulder and London: Shambala, 1976), volume 1, 354-371.

To become more aware of the light, we must pass through our own darkness—our neuroses and fears. Both our light and dark emerge from the fact that we are social animals. Mirror neurons in our brain allow us to imitate what others do and to understand others' mind-states. When this ability is turned inward, these neurons are involved in self-awareness.[25] Being social has led to the development of this capacity for self- awareness and has also made us ever more conscious: it has literally enlightened us.

However, the fears and neuroses in relationship to ourselves and other people (including society at large) also stem from being social, and these keep us in the dark. The understanding that the self is a tool to see the non-self (a unified consciousness if you will) is what actualizes the awakening experience. We all have the potential to awaken, but our self-absorption in the ego and its objects hides the non-self-aspect that reveals the awakening we all long for.

Only by reaching out and stepping over unnecessary defenses can we prevent ourselves from committing psychological suicide. By "psychological suicide" we mean a refusal to reach one's core which includes touching and being touched by others, deeply and sincerely. This includes the emotional and mental aspects of allowing ourselves to be seen/known, and to really see/know other. We must transcend our fears and channel our social instinct to join with others and explore within and without. We could also call this transmission mind: humanity on the same wavelength. This allows us to live a life of passion, commitment, and intensity. We could also call it meeting one another beyond our ego-oriented sense of self.

A vision is both a path and a result. If humanity is going to evolve, we need to awaken. By holding a vision of awakening, we are driven to seek that which currently lies outside our grasp. We continually do this already, seeking that which is missing, albeit with less lofty aspirations and through less satisfying means.

---

[25] Bruce Hood, *The Self Illusion: How the Social Brain Creates Identity* (Oxford: Oxford University Press, 2013). 59–60.

Spiritual awakening involves abiding in a unitive state that allows us to act with loving-kindness and compassion. It also involves exploring and discovering our inner and outer worlds. Some people think that if we figure out how to build a better world first, then compassion will follow, but putting the ideas of the ego (for example, a better world—it's a good idea, but still an ego-based one) before love and compassion is like putting the cart before the horse.

Only when we put love and compassion first can we go forth and manifest in the world in an integrated manner. However, that does not mean that we must have perfected love and compassion before we act. It's usually when we try to act with love and compassion that we learn what this actually means.

DANCING WITH THE QUESTION

To explore the inner and outer worlds, one must also explore doubt. If one is too comfortable with the status quo, no questions can arise, and therefore, there can be no growth. If one has questions and actively investigates doubt, then revelations occur. There's a fundamental difference between skeptical doubt—that says, "This doesn't make sense, forget it"—and questioning doubt, that says, "Let's find out more." The former is a dead end; the latter leads to interest, growth, and unfoldment.

Evolution is a state of questioning, it is an act of investigation, it is a practice of experimentation, and it is a communion of discovery and sharing. This process takes us beyond ourselves. In this "Let's find out more" sense, we must doubt God to discover God. God would have to be a very strange creator to just want his or her creations to nod and obey. This would not be very creative behavior for creation! Doubting God, questioning, and exploring what "God" means, is a compliment, a testament to our creative natures. It means we are asking, searching, and discovering. Instead of the idea that God is an entity in the sky, a being, or a concept, we can see it as a name for a type of experiencing and a way of exploring.

It may seem like a paradox, but this is a type of faith. In Sanskrit, the word for faith, *saddha*, also means "confidence." When you have faith, you may simply "Ask, and it will be given to you; seek, and you will find; knock, and it will be opened to you."[26] Trust in this process reveals the love of God through our own discoveries. Questioning doubt presses us to find out more, experience more, learn more and trust more. This implies a faith that, "if I ask, I'll learn," that questions lead to revelation. Our proof lies in our deepening understanding of our question: we ask the question behind the assumptions of the first question. We can call the ongoing questioning a leap of faith, not unlike the sperm plunging toward the egg or the lotus or water lily reaching up through the mud and water to reach the light.

The faith of seeking, asking, also points to what spiritually enlightened beings have been telling us for eons: transcendence is the most beautiful result for the least effort. All we need to do is ask, seek, and knock at the door.

Awareness of this process reveals another thing we've both always longed for and known: that we are free. We still must obey the laws of Newtonian physics, of course, but it is from the understanding of these laws that we were led to relativity and quantum mechanics. That is, new revelations are based on the groundwork of what comes before, and with each new learning our degrees of freedom increase. First the wheel, then the cart, then the chariot, and so on, until eventually, we have spacecraft. Each new discovery increases our degrees of freedom. And the journey continues.

This is why we like stories and games: because the end is unknown. The unknown excites and enlivens us. The function of the familiar is to be a support and a starting point, not a prison. And it does take effort to go forth into the unknown because our habitual mind prefers the familiar.

How do we measure degrees of freedom to continue the exploration and awakening? We need to be calm and methodical

---

[26] Matthew 7:7 (ASV).

like a scientist, so we can continue to promote and integrate our discoveries. We also need energy and focus to keep our questioning active and alive. If we feel a lack of energy, anxiety and so on, it is because we are in a prison of our own habitual ego, clinging to the known and familiar. There are always reasons for this, and they may seem like good ones. But in the end, humanity's survival and thriving have come from reaching beyond the known.

Greater freedom requires joy, awareness, and equanimity. It has to be fun or we get bored. Awareness is necessary because, if we get too tied down to a particular way of seeing or doing things, we might miss the joker card that opens new possibilities. Equanimity allows us the space to let go. In Buddhism, these six assets (calm, interest, concentration, energy, equanimity, and joy) are called the Bojjhangas, the Seven Factors of Awakening.

In this sense, the kingdom of heaven is taken by storm! We can't experience the transcendental with mere passivity or obedience. We must reach into our own shadow to find and liberate whatever demons lurk there. Our psychological shadows require a tremendous amount of our energy and power to stay under wraps. To be able to integrate them, we need solid support provided by cultivating the Seven Factors of Awakening as well as the Six Paramis or virtues.[27] The Paramis are our moral or ethical compass; they create a wholesome base in our being that is then capable of meeting some of the "demons" lurking in our psychological shadow. Once these are integrated, all that vitality can be channeled into greater discovery and freedom.

CURIOSITY AND OUR QUANTUM LEAP

Vision needs a vehicle. Christianity, Buddhism, and other religions have served as vehicles for humanity's vision in the past. In some countries or communities, science, intellectual pursuits, and the arts may now serve that function for many people. Whatever path

---

[27] Traditionally they are: generosity, ethics, patience, energy, meditation, and wisdom.

we choose, to embrace the vision well, it's important to value diversity and be all-inclusive. After all, how can we be in a unitive state if we say that everyone needs to be the same? Exclusivity is not unity. Krishnamurti taught that awareness is choice-less, and Namgyal Rinpoche talked about choice-full awareness. By this, he meant we grow the most when we are both open to all possibilities while also interested in examining the specifics. In a sense, choiceless awareness is passive; it rests in what is. Choiceful awareness asks questions, examines possibilities, and probes for insight and understanding.

In this sense, once we can remain open to all possibilities, curiosity becomes the vehicle for awakening. Curiosity transcends the apparent splits in our being and unifies all fields of discovery. Curiosity implies overcoming a limited self-view. "I'm good at this, I'm not good at that" is too limiting. We must have an open view of ourselves, appreciating that we don't benefit by pinning ourselves down to any single identity for too long. This of course also means we overcome limiting views about others.

Curiosity lends us courage. Courage comes from a sense of being blessed, not damned. It is, in fact, the sense of being blessed that allows us to dabble in what may feel frightening or even potentially harmful, empowering us to trust we'll get through it somehow. Imagine the first parachutist. If you've ever stood in the doorway of an airplane with a parachute on, the instinct to close the door and sit back down is overpowering: every cell in the body urges us not to jump! Still, we do it, and we survive. Not everyone every time, but often enough for many of us to successfully overcome our fear and even enjoy it.

Humanity is innovative, and we're on the edge—if not in the middle—of a quantum leap. As a species, we are learning many profound and game-changing truths: that selfishness and capitalism are poor substitutes for security and economic sustainability, that environmental obliviousness does not create more luxury, that social connectedness relies on open communication and interpenetration of being, and lastly, that spiritual maturity is not about rules and regulations, authoritarian figures in the sky, nor a new age fantasy of self-indulgence.

How so? We'll address these ideas throughout this book. Simply put, seeing ourselves as separate individuals makes for one kind of life, but seeing ourselves as different facets of a unified consciousness creates an entirely different reality. And more importantly, each creates very different ways of interacting.

For instance, depending on which orientation we adopt, it's completely within each of our power to transform competition into cooperation. We can morph ego positioning into team building that also supports the success of the individual. For the independently-minded Western ego (and particularly in North America), the group often feels more limiting than enriching. The strength of the East has been the reverse, the recognition of the value of the group. In the West, we're learning that community is what has made us such a successful species. The great Western ego often loses track of this!

In *The Necessary Revolution*, author Peter Senge points out that in "creating a sustainable new future three guiding ideas stand out: 1. There is no viable path forward that does not take into account the needs of future generations. 2. Institutions matter (today's world is not shaped by individuals alone) and 3. All real change is grounded in new ways of thinking." In regard to this last point, Senge quotes Einstein: "We can't solve problems by using the same kind of thinking we used when we created them."[28]

When we see our own being in another and realize that we are not separate from each other, clear communication becomes possible. We are learning to understand how it is that we can meaningfully come together. This is the quantum leap we're approaching.

For example, the current philosophy of social organizations tends to embrace the triple bottom line of economic, environmental, and social responsibility, and unfoldment. We include

---

[28] Peter Senge, *The Necessary Revolution*, (New York: Doubleday, 2008), 9–10.

the spiritual bottom line as a fourth element, though, we feel it is the most important; spiritual clarity and integrity are a fundamental aspect of a fully integrated life. As we integrate these elements, the energy and power of a unified field of engagement in our lives will foster a quantum jump throughout our lives and our consciousness.

Through therapy and/or spiritual practices, we recognize that our ego makes us feel separate and isolated, and we become very motivated to move past this. Then, we can experience both unity as well as the rich distinctiveness of each being. We can come together to produce an over-mind, a mind generated in the unitive field, that will take us to a new order of consciousness. This evolutionary leap might be compared to the jump from ape to human, or from Neanderthals to us.

At the moment, numerous beings are becoming enlightened in isolation from each other, just as Buddha, Christ, and Igjugarjuk did. But, as our collective sense of the unitive mind grows, we'll emerge together at a much higher level. It is a defining quality of the Aquarian age that fosters this "group guru," or collective awakening. This group mind will generate a new space, or rather, more readily tap into a vibrant field of consciousness that already exists. We see this at our retreat center Clear Sky where we're creating a field of spiritual awakening that new people can grow into more and more quickly. Many people are already becoming aware that there is nothing better for us to do than join together and collectively tap into our powers—such as empathy, telepathy, clairvoyance, and telekinesis, as well as perhaps traveling through space-time in a "mind capsule"—for the benefit of all beings. We are becoming both psychonauts and astronauts.

GOING WHERE NO ONE HAS GONE BEFORE

In this sense of discovery, our metaphorical bible should be science fiction. Science fiction shows us what we can imagine; therefore, it shows us where we can go and what we can do. It's a natural law that if we can imagine it, we can eventually manifest it. Think of Jules Verne's submarine and helicopter, which inspired both Simon Lake (father of the modern submarine) and Igor Sikorsky (inventor of the modern helicopter). When Martin Cooper at Motorola created the first cellphone, he credited the Star Trek communicator as his inspiration.

Science fiction also tells us about our fears and terrors, often symbolized by monsters and aliens, representing the shadow elements of our psyches. To manifest positive aspects of the future, we need to come to terms with the shadow. Integrating our shadow opens up a greater ability to love, which supports greater compassion *and* exploration. The shadow contains primordial drives and instincts and can manifest like a smoldering volcano that we're trying to keep capped lest it wreak destruction in our lives. We're afraid that these repressed aspects of our psyches will destroy us. But, when we learn to move the energy and integrate the elements of the shadow, all that energy becomes available to us and can be redirected toward the practice of loving-kindness, and its dance partner: creativity.

How are we to do this? Fundamentally it's all about practice, practice, practice. We get better at anything by practicing, and spiritual practice is about learning how to practice love, compassionate action, and recognition of the oneness of all of life. And to get better as we practice, much training is required. If we love what we're doing, training is fun; alternatively, we can get trapped in a view that training is work or obligatory and resent it. But, when we can maintain our interest and engage in the training over and over, the practice leads us to ever greater levels of skill and proficiency.

So, we practice meditation for developing calm and clarity and non-clinging; these then lead in turn to bliss and intuition. We practice communication for better relationships, we practice our skill sets to perform better at work, and we practice loving-kindness, compassion, and generosity for a healthier society.

This love springs from the heart, the head finds ways to put it to work skillfully, and the body actually implements. This is not the personal love of "me and mine," particularly, but of seeing divinity in another, as well as unity: "thou and we."

Neuroses and clinging are what create a sense of separation. When love overcomes these, the power of humanity emerges in new and amazing ways. The collective vision to help humanity evolve is emerging. In spite of much evidence to the contrary, humanity is becoming ever more sensitive and compassionate. We see this in the advances in equal rights for women, civil rights for many marginalized people, environment laws and consciousness, and the democratization of information on the Internet.

We feel better when we embrace these transcendent values. And when we feel better, things in life come more easily and joyfully. This is why this state of awakening really is the most beautiful result for the least effort.

REFLECTION 2

SPIRITUAL AWAKENING IN THE MODERN AGE

A Planetary Vehicle

Historically—and still today—spiritual seekers retired to the forest, the desert, mountains, or caves to seek a kind of freedom they felt they couldn't find in their day-to-day lives. These spiritual seekers lived in isolation or semi-isolation from the bustle of life in towns and cities, instead choosing to meditate or reflect in a state of question and investigation, looking for greater meaning or purpose beyond the daily routine. They traditionally worked with a teacher in a close personal relationship that lasted years or even a lifetime or multiple lifetimes.

These spiritual seekers found something: awakening. This message and way of being has fed and sustained humanity since time immemorial. There have been some misinterpretations of this message by people who haven't undertaken the same inner and outer explorations, but these have not obscured the illuminating effect that bona fide awakened ones have had on human consciousness, culture, and civilization. Besides the obvious examples of Buddha and Christ, numerous beings of every tradition—such as Santa Rosa of Lima, the Dalai Lama, Hazrat Rabia Basri, St. Moses the Black and Gauri-Ma, to name a few—have shown us the way to a clearer, more radiant consciousness, and therefore a more integrated life and experience. Of course, today we're also fortunate to have awakened beings among us.

And, perhaps most significantly, every spiritually awakened being has clearly stated that any of us could have the same experience. Christ said, "The kingdom of God is within you."[29] The prayer *Homage to the Dhamma*[30] explains, "The Dhamma . . . to be seen here and now; . . . inviting one to come and see; onward leading to Nibbana; to be known by the wise, *each for himself.*"[31] The implication is clear: if they can do it, we can!

If each of us could experience awakening, then why don't we? For most of us, "The spirit indeed is willing, but the flesh is weak."[32] That is, while part of us longs for spiritual fulfillment, another part clings to our creature comforts. We're human: we'd like to have our cake and eat it too. It's true that we desire the best result for the least effort, and this is both smart and efficient.

Nevertheless, the Holy Grail of human existence is typically missed because we don't accurately recognize what "the best" actually is. If you consider the paragons of humanity throughout history—Christ, Buddha, Yeshe Tsogyal, Hildegard of Bingen, Gandhi, and many whose names we'll never know—they have all been spiritually awakened beings.

What does this mean exactly? Simply put, "awake" is the opposite of "asleep." Our *habitual* pursuit of comfort—bread and circuses—puts us to sleep. It does take effort to wake up. But once we are spiritually awake, life becomes so much better and so much easier. It is the most sustainable, ethical, efficient, fruitful, and joyous state available to human beings. It takes far less effort than all the other pursuits of the self-referencing ego identity because we are no longer attached to the struggle and concomitant pain of chasing them.

---

[29] Luke 17:21 (KJV).

[30] *Dhamma* is the Pali word for the teachings of the Buddha or of awakening.

[31] Narada Thera and Bhikkhu Kassapa, *Mirror of the Dhamma* (Kandy: Buddhist Publication Society, 2003), 7. (Italics ours.)

[32] Matthew 26:41 (KJV).

Note that struggling never goes away. This is the Buddha's First Ennobling Truth: Life is struggle. However, with awakening, we're no longer *subject* to struggle; this means that the struggle still happens, but we don't get upset or otherwise disturbed by it. We don't struggle about the struggle. This is the difference between necessary suffering—being corporeal, subject to birth and decay—and unnecessary suffering. The latter's based on maintaining a particular self-image and ego clinging rooted in transient desires. We'll explore this more later.

Realized beings and sacred texts such as the fifth-century *Visuddhimagga*[33] tell us that when we are no longer subject to struggle, four special qualities remain:

- A kind, loving disposition;

- A willingness and motivation to be compassionate;

- Joyousness in our and others' successes and discoveries; and

- A great sense of equanimity (not to be confused with indifference).

In Buddhist philosophy, these four qualities are celebrated as the Divine Abidings: the feelings in which we abide when we are in a state of divinity. On the outside, this state can look and act like everyone else, though friendlier, warmer, and brighter. On the inside it's an ongoing experience of joy and wisdom.

---

[33] Bhadantacariya Buddhaghosa, *The Path of Purification: Visuddhimagga* (Boulder: Shambhala Publications, 1956), 1, where it's described that struggle in the Buddhist sense comes from clinging (in this text "clinging" is described as "entangled"). See also I.B. Horner, *Majjhima Nikaya,* vol 1 (London: The Pali Text Society, 1987), 9. Here struggle is defined by the four cankers or mental pollution.

How to Get There From Here:
The Classic Approach

The big question, of course, is how do we realize this ongoing state of bliss and clarity called awakening? To get good at anything, we need to study, train, and practice. The study and practice we can, to some extent, do on our own. But to go deeper, to test our learning and our skill, and to receive training, we need other people who are more experienced and accomplished at this spiritual awakening than we are. We also need methodology. The dynamic duo: training and method!

Traditionally, there have been two main training methods for spiritual aspirants: the yogic model and the monastic model. In the yogic model, one retreats from the world (part of what's known as renunciation) and studies and meditates in semi-isolation with one's teacher or guide. An aspirant may undergo years of dedicated training and practice to clearly uncover the awakening experience. The role of the teacher/trainer is central to help reveal the aspirant's unconscious clinging to culturally biased viewpoints, manifesting as conditioned habits rooted in conflicting emotions and primitive views. These blind us to the suffering clinging entails. The nature of a blind spot is that it is blind!

A skilled and experienced teacher demonstrates how to get out of our conditioned blindness into awareness. They act as a role model and also train us to do it ourselves. They may test our awareness and our ability to keep cool under pressure. After all, this is how we learn to improve.

The yogic model is unstructured and free in the sense that it is not a formal program and doesn't involve an institution. But life with a teacher in a yogic situation can be extremely demanding: it is a face-to-face, moment-to-moment, highly customized training between teacher and student day in and day out that can last for years. It is often an itinerant lifestyle, and even when not, the living conditions tend to be basic as the practice requires isolation and quietude to focus on practice. Christ wandered from place to place as did the Buddha, who only stayed in one place during the rainy season, undertaking retreats during that time. Following this model, our years studying with Namgyal Rinpoche took place in Europe, South America, Africa, and Asia, in addition to North America.[34]

Livelihood and relationships are put on the back burner with this yogic path. The Buddha and the Tibetan saint Milarepa are some examples of followers of the yogic path, and they too had teachers. Christ also followed what we are calling the yogic path. The word *yogi* refers to a student of a guru (including but not exclusively a teacher of Hatha Yoga). The word comes down to us in English as the word "yoke", as in the yoking of two oxen. Through yogic practices, our body and mind are yoked or harnessed. The body becomes trained with physical exercises and awareness, such as Hatha Yoga, and the power of the mind is developed or harnessed by practices such as meditation. We should note that *guru* means leader, teacher, or counselor, but these days might also be called trainer, coach, guide, or mentor.

Some claim Jesus didn't have a teacher, but where was he between his early youth and thirty when he started preaching? One theory holds that he studied in Kashmir during this time and was eventually buried there. In any case, something triggered the transformation from Jesus the man to Jesus the prophet, and these things do not happen in a vacuum. What makes these yogis and yoginis unique and memorable is their personal transformations, and their re-interpretation or refreshed presentation of timeless teachings. The Buddha did have teachers, and upon his awakening, started sharing what he experienced.

The second kind of training method for spiritual aspirants is the monastic model. In this model, one lives in community. The teacher still plays a central role, but so does the community. One must also learn to live, practice, and work well in partnerships, teams, and groups. The added complication of numerous egos creates more struggle as they jostle up against one another. This

---

[34] Namgyal Rinpoche passed away in Switzerland in 2003 at the end of a retreat he'd led.

also creates potential for greater and more complex creativity, connection, and spiritual unfoldment.

Monastic life involves daily interactions through all the group activities inherent in communal living such as cooking, cleaning, gardening/farming, bookkeeping, and managing the organization. If the yogic path focuses on the practice and living in relative solitude in nature, the monastic path focuses on the practice and living in an organization.

Every spiritual tradition has, in some form or another, drawn on these two systems. Teachings are received and then applied while going about one's daily activities. We receive training to learn how to become more and more skilled at incorporating the teachings and realizations in daily life. Regular interaction with a teacher(s) and a community means that we have feedback loops about how we're doing and can refine and improve our practice. This is essential for progress on the spiritual path—or any path.

Some people are drawn to practice without a teacher or feel they haven't found the "right" teacher yet. It's definitely beneficial to be learning and practicing a spiritual path compared to not practicing at all, and some progress may be made. But it is hard to transcend the ego if the ego is in charge!

The nature of the spiritual path is to move beyond the sense of an isolated self, and the best—perhaps the only—way to do this safely is to work with someone who has done it already. Ancient wisdom masters—and contemporary masters too—have agreed on this point. Since awakening explicitly transcends a fixed or attached view of self, *Do It Yourself* presents an inherent contradiction. *Do It Your Non-Self* might have a better chance at success!

TRAINING DAYS

One theory holds that it takes 10,000 hours of training to get good enough at something to really begin to master it.[35] While

---

[35] Malcolm Gladwell, *Outliers: The Story of Success* (New York: Little, Brown and Company, 2008).

there may be debate over the number of hours, there's no doubt it takes long periods of time, focus, training, and integration to master a field. It is *engaged* practice that predicts success, persistent training to which we give our full concentration, guided in some way by a skilled expert or mentor. As mentioned, the Buddha was called a trainer. A trainer helps establish and maintain a high standard regarding the breadth and quality of *how* we pay attention, rather than simply clocking in some hours. In other words, a trainer helps ensure the *quality* of actual mindfulness or attentiveness.

Naturally, we don't need to be a yogini or monk to be mindful. Laypeople can also have a focused practice and receive training. However, if our lives are driven by the day-to-day cares that cause us to ignore both practice and training in favor of a largely self-focused pursuit of happiness, we probably haven't yet realized that the objects we pursue are mere shadows of what we are longing for.

For instance, we need to realize that happiness is not an object we can get; it is a byproduct of interest and engagement. Objects we pursue to be happy—for example, money or relationship—don't yield happiness directly.

Using money as an example,[36] most of us never feel we have enough, and studies have shown that after the basics are covered, more money doesn't make us happier. However, the *way* we make money might make us happy if it engages us, is interesting, and is basically wholesome. By wholesome, we mean leading to greater awareness and unfoldment, to wholeness. Something that's unwholesome leads us to more fragmentation: conflicting emotions, mental models, and opinions that trigger suffering. Thus, the *nature* of the engagement is what makes us happy, while the money made thereby is a nice side benefit.

So, if we're seeking happiness in objects, we'll surely benefit from receiving teachings and attending retreats, but we're not yet ready for more formal training. We may live our lives in the

---

[36] We explore relationships as part of our spiritual practice in Reflection 11.

world of physical, emotional, and mental objects and try our best to apply the teachings to our daily life. This is good, and definitely better than not applying the teachings!

Ultimately, even if the yogic or monastic paths appeal to us, most of us don't feel we have the time and other resources available to follow them. Does this mean we can't have a serious practice? Can't attain spiritual awakening in this lifetime? Not necessarily. It's our extremely good fortune that these precious gems are still available to us.

ADAPTING TO THE NOW

One of the greatest challenges for a layperson is developing and maintaining a commitment and dedication to the continual training process that's essential to the yogic and monastic models. The commitment may be there in aspiration, and the dedication may be present in theory, but the world is full of distractions, and there's not a lot of support for maintaining a serious practice in the ordinary world.

This is why, in the past, the yogic and monastic models entailed renunciation, removing oneself from the usual world. Living as yogi or yogini[37] or in a monastery or convent required the spiritual aspirant to live in service to the teacher and community as representations of the awakening mind. Part of the process entailed learning not to live just for himself or herself, or for one's family as an extension of that self.

In the West, many contemporary practitioners have become suspicious of spiritual teachers and organizations. We feel this is largely a hangover from corrupted teachings and practices in standard organized religion, and a fair bit of cross-cultural confusion as Eastern and Western cultures intermingled in the late 20th century. Yogi Amrit Desai, founder of the Kripalu organization, and Rajneesh are good examples of how translating teachings from one culture to another can go awry. For example, Rajneesh

---

[37] A female yogi.

proclaimed, "All the religions have commanded and praised poverty, and I condemn all those religions. Because of their praise of poverty, poverty has persisted in the world. I don't condemn wealth. Wealth is a perfect means which can enhance people in every way . . . So, I am a materialist spiritualist."[38] However, his Rolls Royce collection didn't help his cause in mainstream Western society.[39]

But our struggles with spiritual guidance also say something about modern egos fighting for control! At the same time, our sincere aspiration combined with our instant-gratification-oriented society may lead us to hope we can find a shortcut to spiritual awakening without dedicating ourselves to these systems of ongoing teaching and training.

The spiritual quest is fraught with tricky situations in part because human egos are tricky. A long-established tradition rooted in cultural understanding and integrated into modern life promises the most optimal growth and unfoldment. These well-tested methods recognize transformation takes time and must be integrated into our daily lives. The quick fix usually doesn't work.

It's helpful to recognize how much Western culture promotes a democratic approach and personal independence, and that this is somewhat unique in human history. We may feel answerable to bosses, spouses, and taxes, so it's even less attractive to have to answer to a teacher who might challenge us at the core of our identity. Besides, we may catch glimpses of spiritual awakening through experiences of oneness while in nature or on psychedelic drugs, so do we actually need a teacher?

The thing is, these feelings of union—while real and wonderful— are usually somewhat fleeting, and not so sustainable. One of the innumerable side benefits of a committed spiritual path as we're

---

[38] Hugh Urban, *Zorba The Buddha*, 12 May 2016, https://thewire.in/books/rajneesh-the-guru-who-loved-his-rolls-royces.

[39] We explore these themes further in Reflection 17 on Money, Sex, and Power.

describing it is that—with practice, of course—this experience of union can be accessed at will.

In developed countries, the culture has become increasingly self-focused: in at least twenty-five developed countries, one-person households are more common than those with two adults living with children.[40] Marriage or relationships may be considered temporary and perhaps not even desirable. We're changing careers several times throughout our life and move from place to place, so deep human relationships can be hard to come by. We seek community but seem to have a hard time living or staying in one. If we're in a community that we feel we can walk out on easily, we don't really have one.

Some consider social media an acceptable substitute for direct personal contact. Social networking sites enable users to "type oneself into being," as social media expert Jenny Sunden describes. If we design who we are in the isolation of our keyboard, we are who we dream up independent of who we're chatting with. In other words, we are becoming avatars to ourselves: our social image and presence in society are being shaped as a product. This product may not truly meet what is in our and others' best interest as people and may be quite different from who we show up as in person. We need face-to-face contact to learn empathy and compassion because our mirror neurons fire in connection with others. We need physical proximity to foster this learning. Without it, we start to look more like computer icons, and our avatars live in isolation and fantasy.

When we can access a state of union at will, we have compassion for the beings we share the planet with, and the motivation and discernment to undertake skillful action or *not* to take unskillful actions. The Dalai Lama, for instance, has often advised compassion for the Chinese in spite of (or because of) their invasion and atrocities committed in his homeland of Tibet.

---

[40] Joseph Chamie, *The Rise of One-Person Households,* Interpress Service News Agency, Feb. 22, 2017, http://www.ipsnews.net/2017/02/the-rise-of-one-person-households/.

Former Zen Roshi Bernie Glassman's pioneering social venture, the Greyston Bakery in Yonkers, New York, is an excellent example of compassionate and enlightened activity.[41]

Because of all the global challenges we face, it is precisely now that the future calls on us to revive these old yogic and monastic models, re-modeled and adapted to our modern world and sensibilities. Most of all, it's time to develop our ability to serve one another and something larger than ourselves.

In essence, the realizations and understandings of spiritual awakening have remained the same across many traditions throughout history, although the forms manifest differently, and incorporate what came before. When Buddhism moved from India into the Himalayas and Japan in the 6th and 7th centuries, it adopted many elements of the native animistic or shamanic cultures and integrated them with Buddhist realizations. Christianity incorporated spiritual traditions that existed before it arrived, such as Roman mythology, Celtic culture, Mayan belief systems, etc. The expressions changed while the heart and wisdom remained, albeit hidden and sometimes repressed.

We now propose a new form of spiritual community, a Planetary Vehicle. In this model, the yogic and monastic traditions form a foundation for integrating spiritual practice with modern sensibilities and lifestyles.

FOUR STREAMS OF CONTEMPORARY PRACTICE

How does this work? We divide the teaching and practice into four streams:

1. the listening stream;

2. the training stream;

3. the meditation stream and

4. the hybrid stream.

---

[41] See Leigh Buchanan, *The New York Bakery That Hires Everyone, No Questions Asked*, Sept. 21, 2015, https://www.inc.com/leigh-buchanan/greyston-bakery-hires-everyone-no-questions-asked.html.

In the listening stream, a student studies, attends classes, and does some retreat work. In other words, they receive the teachings and apply them. As they go about their daily life, they're encouraged to share what they've learned and experienced with other people. But principally, they have a more casual and intermittent approach to unfoldment; it may not be their central focus.

In the training stream, the practitioner also works with a trainer, someone who has already been trained by a more experienced practitioner, who was trained by someone else, and so on. What do we get trained in? Awareness—some call it mindfulness—in every context and every moment. We call it attentiveness, which is mindfulness with applied focus.

The training stream is about learning to make effort with our best dedicated engagement, and without a strong self-interest. In other words, we learn to serve without expectation of reward, and thus free our energy from the grasping and clinging that our standard results orientation usually implies. We learn about the true meaning of service, helping us build much improved communication and cooperation skills. Ironically, but not surprisingly, in learning to give up clinging to self-interest, we've seen that this training greatly improves the professional careers of people who have trained in this way.[42]

This is one example of the myriad ways this path helps us mature as human beings and as spiritual practitioners. It empowers us to work more closely with others and with greater depth.

Through your own experience, you have probably noticed by now that all relationships contain elements of manipulation and control. Even our cat can manipulate a person to open the door for her within a few minutes of meeting that person so you can imagine the artistry that people bring to these dynamics. This is human (and feline) nature, so we are not trying to eradicate these inclinations: rather, the key point is *what* we manipulate and control *for*.

---

[42] For more on this, see Reflection 6 on Karma Yoga: Awakening Through Action.

In the listening stream, this is constantly addressed through the teachings and practice, and it's largely up to the practitioner themselves to pay attention to it in their daily life. The training stream, on the other hand, is designed to provide opportunities to study—together with our trainer—both our efforts to manipulate and control and our responses to being manipulated and controlled. This is fascinating and not for the faint of heart.

When I (Doug) was working with my teacher, one way he taught me about control was through service, a code word for therapy. In this situation, the control was related to sleep. After a day of teaching, he would retire to his room to read, and my job was to get him a sandwich, coffee, or whatever. We would wake up around 6:00 a.m. and had full days, so after serving him tea around 11:00 p.m. he said I could retire. I was just getting undressed when he called me back to get him a sandwich, which I prepared and delivered. Again, he said I could retire. This time I'd just gotten into bed when he called me back. Putting on my clothes and returning to his room, he wanted a glass of water—and on it went. I finally didn't bother to undress and just lay on my bed waiting, and that's how I finally fell asleep around 2:00 a.m.

The point of this was to watch all the arising states and emotions and learn to let them go. As I finally approached sleep, I realized that it didn't matter who controlled you or what your condition is; the power we all have is the state we can rest in. I surrendered, and the subsequent feeling of bliss and clarity and power I felt was exhilarating. I realized that I could choose my state: resentment or exhilaration. The next day, he smiled and said, "You now have a direct and personal experience of the four efforts.[43] In a sense you own them, you have made them yours."

Training helps us see how much of our ego gratification is hidden in unconscious habits of manipulation and control. We

---

[43] Buddhism's Four Efforts are: 1. Recognize the unwholesome (state) for the unwholesome and end it. 2. Make efforts for it not to arise again. 3. Recognize the wholesome for the wholesome and make efforts to support it. 4. Make efforts for it to arise in the future.

also begin to perceive how it's these very habits that are interfering with our desire and ability to experience spiritual transcendence. On the more mundane but very significant level, they also hinder our ability to craft a satisfying career and life. For example, my (Doug's) habit of ignoring grammar could cause this book to be far less acceptable to the reader. By accepting our editor's and Catherine's wonderful advice, I'm learning to overcome this bad habit and you, dear reader, have a more enjoyable read.

The third stream of contemporary practice consists of meditation, including prayer and contemplation. This suits people who are more introverted or those who are interested in studying the nature of mind to a depth not otherwise possible. While neuroscience is making astounding discoveries about the characteristics of the brain and how it functions, the *experiential* study of the mind is a distinct pursuit of its own and of consummate benefit.

All kinds of mental and physical states can arise that are difficult to conjure up without meditation. The inner world is as rich and as diverse as our outer world, but it does take work to break through the atmosphere of our typical orientation toward external objects to access it.

As the name indicates, the fourth, hybrid stream of contemporary spiritual practice is a combination of all three previous ones. People on this path receive some teachings and some training and have a regular meditation practice that is central to their lives. Needless to say, the practitioner benefits most when all three are undertaken as a committed, combined practice, rather than as a dilettantish lack of commitment to any one in particular.

THREE PRACTICE CONTEXTS

There are three ways we see these four contemporary streams of spiritual practice manifesting with strong potential. One is at a meditation center. Many meditation centers around the world offer in-depth meditation instruction and teaching and training in person. This ability to practice in person over a long period of time allows one to develop with precision and refinement the principles and practices leading to spiritual unfoldment. Moreover, the meditation stream requires occasional withdrawal from the status quo world, and unless you have a favorite quiet cave and are able to forage for yourself in nature, a retreat center is an invaluable support.

Doug, in particular, has done many three-month retreats through the years in different parts of the world. When there's external support for meditation retreat, it allows us the time needed to truly let go. We carry the world with us, and like old skin, it takes time to fall away while the new emerges. The deeper one goes in meditation, the quieter and calmer one becomes. This takes time, at least for the beginner. At the same time, energy surges: one becomes very awake. Some of my (Doug's) first long retreats were in Crete, others at Wangapeka in New Zealand, the Dharma Center of Canada near Kinmount, Ontario and at the Malaysian Buddhist Meditation Center near George Town, Malaysia. As we settle into being alone in retreat, all of our programming comes to the surface: we could sum the experience up nicely as "the agony and the ecstasy."

Hopes, fears, and everything between arise in meditation, and as we watch them come and go, and repeat, and repeat, we begin to see their coming and going as impermanence. Since they repeat, we begin to see them as patterns; in a sense, they have nothing to do with "me." They are like movie scripts with characters, and one starts to relate to them less personally. This letting go opens the door to radiant spaciousness. Only in retreat can we learn to cultivate the calm and quiet necessary to hear the depths of our mind as it connects to the Universal Mind.

A second context in which these various streams can manifest is when practitioners live in community in larger urban centers. The community grows up around journeymen trainers: people who have received a solid amount of training themselves and who have been directed by their own trainers to begin training others. Living together with other practitioners forms a basis for mutual support and also for mutual training in mindfulness.

This is a new way of living together, and since most of us come out of a nuclear family, living in community can be a difficult adjustment. Based upon Namgyal Rinpoche's idea of group houses centered around teaching, learning, and meditating together, we and/or our students have lived in group or community in Toronto, Kyoto, and Calgary, as well as at our retreat center, Clear Sky, and have benefited immensely from that.

This keeps the practice alive amidst the necessities of daily life which—without support from other spiritual practitioners—could become major distractions from our spiritual practice, such as our livelihoods and relationships. Instead, living in a spiritual community helps remind us to use these important parts of life as part of our practice, which tends to keep them more vibrant. Additionally, basic needs like cooking, cleaning, and household finances are shared, making these part of the spiritual practice while also liberating more time for meditation. Also, a spiritual community can help buoy us on a bad day, drawing on the power of the group to balance individual trials.

A third context in which the streams of practice may manifest is in the virtual space. Many spiritual teachers and communities use websites to offer online webinars, courses, videos, podcasts, blogs, and so on, and to meet with students via video conferencing. We do this as well. This allows students who are physically distant to stay in contact with their teachers and teachings throughout the year. It also provides various entry points for people to become engaged in new and accessible modalities. In some ways, these emerging services and applications make maintaining a solid spiritual practice far easier than ever before.

However, the conveniences of modern life also tend to facilitate many distractions from our practice. In our experience, some of the greatest challenges to integrating the spiritual life nowadays are continuity and consistency. When we leave the retreat environment and return to daily life, old habits may take over. We tend to lose the clarity and focused bliss that we contacted in retreat or at a live course at a retreat center. We make the mistake of thinking of daily life as "the real world." When inundated with the sensations and appetites of this world, the habitual mind-states and heart-states of the general population can become contagious. Facing these daunting conditions, we may forget to stay mindful.

Regular, engaged connection in person with teachers, trainers, and other practitioners is clearly the easiest way to maintain a vibrant practice and progress in one's spiritual development. This being said, for someone with fierce determination and commitment, virtual connections offer a good alternative. Here's a short list of recommendations to help keep a spiritual practice vibrant in contemporary life:

- Engage regularly online with living spiritual teachers and teachings;
- Seek, join, or co-create centers where people can practice, live, and work together and share spiritual teachings and practices with one another and a broader community;
- Engage consistently with trainers who are also working in the world so they can help us navigate how to integrate practice with daily life and vice versa. Ideally, this happens in person, but online can work too. This may take place during courses or as part of a regular schedule.
- Finally, no matter what the tradition or practice, lineage or an unbroken line of credentials from teacher to student[44] is of utmost importance for verification and confidence. These form our credentials. The Dalai Lama's compassion and wisdom is the fruit of what he learned from his teachers and trainers, and they from theirs, and so on. To our knowledge, there's no real equivalent to this system in the West. Nonetheless any field of study or function—science, the arts, engineering, philosophy, etc.—builds on the best of what has come before, lending

---

[44] In our tradition, we trace our teachers back to the Buddha in two lines: the Theravadin tradition through our teacher's ordination as Ananda Bodhi by Burmese insight master Sayadaw U Thila Wunta, and the Vajrayana Karma Kargyu tradition through Ananda Bodhi's subsequent recognition as Namgyal Rinpoche by and transmission from H.H. the 16th Karmapa. See http://www.planetdharma.com/lineage.

credence while also supporting innovation and discovery. The same is true of spiritual awakening.

When we bring focus and consistency to our lay spiritual practice, and integrate it with our daily life, today it's possible to enjoy the same benefits as from yogic or monastic training. Some of the strict conduct codes and relatively narrow involvements of monasteries and convents of yesteryear are being adapted to our contemporary lives: careers, relationships, and other forms of exploration can enhance our spiritual lives with creativity and richness and vice versa. In 2009, more people lived in urban areas than rural environs for the first time.[45] Cities are full of diversity, resources, and potential explorations through museums, the arts, and intercultural stimulation. Since people are choosing to live in these massively stimulating environments, how spiritual unfoldment happens must adapt to integrate this. One of our contemporary challenges as awakening beings is to adapt the monastic or yogic model into engaged urban cooperative training programs.

While spending time at retreat centers like Clear Sky remains a necessity for deeper practice, conjoining the benefits of both a spiritual center and daily life in the world offers opportunities for spiritual development to a broader range of people than convents and monasteries could in the past. We're adapting those august institutions' excellent methodologies and technologies so that far more people can undertake a spiritual practice and realize the awakening mind. It's our vision that these four streams and three contexts comprise an effective methodology worthy of a global teaching that transcends cultural, racial, gender, and religious biases. We call it the Planetary Vehicle.

---

[45] "World Urbanization Prospects: The 2009 Revision," United Nations Department of Economic and Social Affairs, Population Division, accessed Oct. 24, 2017, http://www.un.org/en/development/desa/population/publications/urbanization/urban-rural.shtml.

REFLECTION 3

IF YOU WANT THE PRESENT YOU HAVE TO OPEN THE BOX

Getting the Horse in Front of the Cart

Curiously, people tend to fear loss more than they value gain. Research shows that it takes two dollars of gain to compensate for one dollar of loss.[46] We can see this reflected in the tendency for our view of the world to tilt toward the negative.[47] Life is all about security: loss of the basic elements for sustaining life results in death. Given that most of the time we are not in a life-or-death situation, gain is worth less than risking what we have. But as everyone knows, if we have nothing, if we are desperate—or perhaps more to the point when we *feel* desperate—we can be very aggressive about scrambling to fulfill our needs. Consequently, our survival needs must be met before we can progress in the spiritual life. The challenge is, many people

---

[46] Daniel Kahneman, *Thinking, Fast and Slow* (New York: Farrar, Straus and Giroux, 2011), 28.

[47] Alison Ledgerwood, "Getting stuck in the negatives (and how to get unstuck)," filmed June 22, 2013 at TedxUCDavis, Davis, CA, video, 9:59, https://www.youtube.com/watch?v=7XFLTDQ4JMk.

never *feel* they have met those needs sufficiently enough to get established on the spiritual path.

When a person enters a monastery or convent, some of the first things the resident abbot or abbess asks are: Do you have enough to eat? Do you have proper clothing? Are you basically healthy?

If you answer yes to these questions, they surmise that you can devote yourself to the practice without hindrance. If the four prerequisites are met (food, clothing, shelter, and medicine) they expect that you can get down to the work of spiritual awakening.

As the reader might guess, this is not always true.

Why not? Because we tend to be driven to *more*. This is what we call "the upgrade motif." When offered a hotel room, most of us will choose the best one available at that price. As teachers, we've noticed that when students share a room in a retreat center or hotel, the first person to arrive will choose what they feel is the best bed. They may spread their belongings out around the room, maximizing their footprint. Similarly, in restaurants, movie theaters, on trains and in planes, we seek the best seat we can find. There is an intelligence to this, and it can quickly become a habit or even a preoccupation. Perhaps our fundamental insecurity as a separate ego makes us hoard metaphorical acorns lest we starve. If our culture also worships the "great individual," this grand sense of me, myself, and I gets magnified. In contrast, in a world where a more cooperative, "I've got your back, you've got mine" kind of mentality prevailed, perhaps our need to *always* take the best would lessen.

Where does this self-interest, self-protection, or self-promotion come from? We're born as dependent creatures, fully reliant upon our mother and other caregivers, incapable of supporting ourselves. Thus, from our earliest aware moments, we feel completely at the whims of our situation and the people in charge, usually our parents. We can sense that our survival is conditional, and out of our control.

We feel that our survival somehow depends on pleasing or satisfying the people who are taking care of us and ensuring our survival. We learn to be what we need to be and behave the way we are supposed to behave, according to the ongoing expectations or paradigm we are born into.[48] Even the rebellious child—let's say one in the terrible twos—is caught in this dynamic, or there would be no need to rebel or nothing to rebel against. For almost all of us, unruliness is merely one step in the process of adapting to the norm. Even in a counterculture, one still needs to somehow fit into the group that is being different. Only the fully awakened have stepped out of this phenomenon, which interestingly, allows them to fit in to any situation or community more seamlessly.

Naturally, fitting in means different things for different families, people, and circumstances. Expectations will vary: perhaps to be charming or intelligent, strong, helpful, or what have you. Whatever the qualities, as the years pile up, so does the operant conditioning. We take on our parents' and our society's value structures, styles of communication and interaction, appetites, and proclivities.

By age five, the basic parameters of our behavior and character are established. In teenage years, we may rebel and choose other alternatives. As mentioned, if we look closely, we see that rebellion and alternatives are rooted in the same group ethic: we're still tied somehow to the paradigm that we're rebelling against or we wouldn't be rebelling. Whether it's beatnik or hippie, punk or goth, grunge, hip hop or hipster, there is still a group dynamic at work.

Note, too, that if or when rebellion happens, our ego is already well-formed because it is only the ego that can rebel. Before age two, there is not yet an ego, and therefore rebellion is not really possible. This is in part because we are dependent, but also because we aren't yet conscious of the programming that gets laid in. We have to be somewhat aware of something to rebel against it.

Even as adults, our well-functioning ego isn't able to explore what our life was like pre-ego, before age two. This is why we

---

[48] We go into this topic of our earliest years and ego formation more extensively in Reflection 14: Spiritual Energy Traders.

have so few memories from that early time. However, there *is* a consciousness that can explore those first few years because, of course, we were conscious beings at that age. This is the meditative mind.

Once skilled, the meditative mind is able to leave the self (ego) behind, at least temporarily, and therefore can reach back before age two. What's more, the meditative mind can explore even further back, into the womb experience. Meditation masters can explore "out the other side," before conception. Similarly, consciousness extends beyond the grave, into the realm between death and birth that Buddhism calls the *bardo,* and on to rebirth of the next formation.

In other words, once the ego-referencing mind has been transcended, if only temporarily, time/space dissolves, and consciousness is free to move anywhere or in any time, as it were. Consciousness is always and everywhere, while the ego has a beginning—around age two—and an end—when this organism expires.

In contrast, the ego has the sense that it is totally reliant upon many things that are beyond its control, starting with the parents, and continuing with entities like partners, bosses, the economy, etc. This distressing awareness results in countermeasures: the ego's primary mandate is to try to do the impossible, to make itself fixed and permanent, to shore up some kind of security. Since it's cognizant on some level that it is a separate being, an "I," alone and dependent, this is a terrifying state of affairs. So, the ego tries its best to remain in denial about this vulnerability.

How many of us seek larger incomes, better partners, or more stuff to feel more secure? If it worked as a strategy, this impulse might be understandable, but the problem is it doesn't work. By its very nature, the ego can never feel safe and secure.

THE FOUR DEEP EGO FEARS

We've found that the early experience of the toddler becoming aware of its separation from mother results in universal concerns that we call the Four Deep Ego Fears. These are:

1. The fear of being abandoned.
Our separation from mother felt like an abandonment, the proverbial banishment from the Garden of Eden, when we went
from a state of bliss-union with the mother to the fear of being
alone in an unsafe world. This feeling of abandonment can be
triggered throughout our lives, arising from minor experiences,
such as when a friend doesn't show for coffee, to major ones
like when a partner has an affair with someone else or wants a
divorce. The triggers differ, but the root feeling of abandonment
is the same: terror.

2. The fear of being annihilated
If we're alone, we're vulnerable: we might get injured and die or
otherwise be destroyed. This fear results in ongoing efforts to feel
safe, secure, and unassailable. We also see this fear reflected in
our apprehension about being "taken over," for example, being
invaded by foreigners or brainwashed by a cult of some sort. This
fear has provided tremendous resources for the film industry,
the *Alien* series being one outstanding example. Classically, this
movie features the monster entering a human body and bursting
out from the inside, destroying its human host.

3. The fear of insanity
The ego needs to feel it has a handle on things. Losing the sense
of self can feel like losing control. This is the case, sometimes,
when someone's taken hallucinogenic drugs, but the ego is not
prepared to lose its coordinating function. The sense of expansion
or alternate universes can overwhelm the ego's sense of order and
control. The potential impairment or loss of the ego's coordinating
function, sanity, is distressing.

4. The fear of being evil
This might be more easily recognizable as fear of being a bad
person or of doing something bad. Generally speaking, we do a
lot of things contrary to our desires because we're afraid that if
we did what we'd like, it would demonstrate that somehow we're

bad. One example would be choosing to stay in a relationship that's not growing because separating would mean I'm selfish, or it would hurt them too much (making me a hurtful person).

Additionally, we may fear that if we lose control, we might do something reprehensible, revealing ourselves as a bad person. What constitutes a bad person varies according to family and tribal conditioning, environment, and time in history. For example, on one end of the spectrum, we might fear becoming a fascist dictator, criminal, or abuser, or on the other end, we might fear that we'd have extramarital or aberrant sex. Fundamentally, we may see anything that remains hidden in the shadow of our psyche as "evil."

Integrating our shadow through therapy and meditation helps us transcend these fears. Etymologically the root of "sin" means, "to miss the mark," and to us, sin is about non-love: generally, we would all like to be loving, but it doesn't always work out that way. What's more, love is not always nice. Typically, the shadow hides issues around sex, power, and control. So, releasing the energy locked up in the shadow may also redefine what we see as moral or ethical or how that's been defined for us by our cultural or societal conditioning.

For instance, it wasn't so long ago that homosexuality was a criminal offense, or that masturbation was believed to cause a wide range of physical and mental disorders. Liberating the shadow around these and other mistaken beliefs allows us to reconnect with our "natural" being minus the guilt, shame, and low self-esteem that come from repressing it. In other words, with increased acceptance, we gain increased capacity to love ourselves and others.

Our ego convinces us to expend a lot of resources trying to avoid these feelings of shame, guilt, and low self-esteem. This entails shutting them out, trying to make the self feel inviolate, which also means permanent and independent and not alone. The ego has various strategies, and if we don't do the inner work required to uncover these, they can determine much of the course of our life.

For instance, to protect against abandonment, the ego may choose to try to make a relationship solid and unchanging and maybe use marriage as a way to try to do this. An unintended consequence is that this also usually leads to some stagnation. Life is about growth and learning, but we might try to keep our partners as they were—or as we *thought* they were—when we first got together. Relationship, at its best, is meant to foster unfoldment in our being, which implies ongoing change.

To protect against annihilation, the ego tries to control everything. To protect against insanity, it tries, in some form or other, to fit into the status quo. Despite evidence to the contrary (e.g., the holocaust or our unsustainable resource use), we feel that sanity can be found in the majority. To protect against being a bad person, we may live a life that on some level we don't really want, or perhaps—due to a buildup of frustration and aggression from this—we overdo measures to ensure we don't lose control.

One common strategy to avoid losing control is to try to amass more and more stuff,[49] which, in turn, creates ever-increasing pressure to obey the conditioned programming: to acquire the stuff, we need to fit into the models that generate it. Our consumerist society has evolved to exploit this fundamental ego insecurity. The cost of living within this paradigm is the feeling that something is being missed in life, a longing for true meaning or connection. At the same time, there's an intuitive sense that if we step out of this dynamic and begin the quest for something deeper or more substantial, it means leaving behind the whole matrix of our life as we know it. The only people we know who have done this seem to be saints or the insane. Throughout most of history, it has been difficult to distinguish between those two.

---

[49] The documentary film *The Queen of Versailles* is an excellent if perhaps unintentional study of this phenomenon. Written by Kenneth Chisholm, directed by Lauren Greenfield, released by Evergreen Pictures, 2012.

IN QUEST OF THE BEST LIFE

Generally speaking, the standard view of how saints (and their like) fare could be improved upon. Think of the crucifixion, St. Francis walking around naked and talking to wolves, and other erratic behavior from the lives of the holy that we hear about. Even the good guys in the movie *The Matrix* eat slop and live in gray, dungeon-like environments. The descriptions of beatitude, joy, spaciousness, and their benefits tend to be scanty and two-dimensional—not a great advertisement for seeking sainthood.

But there are other views on sainthood, as typified by the Buddha, for example. He led a good life until he was eighty and taught countless beings for more than forty years. What did he teach? He taught what he'd discovered, as many beings had before him, and have since—the solution to the sense that we're missing something: the bliss emptiness of the awakening mind, the feeling of coming home.

How do we discover this for ourselves?

Let's work it backward. To feel more secure, the ego wants things, objects, including emotional and mental objects like a good relationship or happiness. We all know that objects don't really make us happy for very long. A child can tire of a new toy pretty quickly, as can an adult, at which time more new objects are needed. The ego may be temporarily satisfied but never satiated. Moreover, happiness is a *result* of living a good life that we love and feel fulfilled by, not an object to get to help us feel fulfilled.

And if happiness is a result, it begs the question: a result of what? If objects don't make us reliably happy, what does?

The short answer is that focused absorption makes us happy. In Sanskrit, it's called *samadhi*. All the most wonderful states we get into are variations of samadhi. Think of that beautiful sunset, that breathtakingly poignant space when you were holding your newborn baby, a magical moment in nature, or that time of athletic achievement. Each of these and other experiences or objects can trigger a samadhi, but the bliss is in the state of mind, not in the object or experience itself.

If this were not the case, then every time we held our newborn or watched a sunset we would feel satisfied and blissful. But we know it doesn't work that way. This proves that the pleasure is not in the object: it's in the state of mind.

Our teacher Namgyal Rinpoche taught that there are five factors in a wonderful state, a bliss state, a *samadhi*. They are:

1. a feeling of calm;

2. a sense of unity;

3. less internal dialogue;

4. joy; and

5. an evenness or composure that Buddhism calls equanimity.

As these five factors grow stronger, the ego is quieted. When the ego moves from identifying with objects to identifying with the state, the state becomes a kind of non-ego zone. The difference is significant. The ego, in pursuit of desired objects, is subject to struggle and suffering—*this object doesn't interest me as much as I thought it would; I need a new object*—whereas the non-ego dwells in spacious emptiness and has the feature of equanimity. Even if struggle and suffering arise, equanimity gives us a buffer, meaning we're not so bothered by them. What's more, our brains and our hearts are still fully functional, so of course we do what we can to ensure less suffering in the world.

This joyful, ongoing effort is called "the Bodhisattva vow" in Mahayana Buddhism.[50] The Bodhisattva vow comes from the understanding that we're all in this thing called life together, so I can't really be happy if you're suffering. For me to be at ease, I

---

[50] It begins, "However innumerable beings are, I vow to meet them with kindness and interest." See Reflection 10 for the entire Bodhisattva vow we use, under the subhead *Forewarned is Forearmed*.

need you to be well, and vice versa. Therefore, the Bodhisattva dedicates all their life energy toward benefitting all beings, all the way through to helping all other beings attain enlightenment.

Our mirror neurons allow us to feel what others feel, but we can learn not to suffer about suffering. We let it stay just one layer deep without adding our own second or third or fourth layer of suffering about suffering on top of it. For example, imagine that a friend of someone close to you has died. Obviously, you would feel sad for your friend and for the deceased and his family as well. But, we know we are all going to die, it's part of life, so remaining in a clear blissful non-clinging state is the most compassionate thing we can do. The radiant, spacious state is more support for your friend than pulling our hair and wailing.

The freedom of energy that ensues allows us to be more effective to actually do something about the suffering and to enjoy life's wonders as we do it. This is a life worth living.

Attaining true happiness in life boils down to a cart and horse argument. If the ego takes precedence over the samadhi state, then the cart is in front of the horse. In essence, the ego gets in the way of the samadhi experience that nourishes us so deeply. The ego still seeks a good life and happiness, but it looks for them in all the wrong places. We end up going in circles, turning around on ourselves, and don't understand why we can't seem to get where we'd like to go. In contrast, when the samadhi state leads the ego, then the horse is in its optimal place: in front of the cart. A mind thus liberated is able to do things that an ego-bound being prevents itself from doing.

THE EGO IS A HOUSE ON FIRE

In the *Burning House Parable* in the *Lotus Sutra*, the Buddha talks about the ego (an average person, let's say) obsessed with objects and compares that to being in a burning house. Since most people are obsessed with objects—remember, this includes mental and emotional objects, such as our relationships or our ideas about who we are—he is in fact, addressing each of us. Meanwhile, the Buddha is outside the house, outside the ego, calling us to a state of clarity, awareness, and bliss that is *not identified* with the objects. He is, in fact, asking us to embrace the non-self, that state of awareness in which there is no permanent, inherent self; there are simply a collection of patterns shifting in response to ever-changing circumstances.

It's important to note that when Buddhists refer to non-self, we're not advocating obliteration or nihilism. Non-self is an attempt to indicate that the idea of our self is rooted in our attachment and identification with the objects of our minds, and by extension, the outer world. After all, everything we perceive in the outer world (including our body) is interpreted by our mind. These objects and interpretations in our mind are, by their very nature, ephemeral: they are constantly in flux, in no small part due to our faulty memories![51] By letting go of the clinging to these transient and impermanent arisings, we let go of a fixed sense of our self and open up, in that sense, to a non-self.

Embrace non-self? For many of us, this is too much to fathom. So, we remain in the burning house playing with our objects while everything around us is going up in flames. This is a metaphor for death inevitably approaching, at which point all our objects must be let go of, without exception.

But the Buddha is compassionate and wise. In the *Burning House Parable*, he promises that if we come outside the burning house, he has even bigger and better objects for us. In essence, he is pulling a Buddhist ninja move, called "using the poison as a cure." In this case, the poison is the ego's greed for objects; he's using that very poison to tempt us to come outside the burning house/ego, knowing that once we are outside, we'll see the burning house for what it is. We'll naturally recognize that our well-being is based on our liberated state—in this case, the non-self, the freedom from the burning house/ego—not in the objects.

---

[51] For more on our remarkably unreliable memory, see Hood, *The Self Illusion*.

In a sense, we could say that the Buddha is offering us a gift. To get the present, we must come outside the burning house. Using our metaphor, getting the gift implies opening the box of ego-clinging. When we open the box, what we find inside is not an object, per se, but a state of radiant, spacious clarity. This state is not subject to the vicissitudes of the mental, physical, and emotional objects to which we normally cling. This is the present.

With this understanding and state of spacious clarity, we move in the realm of absolute truth, even as we live and work in the realm of objects or relative truth. Absolute truth could be likened to a state of spacious emptiness, like a clear sky. Relative truth manifests as the different forms that appear against that backdrop of spaciousness, like clouds. Clouds come and go, they overlap each other and are always shifting around; they may be beautiful, gloomy, stormy, spectacular, or have many other qualities. Meanwhile, behind the clouds, the clear sky remains constantly pristine.[52] A spiritually awakening being is one who abides in the clear sky realization, even as they live and relate and work in the world with clouds.

We know that in the realm of relative truth, the cart, there are going to be issues from time to time, if not all the time. But the awakening as represented by the horse is forever free-spirited. In our metaphor, it pulls the cart but is not limited to doing only that; it also gets its moments of galloping around the field. The ego still gets to hold and use the reins, but the horse pulls us to where we really want to go. The horse represents the freedom of open spaciousness pulling the cart containing our career, relationships, and other aspects of our object world. And when they're in the proper arrangement, the horse of awakening consciousness pulling the cart of everything in our life, we have a tremendous opportunity.

What opportunity? If we want to be more than we think we are, then we have to become what we're not. When we embrace an other self, versions of our self that we haven't embraced before,

---

[52] We named our retreat center, Clear Sky, after this radiant state of mind.

eventually we find non-self. We're not limited to our ideas about who we are; such an idea is merely another object we hang onto unnecessarily.

A non-self doesn't suffer from the same feelings of insecurity that the ego inherently does. Without feelings of insecurity, imagine how problem-free life becomes for someone who's dwelling in their sense of non-self! Problems still happen, of course. Our loved ones still pass away, for example. But even as we weep for them and our loss, in our core, there is only spaciousness and peace. Such a person can still function in the world, and the lack of insecurity and associated problems make it far easier to work things out in relative truth.

This is the present we all long for. By opening the box of the self, we get the freedom to put on any self as we wish and as appropriate for the situation. In other words, we don't really have a fixed self: who we are changes with who we're with and what the situation calls for. We may feel that we are the same over time, but that feeling is an illusion. If I change my appetites, my habits, my feelings, my thoughts, I'll still feel like me, but what is a me independent of these things? Nothing really. Where we get into trouble is thinking that if these things are interfered with, then so is my self. But if I can manifest in multiple ways as appropriate, I can't really be disturbed. With this skilled flexibility, imagine how much more helpful we can be for other beings. And how much more enjoyable life can be outside the box.

REFLECTION 4

PROTECTING AGAINST HURT IS WHAT HURTS

Liberation through Letting Go

The feeling of hurt comes from the past. It can be transformed by feeling love in the present. To feel love in the present, the hurt must be let go.

It sounds so simple. But complexity arises because a network of habitual sensations, emotions, and thought patterns forms and, over time, calcifies around our self-protective reactions to past hurt. These, too, must be released.

Where, then, do we start on this path to love?

It starts with the body. If we can let go of the muscle tension related to the past experience of hurt, then emotional and mental models that have been bound up can also be freed. From the perspective of the physical body, letting go often appears as visible or felt phenomena such as trembling, shaking, or shivering. This indicates the release of the muscle tension that has been held, a de-armoring of the body, and a letting go of the hurt. This is a beautiful and important step on our way to greater love.

Such physical de-armoring happens on its own through the process of deep meditation. We can support this process of unfolding more quickly but sustainably through many different approaches developed over the last fifty years.[53] Emotionally and psychologically, we can take advantage of therapy, counseling, family constellations, and the like to release emotions held in the body. Physically, massage, yoga, traditional Chinese medicine, tai chi, and related therapies are very helpful.

Why let go? After all, each of us has good reasons to feel hurt. The key thing is, it's this very act of letting go that liberates us. And, since hurt is one inevitable aspect of life, we would benefit from letting it go again and again. Letting go is a skill that we can develop through deep meditation practice over years and through the methodologies described above. Modern approaches continue to emerge in different modalities, including reframing techniques and our *Going to the Core* exercise.[54] Imagine the amount of energy that becomes available to us when it is no longer tied up in hanging on to past hurts.

And the liberating journey continues. Once we get good at letting go, we let go of letting go. Then, we experience the liberation of *transcending*: it is a gerund, an active and continuous happening. After letting go of the emotional tension of hurt, we then allow the energy that was stymied by clinging to being hurt to then move toward forgiveness or other emotional release. Then, the mind's and heart's energies are opened up, and we can naturally embrace equanimity. Equanimity is another word for peace of mind and heart.

Now the former emotional tension is available to be transformed into creative tension.[55] When there is a gap between the

---

[53] See, for example, Alexander Lowen, *Bioenergetics: The Revolutionary Therapy That Uses The Language Of The Body To Heal The Problems Of The Mind* (London: Penguin Books, 1976), and Wilhelm Reich, *The Function of The Orgasm: Sex-Economic Problems of Biological Energy* (New York: Farrar, Strauss and Giroux, 1973).

[54] See more about how we use reframing and our *Going To The Core* exercise in Reflection 15: Only the Shadow Knows, under the subhead *Using the Shadow as a Resource*.

[55] Peter M. Senge, *The Fifth Discipline*, (New York: Currency Doubleday, 2006), 139-44.

vision of how we'd like our life to be and how we experience our current reality, there is a lot of energy held as tension in the dynamic of that gap. We can respond to this gap with either emotional tension or creative tension. We tend to experience the former as stressful and the latter as a source of tremendous inspiration and motivation to action.

How do we make the move from emotional tension to creative tension? By making a plan and developing step-by-step actions that address the situation we can accomplish the transformation from one to the other. Depending on the situation, our plan of action may be a note to our self to, say, listen more and speak less, or it may be a more complex process involving input from multiple stakeholders.

Our emotions provide us with important information regarding energy and other blocks in the body: the body holds the tension, and the emotional tension manifests in tandem as a cover over the physical holding. To release tension and other energy blocks in the body, we often need to release the emotions first, and to do this, we must get past the stories, excuses, and distractions that the mind creates to protect and hide from the hurt and trauma itself.

One tactic we may use to hide is to pretend (and even believe) that there is no trauma. Often, we can't remember it because the emotions are acting as a layer of protection, blocking out the hurt and obfuscating the facts. So, we pay attention to the emotions, rather than the words or ideas. For instance, if Cheng feels hurt by Marguerite, he may feel inclined to recount all the reasons and stories of how she hurt him. The hurt he feels now is an elaboration of previous hurts, often from early childhood,[56] that we each carry and that get triggered whenever we feel hurt later in life. The stories we tell now actually obscure the earlier hurts which are the core of our current pain. If Cheng gets in touch with just his emotions here and now (and if we support him in this as friends bolstering his unfoldment), he has a better chance of unlocking the stored patterns of hurt. Once the emotion is released, then the body naturally begins to let go of the energy

---

[56] See more on this in Reflection 3, under The Four Deep Ego Fears.

blocks it has been holding to store that emotion. Our role is to bring intention to the process.

Our first and biggest trauma as an ego is the feeling of separation, of the vulnerability of aloneness. We first experience this around the age of two when we realize that mother and I are two, not one. Moreover, it becomes apparent to each of us as two-year-olds that mother is not under my control, and therefore, I experience my basic defenselessness with, naturally, some terror and even anger: hence the Terrible Twos.[57]

We've all had this experience, and thus, we've all been traumatized. We can also be sure that we will all experience some kind of trauma again in our lives. The degree and intensity may vary, but what's important to note is that the core issue with any trauma is the hurt of separation and the shock it brings. These are the basic feelings that cause us to shut down in an attempt at self-protection. Our journey to a more joyful life and relationships begins when we realize that this strategy simply doesn't work.

FREEDOM FROM TRAUMA

There are two main paths we can walk to arrive at an ongoing state of spiritual liberation and freedom from trauma: therapy and meditation. We believe that we need to embrace both of these paths together to make true breakthroughs to spiritual liberation.

While they can be helpful under some circumstances, we don't consider psychotropic drugs (i.e., hallucinogens) a path to effectively healing trauma in and of themselves. Although we've found that they can liberate the ego to some degree, they cannot liberate the organism, the body. Nor do we include forms of physical exercise. Though physical exercise is essential for holistic health and can release tension, it cannot release the *sources* of tension on its own.

Therapy, including body-based therapies, can reveal and even help de-armor the defenses around old trauma, which is of

---

[57] See Reflection 14: Spiritual Energy Traders for more on this important topic of ego formation in our earliest years.

enormous significance. However, most therapy can only go as deep as ego awareness goes because most therapy takes place in the context of the ego's understanding. This can help free some of the trauma but not all of it. Some somatic therapies or dream work can work in realms where the ego is not in charge, but getting to the root of the traumas entails reaching back to the hurt that took place before we were two years old, before the ego was formed.

And *full* liberation requires going past the ego into spacious emptiness, the realm of the spiritually awakened. This involves the path of meditative practice. One of the things this path explores is what took place before our ego coalesced. This is one of the things that's meant by the phrase, "transcending ego." When we understand what happened to our being before our ego was in place, and how our ego has been shaped, then we have more choices about how our ego can function optimally in our daily life. In other words, our ego doesn't have to automatically interpret and react to every situation from its own limited vantage point, which is what non-transcending egos tend to do.

In our experience, to gain greater freedom from an overactive ego (often called "ego-clinging" in Buddhist philosophy) and from the associated trauma, a combination of both therapy and meditation provides us with the most tools and opportunities. Therapy helps us to dismantle and clear out old conditioned patterns that don't serve us well anymore. Meanwhile, the meditative path helps build a healthy, vibrant, and resilient being from the ground up. By "healthy," we mean one whose natural manifestation is loving-kindness and compassion and is naturally interested in the well-being of the whole of life.

Our teacher Namgyal Rinpoche posed that the ego typically experiences a few traumas in a lifetime and that each trauma typically gets triggered again three to four times—resulting in shock waves stemming from the original trauma—before the trauma is finally and naturally released. Each subsequent wave is a little less turbulent than the previous one, like ripples from a rock dropped in a pond, gradually dissipating altogether.

As a result, protecting against hurt and thus shutting down

one's life force in some way or another only serves to maintain the trauma and continues to reflect and manifest as feelings of separateness. It's why so many of us feel lonely, sometimes even in a crowded room full of people we call friends. The original separation trauma related to our mother is a leitmotif held in our body, emotions, and thoughts, and can be triggered at any time.

For example, if my mother was not a very physically affectionate person, and I now have a partner who is also not very physically affectionate, every time I feel unloved by my partner's infrequent hugs, caresses, or other kinds of touch, it's a trigger for feelings from infancy. That is, regarding this phenomenon of response to a lack of physical affection, I'm really in a (usually unconscious) relationship with my mother. My partner, in a sense, isn't even there.

The irony—or we could say karma—is that I have been attracted to a partner or partners who have the conditioning to not be very physically affectionate. My partner helps me to see what's required to learn to recognize my needs and figure out how to have them met. It may be good communication and mutual support with my partner or it may be learning to let it go.

Therapy and meditation practice help us learn to let go of the habitual patterns that have been laid down over a lifetime in response to the trauma. However, only the transcending state can overcome this feeling of separation completely because it gives us the strength to let go of the last bastion of our trauma: ego clinging.

We can think of our being as a series of concentric circles. In the outer rings are protective patterns, casual ones, becoming more defensive as the circles get closer to the vulnerable core of our being. At the center is our ego, the inner fortress, most heavily guarded when under threat. Through therapy, meditation, and other spiritual practices we describe in this book, we realize that the ego doesn't need protecting after all because it's merely a concept we've built to protect against trauma.

We could call the release of this protection the transcendence of ego clinging. Buddhist traditions refer to the experience as spiritual awakening, a.k.a. recognizing the non-self, or a lack of a permanent, inherent self. Instead, we clearly perceive that we are an amalgamation of patterns that have been conditioned by our environments, experiences, and choices. The accompanying mind-state and heart-state of non-clinging awareness is always clear, radiant, blissful, vibrant—and empty.

"Empty" is the best English translation for the Sanskrit word *sunyata*. This is not the negative emotional emptiness that causes us to feel things like "my life is meaningless," which is a state that's rooted in ego identification. (It's about *my* life and therefore *me*.) Instead, emptiness here refers to a full, joyous, spacious state of potential and possibility. It's a state that's available to all of us at any given time; all we have to do is choose it.

If emptiness is available all the time, then why do we hurt? We hurt because we feel alone, isolated, and insecure. This makes perfect sense: as egos, we *are* alone, isolated, and insecure. We need to get past the ego to get past the hurt.

There are many reasons to feel motivated about this. For one thing, when we feel hurt, we act badly toward ourselves and others. Similarly, if someone does us wrong, it's because they feel hurt. While retribution may seem just and necessary, ultimately, it only spreads and deepens the hurt. No amount of vengeance makes us feel good. As the saying goes, an eye for an eye only ends up making the whole world blind.

MOVING BEYOND PAIN

To move past ego-bound trauma, we need to see our own reaction patterns and how we react when the hurt is triggered. These patterns are not so easy to observe, since by its very nature the ego protects itself. One way it does this is by keeping these patterns obscured. The ego is built on hurt, primarily the trauma of separation from mother. However, a tremendously powerful and amazing characteristic of the ego is that it can come to know its own pain. What's more, it can also do something about it.

How does this work? We know that the ego is able to cultivate self-awareness. It's also worth noting that we can be aware—for example of our surroundings—but not be self-aware. The reverse is also true, so cultivating both awareness and self-awareness is important. Self-awareness offers us vast power because it allows us to know we are separate, and also empowers us to transcend this separateness to experience unity. This feeling of unity is what we call "transcendent awareness."

We can use the metaphor of looking into a mirror. We need a mirror—something separate from our self—to see our own face. Our ego is akin to our face, and the mirror is like awareness; the image in the mirror is self-awareness dawning. The ego has the ability hold up a mirror to itself, to become self-aware.

Once we know we are separate—we know that there is a face, and it is separate from the mirror—we can consciously choose to override the separation and choose to see the unity instead. We can see the image, the face, and the mirror as one entity while still maintaining the ability to perceive the component parts. We have the power to see what we choose.

This is transcendent awareness. As far as we know, no other living creature has both self-awareness and the power to transcend that separate self to experience unity.[58]

---

[58] A number of animals besides humans—including great apes, Asian elephants, dolphins, rhesus macaques, and, curiously, European magpies—have demonstrated self-awareness through the mirror test which continues to evolve to broaden human ideas about self-awareness," according to Virginia Morell, "Monkeys master a key sign of self-awareness: recognizing their reflections," *Science*, Feb. 13, 2017, http://www.sciencemag.org/news/2017/02/monkeys-master-key-sign-self-awareness-recognizing-their-reflection.

However the jury is out on animals' capacity for spiritual transcendence as we don't yet have any data on their interior life. That said, it is an intriguing subject worthy of ongoing investigation, and we are very interested in the consciousness of the animals in our lives, and in supporting one another to explore the nature of consciousness.

Meanwhile classic Buddhist texts describe the six realms of existence—the god realm, jealous god realm, human realm, animal realm, hungry ghost realm, and hell realm—and maintain that spiritual awakening is only possible in the human realm.

With self-awareness, with knowledge, we come to know the edges that arise out of separateness. We can only perceive something if we are able to stand apart from it to apprehend it: thus, knowledge requires a divide. Separation is both the innate state of the ego and one of its Four Deep Ego Fears.[59] The wonderful thing is that, once we resolve the ego fears by letting go of them, this separation is precisely what drives us to the Holy Grail of a human lifetime: spiritual awakening. The power of the fears of the ego comes from trying to ignore or avoid them; only by transcending the fears can we render them powerless.

Hurt is a reaction; love is a decision. Hurt brings paralysis or stuckness, while love offers us greater freedom.

One of the meanings of the Sanskrit word *karma* is *action*, referring to the law of cause and effect. The Sanskrit word *cetana* means *decision*. Buddhist philosophy holds that karma is cetana; actions are based on decisions, as is our karma. If we are just reacting, going in the same flow with the hurt, then we will only get more of the same hurtful karma we've had so far. By choosing love, we make a decision that leads to good actions, good happenings, and good karma.

As mentioned, we each have lots of good reasons to feel hurt, starting with that original separation anxiety, usually related to recognizing our separateness from our mother in our first years. That's an extremely painful experience. More good reasons to feel hurt pile up in our life as our individual ego bumps and jostles with other egos. Egos are driven to self-preservation and self-promotion, basically to protect themselves. Fortunately, egos are also driven to wake up!

If we know that our own suffering is an unavoidable part of life—this is the Buddha's First Ennobling Truth, after all: "Life

---

[59] We go into the Four Deep Ego Fears in more detail in Reflection 3: If You Want The Present You Have To Open The Box. Briefly, they are: abandonment (separation), annihilation, insanity, and being evil (a.k.a. being a bad person or doing bad things).

is struggle"[60]—we soon realize that everyone is in the same boat. We then see that our ability to transcend *our* personal suffering depends on us helping others transcend *their* suffering. Since we're all in the same boat, the boat only serves its purpose if we're all pulling in the same direction. Otherwise, it goes in circles and eventually tips or sinks. This is the wellspring of the spiritual life—raising up others and ourselves to a better way of being.

The origins of the word *spirit*[61] include "animating or vital principle" and "breath," so it has a feeling of vivacity and flow. Suffering is more like stagnation. In this sense, the self-interested ego is a form of dullness trying to maintain a protective status quo to avoid more hurt.

Another effective way to foster the transcendence of trauma or other hurt is to put things in perspective. We are not alone in our pain. We live and work and relate to others continually, and everyone is struggling with the same dilemma: do I choose to open up to love or to protect myself from further hurt? Our experience, in fact, co-arises with others' experience; we need others to find our place in this world, and they need us for the same reason. In other words, we're all interdependent.

So, when we make the decision to choose love over suffering, we help ourselves as well as others. This does not make us naïve or a Pollyanna. Letting go of hurt also empowers us to move into a better, more functional, and ultimately more successful state of being. When we let go of the trauma, and with it, ego clinging, we don't lose intelligence, memory, the ability to make a good living, relate to other people, or anything else. In fact, we gain. We gain the ability to meet the reality of any situation and respond accordingly. We also gain the heart of loving-kindness

---

[60] The second is that this struggle has a cause: craving. Thirdly, the struggle has an end. Fourthly, the end of struggle lies in the Eightfold Ennobling Path.

[61] According to https://www.etymonline.com/word/spirit: "mid-13c., 'animating or vital principle in man and animals,' from Anglo-French *spirit*, Old French *espirit* 'spirit, soul' (12c., Modern French *esprit*) and directly from Latin spiritus 'a breathing (respiration, and of the wind), breath.'"

and the mind of compassion. These are qualities of inestimable value, to ourselves as well as every being on the planet.

Take the case of an adult who was sexually abused as a child; we'll call her Maxine. Through much courage, therapy, diligent spiritual practices, and other inner work, Maxine has processed the pain of non-support and lack of trust, as well as the rage stemming from her history. Through cultivating non-clinging and loving-kindness (toward herself and others) she's found release, what we call spiritual liberation.

Now, when Maxine encounters sexuality in her own life, and even abuse in others' lives, she can meet these events as a compassionate supporter and empowerer, rather than as a reactive victim. She's turned her suffering into a source of hope and strength for herself and others.

We must be clear though: the pain and sadness Maxine experienced—that each of us has experienced—will never go away. We could say that our protected hearts of stone only grow softer from the rain of millions of tears. Each of us can find a place that transcends our hurt and sorrow and from where we can live and engage in beautiful ways. From this space, we're not only unhindered by our past experiences, but wiser and more compassionate due to our journey to overcome them.

LOVE VS. MISERY: LOVE WINS

Our strength comes from confidence, and confidence is built on experience. We need to ensure that our confidence is growing in healthy ways, not eroding. If our experience says the world is a hard and difficult place and that we are in decline, then we adopt that perspective, that belief, and it will determine how we feel, think, and act. The messages we get from those around us also influence what we believe. Alas, modern media feeds us unlimited examples of difficulties and horror. There is a kind of unholy glee, an almost compulsive sado-masochism in narrating how terrible everything is.

There are many reasons for this, and they are all rooted in the Four Ego Fears. What we fear draws us as well as repels us. We're drawn to death and destruction in part because we know we must die and thereby be "destroyed." Significantly, we're also drawn to these things because we instinctively know that if we face our fears, we can transcend them. However, we have to consciously choose to make the considerable effort to do this. Otherwise, we are likely to stay in a limbo of ongoing anxiety.

Since we all read, watch, and repeat the same fearful messages to each other, it can build a group ethic of impending disaster. Though there are wonderful things happening every hour of every day, 24-hour news channels narrate a globe in constant crisis; is it any wonder that anxiety and depression are so widespread? We are being inured to misery and disaster as the norm, rather than being educated about it being a choice. Victor Frankl contributed enormously to our understanding of this when shared how he survived the holocaust by consciously choosing to find meaning in the experience. Similarly, while his country, culture, and people have endured more than a half century of persecution by the Chinese, the Dalai Lama has dedicated his life to promoting peace.

As these examples demonstrate, what good news it is for us that loving, buoyant states are far more powerful than negative ones. A good state can blow a bad state right out of the water, so to speak, or perhaps we could say that a good state liberates innumerable negative states. When we are in a good state, we are open, kind, generous, friendly, humorous, and fun to be with. Other people are drawn to us like bees to nectar. Not only do we feel better, but people around us do too. We also think better and interact with others in more positive ways. Additionally, we're more productive and efficient in our work.

In Sanskrit, *saddha* means both *faith* and *confidence*. By making better decisions than choosing to be hurt—in other words, by choosing love—we build the faith and confidence that are the bedrock of our ability to step beyond the ego to spiritual liberation. Hallelujah.

COST-BENEFIT ANALYSES OF EGO PROTECTION

One way of looking at how the ego protects itself is to use the economic model of cost-benefit analyses. Since finances are the de facto measuring system worldwide, why not try looking at the ego through this lens? We'll look at some of the internalized beliefs that the ego uses to try to protect itself from potential hurt and at the potential costs and benefits. We're adding a third element in addition to cost and benefit that we'll call resolution. This is one way to reframe the dialogue, making sense of the natural functions ego protection is trying to serve, while supporting the transformation of it all into loving-kindness and compassion.

Protective Belief #1: *I need to look out for myself.*

Potential Benefits: A sense of security that comes from feeling in control. If we believe that everyone is in it for themselves, it follows that the only way to get taken care of is to take care of myself. If we believe we're alone, it also follows that we need to protect ourselves against others, who are also protecting themselves.

Potential Costs: Most of our defenses, over time, become habits. We live from habits, and habits are by definition unconscious. Since our defenses are habits, we are therefore mostly unconscious when we're being defensive. Thus, we are often unduly protective.

Furthermore, if we feel alone and unsupported, with the need to be wary and defensive, we're not in a very good state. Since many, if not most, others are in a similar state, there's a status quo of substandard states that makes it challenging to notice as unhealthy; it's just the norm. It also means we are somehow not recognizing all the kind and altruistic deeds that are constantly occurring around us. A murder may make the news but less common are stories about when someone saves another's life, an event worth celebrating that happens regularly.

Resolution: From a Buddhist perspective, the idea of an inherent, independent self is an illusion. Instead, each of us is an ever-changing collection of forms, sensations, feelings, thoughts, and consciousness. Rather than a single self we are more like an aware compost heap of selves! The illusory self feels alone and independent and believes itself to be permanent. This illusory self is also the origin of our self-protective position: we try to protect something that isn't really there.

When we say the self is an illusion, that doesn't mean it doesn't exist, but that it doesn't exist the way we think it does. In this sense, the illusion is that the ego is a raison d'être or endgame. Contrary to our default modus operandi, our ego functions better as a servant than as a master. It is meant to serve transcendence, divine consciousness, or cosmic consciousness, if you will. When the ego's in charge, it's selfish and insecure.

The real raison d'être of being human is spiritual transcendence; it's the ego's job to accept this challenge and undertake its journey to liberation. In this way, the ego is a tool we can use for spiritual awakening. And, the ego comes through this transformation perfectly okay, even relieved that it is no longer burdened by its former selfishness and insecurity. We'll explain.

Evolution created the ego, the sense of self, as a mechanism for making us more intelligent, thus equipping us with greater survival capabilities. The ego is seated in the neocortex and its purpose is higher-order (i.e., cerebral) functioning. This has led to humans' ability to use tools, invent computers, and get us off planet, at least a little. Two approaches the ego uses are analysis and questioning. Questions are the building blocks of discovery: every question makes us a little smarter and more aware.

Being more aware helps us survive and thrive: it allows us to better evade predators and take advantage of opportunities. Being *self*-aware is the next step: self-awareness allows us to override our survival instincts, like fight or flight, when they're unnecessary. It also allows us to choose instead higher qualities, such as empathy, which help us survive as a species and as a planet.

Greater awareness can then also take us to the next step on the evolutionary ladder, namely, the transcendent self-awareness we introduced earlier in this reflection, the awareness of unity.[62]

Most of us spend much of our lives chasing ecstasy and euphoria. Why not? They feel good. Sunsets, lovers, mind-altering or state-altering substances, runner's high, and so on are all short-lived substitutes that bring some baggage with them. These rely on objects, which are impermanent and therefore offer fleeting good feelings at best. What's more, the resulting states, however nice they may feel in the moment, are meager stand-ins for radiant, sublime states that are sustainable precisely because they are *not* tied to objects. This is abiding peace, also known as emptiness or spaciousness.

When we realize the state of transcending self-awareness, we find that it includes ecstasy and euphoria and is more than just these things. It is like a hot-air balloon, where the balloon itself is the ecstasy and the euphoria, and the air inside consists of clarity and spaciousness. The act of transcending is accessing the spaciousness.

Transcendence doesn't mean we get rid of the ego but that it is put into perspective. We begin to use the ego as a tool rather than as the determiner of our reality. When we become alert and awake to our own (and others') defenses, we can use those defenses when they're helpful, rather than allowing them to blindly lead us in unhealthy and unnecessary ways. The misery of our ego is to use these defenses when they don't really serve a wholesome purpose.

For example, we may tense up psychologically and therefore also physically during a bumpy airplane ride. Since there is nothing we can do about the air turbulence, and tensing up makes us feel worse, breathing and relaxing is a better strategy. In a similar way, if we hear a tone of voice that reminds us of our father when he was angry, we may respond defensively and shut off. The person speaking isn't our father, however, and in this case, their tone of voice may be indicating a different form of energy, such as eagerness.

---

[62] Under the subhead, *Moving Beyond Pain.*

In these ways, we can use our awareness to discern our situation, potential responses, and their results, and thereby overcome our ego-based reactions. This helps us move away from unwanted and unnecessary conflict and into creating a more wholesome future that benefits us and others, too.

Protective Belief #2: *If I let myself be vulnerable I'll be hurt or taken advantage of.*

Potential Benefit: By keeping others at a safe emotional distance, we can ensure against being wronged or harmed by them.

Potential Costs: By closing ourselves off, we miss out on learning what true strength is. When we see that another person's hurtful acts are most often unintended—because, remember, they are typically unconscious—and that these stem from their own hurt, we can stop taking it personally. Thus, we also stop feeling that we're being taken advantage of.

On deeper reflection, we may realize that we unintentionally hurt those around us too. For instance, we can all recall occasions when we felt misunderstood and justified in reacting strongly, even harshly. And in some cases, we found out later that we'd misinterpreted the other person's intentions and that they actually meant well.

The truth is, we can only let go of hurt by acknowledging our own vulnerability as well as that of others.

Hurt is the emotion of feeling somehow rejected, and rejection makes us feel vulnerable. If we can rest in the center of the feeling of rejection and let go there, we always have the ability to come to a place of clarity, peace, and compassionate bliss. From here, the hurt can be released. We work with this principle quite intentionally using an exercise we call *Going to the Core*.[63] This exercise stems from the understanding that in the core of our being

---

[63] For details about this exercise see Reflection 15: Only the Shadow Knows, under the subhead, *Using the Shadow as a Resource*.

there is emptiness and, therefore, freedom. From this place, we can be in a far better state and meet others from that place as well.

Resolution: Openness does not have to be weak. In fact, consciously chosen openness is a quality of tremendous strength.

Our egos have been conditioned to act from instinct and habituated reactions, particularly to hurt. Instinct is not bad in itself; it's just a built-in response. If a cat lashes out at you for stepping on its tail, you may get scratched, but your feelings don't get hurt since you understand the cat is just acting from instinct. However, by transcending our own ego's instincts to strike out, while perceiving the instinctual reactions of others, we can remain in a clear and kind state of strength, even when wounds befall us.

Protective Belief #3: *I might be abandoned.*

Potential Benefits: Thinking that abandonment is possible, likely, or even a foregone conclusion, we often try to inure ourselves to it now. This lets us think that self-protection is both normal and healthy and that it actually works. It provides us with some feeling of security.

Potential Costs: On one hand, thinking you will be abandoned can be a self-fulfilling prophecy. On the other, Buddhist philosophy holds that, indeed, everything about existence is impermanent[64] and constantly changing. Nothing remains the same for even an instant. In that sense, everything we try to hold onto is in a constant state of slipping between our fingers.

So, we have two choices: either to take my ball and go home or jump in and enjoy the game while it lasts. When we choose the former, we ensure loneliness, isolation, and probably bitterness. Meanwhile, the latter creates joy, congeniality, fond memories, and

---

[64] In Buddhist philosophy, impermanence is known as one of the Three Marks of Existence. The other two are the unsatisfactory nature of samsara and the lack of a single, independent, inherent self.

the appreciation of the preciousness of each unique moment. We are constantly choosing one or the other; which one is up to us.

Resolution: Suffering doesn't come from the pain of loss; rather it's the result of trying to cling to something, whether we've lost it, or we still have it and are afraid of losing it. We may have conditioned mental, emotional, and psychological habits of overly focusing on what has been lost. The good news is that we can train ourselves to focus instead on celebrating what we have and on new beginnings and adventures. Through this training, we can learn to let go and be let go of without experiencing it as abandonment, without having to suffer about it.

While grief is a normal human response to loss and has its rightful place in a healthy emotional repertoire, it can also contain elements of clinging to the past. When we let go of clinging, we can still love those who have passed through our lives or this world, without suffering terribly about being left behind. In Buddhist philosophy, there is an expression: "There is suffering, but no one suffering." The idea is that, while the ego or self may suffer, there is another part of us that can remain calm, clear, and peaceful. While one part of us may feel sorrow, another deeper part of us can feel immensely grateful for all the positive experiences we shared during our time together and can look forward to sharing these with others.

If we spend most of our lives ignoring impermanence (including death), when we inevitably experience it, we find ourselves ill-prepared for how to respond healthfully. But when we learn to live with death and impermanence as essential aspects of life, we begin to appreciate the opportunities they provide.

For instance, when one thing ends, something else always begins. So rather than clinging to what is ending, we have the opportunity to step into something that is arising or being born. Clinging to what is passing invariably leads to suffering while stepping into what's emerging speaks to growth, potential, and creativity. As Zen teachings suggest, if we see ourselves as already dead or dying, we can really live. That is, if you see this moment as passing away or dying, it inspires us to appreciate the aliveness of the next moment with joy.

Buddhist philosophy holds, "Death is a temporary end to a temporary phenomenon."[65]

Protective Belief #4: *I have trust issues; people need to earn my trust.*

Potential Benefit: If you feel as though everyone you've trusted has turned out to be flawed and that has led to you getting hurt, you might feel that relating with more reserve can prevent it from happening again.

Potential Costs: Defensive behaviors have the unfortunate tendency to spill over into situations where they are not needed or appropriate. In protecting against hurt, we often unwittingly limit our capacity to love. This is bad news for many reasons. Scientific studies have shown that love is good for our health and well-being, and, moreover, that feeling isolated is bad for it.[66] Practicing discernment of character and situations is an important skill, but habitually relating defensively hurts us more consistently and enduringly than the occasional hurt caused by betrayed trust.

Think of a beleaguered air stewardess who tells us to take our seats in an abrupt tone; we may experience her tone as unnecessary, even somewhat hurtful. A short while later she comes and pleasantly offers us a beverage. Due to our prior experience, we may anticipate more hurt: we may have made up our minds that she's an unpleasant person or in a bad mood.

Now, our hurt feelings have been triggered based on the past even though she's done nothing hurtful in the present, and to the contrary, is being congenial. Based on our earlier experience, we may even be triggered to react and attempt to preempt further

---

[65] Ven. Narada Mahathera, *Buddha and His Teachings* (Somerville: Wisdom Publications, 1988), 233.

[66] Rose Palazzolo, *Studies: Love Is Good for Your Heart*, ABCnews.com, May 21, 2017, http://abcnews.go.com/Health/story?id=117439&page=1.

pain by being rude to her first. This simple example shows how karma (cause and effect) is often perpetuated.

Moreover, we glimpse here the Buddhist concept of *non-duality*, that there is really no difference between self and other, subject and object. As we see, there's no end to feeling hurt by her, hurting her back, and it would be very human for her to then want to be rude back to us, and around and around we go. Fortunately, there's also no end to the cycle if we substitute kindness and compassion instead of hurt.

Resolution: By their nature, egos try to maximize happiness and minimize unhappiness. So, when two egos meet, it's inevitable that the pursuit of happiness *for me* will be jeopardized or have competition.

Egos also often attach a feeling of happiness to getting what we want, and the "what" is often an object. Even happiness is an object, in that it's a concept or a feeling. On closer examination, however, we realize that happiness is not an end goal in itself, nor is it tied to any object, whether thing, concept, or feeling. Happiness is one of the many side benefits of a good state.[67] Any object that comes along with the good state—including happiness—is just an accessory. Self-protection cannot produce a good state, but skillful receptivity and openness can.

Protective Belief #5: *Feelings are messy: it's easier to just not deal with them.*

Potential Benefits: Not feeling seems easier than feeling. You can just get on with things and not spend all that time sorting through endless interpersonal issues.

Potential Costs: Nice try. We may think that we're not feeling, but "not feeling" is a type of feeling, and not a pleasant one. Keeping

---

[67] We go more deeply into the characteristics of a good state in Reflection 3: If You Want the Present You Have to Open the Box.

walls up to contain or shut down feelings costs us at every level: physically, emotionally, and even mentally. We know that when energy and breath flow evenly (such as when practicing tai chi or yoga), we are more relaxed and feel peaceful. By comparison, when we put up defensive walls with our energy—imagine some time when your partner corrected you in a way you felt was inappropriate—our breath shortens, muscles tighten, and our emotions get steely or erupt, causing our thinking to become fuzzy. We may even jump to conclusions, such as feeling that our partner doesn't really love us.

Being in touch with emotions and learning to be more and more skillful with working with them is what actually sharpens our acuity and makes us more effective at work and in our interpersonal life.[68]

Resolution: Feeling is one of the avenues through which we learn to transcend the ego structure. Because an ego-oriented life can be painful, painful feelings motivate us to look for a solution. Not feeling doesn't work since it is a type of feeling in itself. What's more, feeling is an essential part of being human, so do we really want to eliminate that richness from our life? It's not possible to avoid painful feelings, but we can learn to transcend them by choosing how we respond. Buddhist philosophy suggests choosing to respond with loving-kindness and compassion.

The standard repertoire of ego-based feelings makes us human. The transcendental move to wider, more encompassing, and less self-centered feelings makes us more divine.[69] Interestingly, this does not cause us to lose touch with pleasant human feelings; it

---

[68] Tomas Chamorro-Premuzic and Michael Sanger, *How to Boost Your (and Others') Emotional Intelligence, Harvard Business Review* online, Jan. 9, 2017, https://hbr.org/2017/01/how-to-boost-your-and-others-emotional-intelligence.

[69] Buddhist philosophy holds that a fully awakened being feels just four feelings known as The Divine Abidings that we mentioned in Reflection 2: loving-kindness, compassion, empathetic joy, and equanimity. All other emotions are nuances of these four or their opposites. It's worth noting that even with just four feelings, the entire range of human experience is still enjoyed in all its richness.

just raises them to a new level of integrity while decreasing the negative ones with patience and forgiveness.

The hallmarks of human consciousness are spacious clarity and light. Consciousness is all-pervading and ever-present. It manifests in a myriad of forms, including blissful emptiness. Only self-aware beings (like humans) can recognize this transcendental experience for what it is. Different cultures have called it different things, such as God, universal love, Christ Consciousness, spiritual awakening, and so on. Self-protection renders contact with this experience impossible.

Choosing again and again to love, to be compassionate, kind, empathic, to forgive and understand raises us above the ego's selfish needs. It opens our hearts and minds to the infinite while allowing us to enjoy the relative—even as it sometimes tears at us and causes us to weep.

After all, the liberation is in the letting go!

PART 2

RIDING THE DRAGON

Spiritual Awakening in Modern Daily Life

REFLECTION 5

KARMA YOGA:
THE PATH OF WORK

How We Got Here

I t seems fairly clear that most of us busy, modern people aren't really geared toward being still and contemplating. This is particularly true in the West where we don't have a millennium or more of history with sitting meditation. But we have good news for people who feel challenged around having a regular meditation practice: there are alternatives! We propose that the path of spiritual awakening for modern beings may well be through action.

Awakening through action, or *Karma Yoga,* is a time-honored, if little-known path. Traditionally, a monk who had newly arrived at a Tibetan monastery would spend two years rotating through various departments one at a time: he would clean the monastery, work in the garden, support in the kitchen, help prepare for rituals, meditate, assist with sacred arts (i.e., ritualistic paintings or sculpture), order and receive provisions, attend to the monastery's financial management, and so on.

At the end of two years, he'd have a good overview of the value of each role, and a long term one would be chosen for him according to talent and inclination. Note that meditation is one of numerous roles. Not everyone in a monastery is a professional meditator! And when they are, it's a full-time responsibility that supports everyone, just as a cook or painter or accountant's duties do.

It has probably always been similar in European monasteries, which likewise require considerable effort, care, and funds to keep operating. Besides tending to the spiritual needs of the community, over the centuries, European monks and nuns have made medicine and cordials, grown and crafted foods like honey and cheese, and have been scholars and publishers. When done well, these products and services were enhanced with the power of prayers that formed the soundtrack during their creation. So, if you don't feel cut out to be a champion meditator, there are other means that countless monastics have used as their practice fruitfully over the centuries.

Let's back up and look at *Karma Yoga* again. Hinduism traditionally embraces numerous kinds of yoga. We're probably all familiar with the physical training path, Hatha Yoga, but there are other kinds of yoga practice as well. There's a path of devotional practice called Bhakti Yoga, perhaps most easily identified by images of Thais or Indians (for example) offering flowers and incense at their local temple. For devotees, this is a practice they may undertake several times daily, rain or shine. Jnana Yoga is a more scholastic practice, developing understanding through the mind, usually through study and reflection on sacred teachings. Karma Yoga is sometimes called the path of work or service and entails serving a teacher or community as a vehicle for spiritual unfoldment.

Most of us understand the Sanskrit word *karma* as meaning *cause and effect*. Literally, it translates to *activity* or *work*; the consequences of our activity are also implied. As previously mentioned, yoga literally means yoke or harness. With Karma Yoga, we harness our self to the path of our work, our vocation, and dedicate the effects or results of our work to the benefit of all beings. This is a very pragmatic path: since we spend so many hours of the day working, integrating this with our spiritual practice feeds several birds with one hand.

When work is not an integrated part of our spiritual practice, it can often be just about making a good income, making ends meet, or attaining status or a particular identity (professional, successful, an artist, etc.). With Karma Yoga, part of the practice is to train ourselves to learn to let go of attachment to results and any related identity and the tendency toward self-interest. For example, when we undertake a project, we naturally hope it will succeed and dedicate our energies toward that. Karma Yoga supports us to reflect more deeply on our work, perhaps discovering that part of us strives for success so that we get praise, love, or a promotion. This is very human, but has inherent problems: if the project doesn't succeed—which is often not entirely under our control—do we lose self-esteem? Feel unloved?

As part of our ongoing spiritual practice, we learn to transform personal motivation into benefitting all beings instead. With self-interest out of the way, our ability to hold this as our aim usually results in the project working out better—and feeling much better, too.

IN THE LAND OF TWO THOUSAND TEMPLES

Karma Yoga may manifest as a multi-million-dollar project, or it may be something more mundane, such as doing the dishes or cleaning bathrooms. This latter kind of practice of doing service had some cachet to it when we lived in Kyoto, Japan, in the 2000s. Doug was invited by some meditation practitioners to teach in Kyoto in 1998, and we met when I (Catherine)—already living in Kyoto for close to a decade—attended one of Doug's classes. Home to more than 2,000 Buddhist temples, the city and culture of Kyoto are veritably steeped in Buddhism like a cup of very fine green tea. There, doing service for a *sensei*, a teacher of a respected tradition like Buddhism, is considered an extremely valuable opportunity.

How so? For one, when we serve a wise being, we get to spend more time in their presence observing how they conduct themselves in various situations. We have daily opportunities to learn from them and perhaps ask questions to clarify. It's a kind of internship in becoming more aware through osmosis and emulation. Over time, with practice, we undertake to grow into at least some of their realization, cultivating qualities we admire in them, such as inner peace, a heart of compassion, and wisdom.

Second, many wisdom traditions embrace a concept that Buddhist thought calls generating merit. This means that by serving someone who is working for the benefit of all beings, we accumulate a wellspring of goodness. Merit could be considered something like a forcefield of good mind states and acts that we tend to so that it grows and grows, benefiting everyone and everything. This field of merit has been called The Blessed Buddha Field or The Pureland. We can then live our lives surrounded by an ever-expanding merit field, and salubrious things are sure to follow for any being who passes through that field.

When Doug came to teach a small community of practitioners (mostly expats) in Kyoto, our practice was supported by this long-standing traditional culture. Usually, if a non-Japanese person lives in Kyoto for more than a year or two, it becomes quite obvious that they have some rough edges that could use polishing. Expats in Kyoto enjoy swapping stories of the mortifying cultural faux pas we've committed over the years. We do things like accidentally eat other peoples' portions of food, wear slippers designated only for the toilet into the living room, wear our kimono the wrong way (Catherine once accidentally wore her kimono the way corpses are dressed at wakes), and so on. American culture in particular encourages breaking rules as an exhilarating expression of independence while Japanese people find such behavior inconsiderate to others. Expats who plan to stay in Kyoto for a while usually start looking for ways to cultivate greater awareness and refinement so that we don't die of embarrassment from repeatedly committing these kinds of gaffes.

There are so many ways to do this. Traditional Japanese culture abounds with meditative practices designed for people who might want to practice mindfulness off the cushion, and Kyoto in particular has been heavily influenced by centuries of Zen practices. "Dō" means "path of" or "way of," and practices like sadō (the path of tea), aikidō (the way of energy meeting), shōdō (the way of calligraphy), jūdō (the way of softness), kadō (the path of flowers), kyūdō (the way of archery), etc. are just some of the better-known options. These all involve apprenticing to a *sensei* and being trained both in the art form itself and the state of being that's required to master it.

The influence of Rinzai Zen has had a particularly strong influence in Kyoto with seven of its fourteen head temples[70] located there. Rinzai specializes in kōans, which are riddles and actions designed to shock our awareness out of habitual thinking into pure perception. As such, Rinzai history is riddled with tales of Zen teachers' shocking behavior and bewildering speech, intended to enlighten their students. Zen has helped mold traditional arts in Kyoto in many ways, and those committed to the arts tell stories of ascetic practices they've endured at their teachers' behest to develop character and hone commitment to mastery. One ceramic artist I knew told me how he kneaded clay in a workshop without heat in midwinter hour after hour and day after day, until finally his hands bled into the clay he was working. This is fairly normal for those on a committed path in Kyoto.

In Kyoto, many practitioners in our community had studied traditional Japanese arts and become familiar with this paradigm of students gladly serving their teacher and committing under challenging conditions to subdue the ego and attain mastery. So, it was relatively easy for us to extend this service to Doug Sensei, our teacher of spiritual awakening, even though he was freshly arrived from Canada. Get up early to make coffee for our

---

[70] "Head Temples," Rinzai Obaku Zen, accessed April 2, 2018, http://zen.rinnou.net/head_temples/index.html.

teacher? Sure. Clean the bathrooms after a retreat? No problem. Stay up all night meditating? I'm there.

Doug, in turn, had done years of service as part of his training under the Venerable Namgyal Rinpoche, who was also born in Canada but had trained for years in Myanmar and Thailand in the 1950s. Doug also had a strong interest in Zen, and that was his central path of teaching and practice under the tutelage of Namgyal Rinpoche.[71]

In Kyoto we lived and practiced in a small house-come-temple we called Yumedono[72] where we meditated, gave and received teachings and training, drank tea, and ate meals together. Residents and attendees varied, but Doug and I remained constant in Yumedono as various students cycled through for periods of teaching and training. Inspired by Kyoto's traditional Zen temple culture, we enthusiastically cooked, cleaned, gardened, organized meditation retreats, and otherwise served our teacher and one another.[73]

Our earnestness felt tempered on occasions when Doug Sensei, our community, and the teachings challenged us deeply, which was a lot of the time. Sometimes (mostly from Doug Sensei) this was deliberate and skillful grist for our spiritual unfoldment, and sometimes (mostly from one another) it felt unintentional, painful, and unproductive. We argued, stonewalled, cried, and pouted. But mostly, we persisted because we had the support of this Zen culture, which features a "Enlightenment or bust!" motif.

We were immersed in the Zen belief that transcending suffering helps purify our minds and hearts on the path to spiritual enlightenment. We didn't quite understand, but it helped us hang in there when training from our teacher bruised our ego

---

[71] If a being has depth realization, all of the different streams of understanding and interpretation are one in their essence.

[72] Named after Hōryūji Temple's Hall of Visions built in Nara by Prince Shōtoku Taishi, the remarkable Leonardo da Vinci-like innovator who first officially adopted Buddhism as Japan's official religion.

[73] For a very humorous introduction to this culture, we recommend the German film, *Enlightenment Guaranteed.*

or when conflicts (usually over pretty trivial matters) within our community, or *sangha*, felt like death by a thousand paper cuts.

Indeed, much of the spiritual path consists of purification; through various practices we purify our bodies, our speech, our emotions, and our minds. Cleaning our little temple in service to our teacher, community of practitioners, and teachings—known in Buddhist philosophy as the Triple Gem—became an important part of our purification practices. The idea was to clean, clean again, and clean some more, until there was nothing left to clean, as a metaphor for polishing the mirror of our hearts. Similarly, sharing tea and food with awareness and care helped us train in nurturing ourselves by nurturing each other. Organizing dharma classes and retreats also became part of our ongoing practice to sharpen our discernment.

When we weren't working as teachers, writers, and artists, we meditated together, gazed on cherry blossom petals fluttering to earth, pondered temple gardens' immaculately raked sand, and drank innumerable cups of tea. All the while, we took to heart Doug Sensei's exhortations to use whatever was taking place in the mundane world as a precious part of our path to spiritual awakening.

Our day-to-day life and practice was punctuated by several retreats a year when we received teachings and practiced many hours of meditation at a time. We organized these retreats, prepared the venues, and cooked and cleaned during retreat as part of our Karma Yoga. While some of us were more inclined toward the activity of Karma Yoga, and others toward the reflective nature of meditation, we generally found that practicing them in tandem was optimal as each one helps integrate the other.

THE WORLD IS MY CLOISTER

During this time, we also traveled together as a sangha with Doug Sensei on annual or semi-annual trips overseas. We traveled to Egypt, Mongolia, Cambodia, Ladakh, Bhutan, South Africa, and elsewhere, exploring the world's wonders together through the lens of spiritual awakening—including challenges to our ego orientation. Organizing these Dharma Trips was and is a fairly painstaking and extremely meritorious form of Karma Yoga.

Even before studying with Doug Sensei, most of us had already been taking advantage of the easy access to other countries in Asia via Japan by traveling often. Japan's robust economy at the time made it easy for expats to do this as there was a reliable supply of well-paid employment. Besides, as expats, many of us didn't have the economic responsibilities that we might have held in our home countries, such as extended families and community commitments.

Our teacher Namgyal Rinpoche, meanwhile, had traveled extensively with students over his decades of teaching. Ongoing outer exploration of this amazing world and universe we live in is the counterpart, the yang, to exploration of the innerverse we undertake on the meditation cushion, the yin. The balance between these two is fundamental to our teaching.

What's more, in terms of methodologies for personal and spiritual unfoldment, traveling is a valuable one. When in an unfamiliar environment, we're no longer bound by daily habits and the usual status quo. A new country, culture, and people displace comfort zones and standard ego defenses—the fridge, our friends, our career, the gym, etc.—so we don't have them to run to or hide behind for a false sense of security.

Travel thus provides optimal conditions for psychological and spiritual breakthroughs to take place. Essentially, our comfort zone can be easily pushed, and we thereby explore the frontiers of what it means to be me. In other words, me starts to take on new experiences and qualities, becoming less of what we thought was me and more of what we thought wasn't me. Since one of the hallmarks of spiritual awakening is seeing through the illusion of a single, inherent, permanent self, this is right on target.

For many people, international travel sounds quite appealing. For some, traveling in a group, maybe not so much, and being on a bus together and following a schedule not completely within our control, perhaps even less so. Herding fellow travelers to the next meal or sight or helping interpret or register everyone in a new hotel was compensated by the tremendous merit we were generating but no material gain. We had to be truly committed to the Triple Gem and the practice of Karma Yoga to see it through and to do it with a modicum of graciousness and functionality.

The usual stuff happens: we misplace luggage, pay too much money for something, get lost, push each other's buttons, and so on. On top of all this, receiving spontaneous and situational teaching and training designed to push our growth envelope can feel like the absolute last straw.

And then what? Then we get back on the bus, because it's leaving.

While we may be tempted to depart (or escape or flee) from the group travel and enjoy our own journey, at our own discretion, usually we can sense that there's some important growth happening. In a sense, the objective with Dharma Trips is to become entirely comfortable with feeling uncomfortable. It's an optimal petri dish for spiritual unfoldment. Ideally, we get so disoriented, annoyed, impatient, restless, and self-conscious that we just can't take it anymore. If our teacher and fellow travelers drive us bananas, the backdrop of the Taj Mahal, majestic wildlife, or the pyramids at Tikal hint to us that there is something grander, more cosmic, than our little egos at play. And then it's time to get back on the bus.

And then we let go.

REPATRIATING

Constant pushing of growth envelopes notwithstanding (or perhaps because of them), we recall those early years in Kyoto and international travel as halcyonic ones. But despite the innumerable temples around us, it was extremely challenging to find venues where we could hold regular meditation retreats. Locating suitable retreat venues and organizing and delivering the retreats thus became an important part of our karma yoga.

However, after the Japanese pseudo-spiritual[74] organization Aum Shinrikyō poisoned the Tokyo subway with sarin gas in 1995, any spiritual group without direct links to well-established Japanese ones became suspect. Standard space rental contracts—including the one for our little temple—included a clause that meeting for spiritual practices was forbidden. As the population of monks and nuns had declined over the centuries, many temples in and around Kyoto were and are chronically underused. But when we inquired about using them for teachings and retreats, after explaining what kind of tradition and practitioners we were, our queries were usually declined without explanation, or our calls were not returned.

We still found venues that we could rent for a week or two of meditation retreat—they tended to be unusual spaces not designed for meditation or events longer than a few days—but as a community, we'd make it work. These spaces were usually in disuse and needing funds. What's more, they needed more funds than we provided. One after another, they were revamped or sold with the new management or owners not envisioning us as part of their plans. Then our search would begin again.

After a decade or so, we realized we'd devoted a sizable sum to renting meditation spaces that kept disappearing out from under us, and that buying our own retreat center made more sense. We started looking around where we were, but it was challenging to find affordable properties in Japan with enough quietude for meditation retreats. Additionally, as expats, our access to financing was challenging. So, we also began looking in North America. After viewing innumerable real estate webpages, and after Doug Sensei and members of the Japan sangha visited numerous properties over three years on both sides of the U.S.-Canadian border, a small group of us finally saw a spectacular

---

[74] We call Aum Shinrikyo "pseudo-spiritual" with the understanding that no genuinely spiritual person would willfully harm other beings or direct anyone else to do so.

property in the British Columbia Rocky Mountains that somehow whispered to us, *This is it.*

The *sangha* from Japan were jubilant, and our celebrations were shared by fellow practitioners from Canada and the U.S. who were happy to welcome our presence in closer proximity. Maybe fifty people or so were keenly captured by the excitement. We finally had a place of our own to meditate, whenever we wanted, for as long as we wanted. We could inquire about local regulations and understand everything they said in response. It seemed so easy.

The land's single dwelling had been designed as a five-bedroom bed and breakfast, but was unfinished. While supplemented by a beat-up mobile home and pole barn, it was largely devoid of furniture, provisions, or plans. We envisioned a bright future: we felt inspired to model Clear Sky after the European monasteries of yore. We aspired to light up the darkness of ignorance as beacons of spiritual, cultural, and academic light, become self-sufficient through farming and healthy micro-businesses like wine and cheese, sources of support to local communities, and so on. Our first two summers were exciting if tiring seasons of working together shoulder to shoulder, contributing countless hours of Karma Yoga to generate mountains of merit and make Clear Sky the retreat center of our dreams to benefit ourselves and all beings. We meditated, attended Doug Sensei's dharma classes, cut firewood, grew food, developed programs, sewed curtains, surveyed the property, and cooked and cleaned for thirty people.

It wasn't long before it dawned on us—with a sinking feeling— that we hadn't just acquired a meditation center. We'd also somewhat unwittingly started operating a business *and* acquired a large parcel of land that needed managing. We felt chagrined and more than a little panicked that our collective clarity of minds had missed this obvious fact. It was clear that, as a community of spiritual practitioners, we were long on enthusiasm, dreams and creativity, but short on business experience, financial acumen and land management skills.

Fortunately, we had already been trained to explore beyond our notions of who we were, so we started to learn about business. How hard could it be, after all?

Our first big learning was during the peak of a busy summer, when we were full of people and activity and receiving abundant finances and other forms of generosity. We'd been awarded a grant (another amazing thing about relocating to North America) to learn about organizational development. We were on it! Together, we crunched the numbers: all these people, all these days and nights at the center, all the meals shared. We drew a bottom line, did our sums and—somehow, we were still losing money. We realized this was more complex than we anticipated. We also realized we had to dramatically change something.

Ourselves.

REFLECTION 6
KARMA YOGA: AWAKENING THROUGH ACTION

A Path for the 21st Century

As Karma Yoga is little known in the West as a spiritual practice and path, perhaps the most effective way to describe it is with a personal account demonstrating how it may be applied to contemporary lives and times.

As mentioned, we originally purchased the Clear Sky property so that we could fulfill our heart's desire: undertake longer meditation retreats, more frequently. But it emerged that to do so we also needed to successfully operate a retreat center. In other words, we'd entered a kōan-like situation: to meditate, we had to become good business people. Some of us were up for the challenge. After all, to become more than what we currently are, we have to become what we are not (yet).

Understandably, not everyone agreed that becoming more business-like was in line with our spiritual values. While our retreats and teachings were, we believed, world class, we still felt challenged to find a way forward together. Thereafter, some members of our community studied up on Business 101, fairly randomly, not knowing where to start. Standard business frameworks of selling to consumers and maximizing profit margins clashed dramatically with our culture of generosity and enlightenment. We couldn't get our heads around considering awakening meditators as customers buying a retreat unit.

We had a core group of about thirty people who'd become passionate about developing Clear Sky. Together, we faced a unique challenge: with all our pooled resources, our creativity, plus our center's 310 acres, we had the opportunity to create the center of our dreams. And we had a lot of beautiful dreams. And plans. And opinions. At least one per person. And we each wanted *my* dream to be *the* dream. Some cracks were showing in our ability to truly embody our spiritual practice.

After an initial honeymoon phase that lasted a summer or so, our ego-based positions combined with lack of experience in teamwork and execution made for a pattern of terribly long and unfruitful discussions about Clear Sky's future. These meetings strained our relationships and kept our goals in a perpetually distant future. We were awarded grants to hire consultants to help us clarify our vision and mission, for example. But we realized that, beyond attaining enlightenment, we didn't really know what we wanted to do or could do at our center all year round. Doug Sensei gave us the task of working it through, but we floundered. Arguing was almost a welcome alternative to the floundering. The disconnect between our values of loving-kindness, compassion, wisdom, and skill in means began to weigh heavily on our hearts, minds, and bodies.

Our scenario was not unique. It exemplifies the human condition, the root of all our suffering. Despite all of our meditation, our purifying cleansing of dishes and hearts, our dedication to the Path, the awareness that we weren't as realized as we thought became painfully obvious.

Our great collective aha moment turned out to be an unwelcome one: we hadn't and couldn't meditate our way to skilled collaboration, nor to a wonderful retreat center. And if we couldn't live and work together, our practice needed to deepen and broaden beyond what we thought it was about.

Maybe we did need to become businesspeople after all. Awakening ones.

In Meditators' $hadows

As we increasingly conferred about how to best adopt better business practices at our center, including revenue generation, some people lost interest.

"We're not supposed to make money; we're a non-profit," was one mental model in the air of those early years. Teams formed to study up on how to run a successful non-profit, but in Canada, many were dependent on government funding, which we were not eligible for. Others possessed robust fundraising departments, which we didn't have. Plus, we were a small community and knew that our nets could only be cast so wide. Our rural region didn't have the population or the culture to support a retreat center, particularly year-round.

In the meantime, Clear Sky continued to offer one or two-month-long meditation retreats in the winter, and a summer season combining spiritual teachings and karma yoga on the infrastructure and land, making for about six months of activity. Organizing and running this was keeping plenty of us fully engaged with Karma Yoga—on top of our day jobs—all year. For some of us, the Karma Yoga was edging out meditation retreat time.

Fortunately, the community was blessed with some extremely generous donors, deeply committed to dāna as part of their personal practice. We were, in fact, highly dependent on the tremendous altruism of a small number of individuals, without a solid backup plan in case their support ended. Inch by inch, we began to catch glimpses of the iceberg below the water's surface: the majority of us had unhealthy and unrealistic attitudes toward money. Nearly all our dream projects entailed expenditure, but few were designed to bring in revenue. Budget drafts came in with detailed expense columns but no income.

The halo we liked to think emanated from our spiritual practices had not yet illumined our views of this essentially neutral energy form. As a culture, our community felt proud to have prioritized spiritual practice over the pursuit of money as a central, orienting axiom in our lives. Together, we'd also chosen not to look at how we were vilifying or ignoring money and how it functions, hoping the universe (or somebody else) would provide. Our relationships with one another became strained over these issues. Our attitude toward finance did not herald well for Clear Sky's future.

It was our interest in grass, of all things, that alerted us to the need to make all these things sustainable, and thus become truly integrated human beings.

THE BOTTOM LINE, FOUR WAYS

I (Catherine) had worked in Japan as a journalist and editor, specializing in environmental challenges and sustainable development for clients like the United Nations. I did some research and discovered that the ecosystem in which Clear Sky is located is extremely biodiverse and endangered, and therefore precious. Though it accounts for less than one percent of British Columbia's land mass, the native grasslands ecosystem is home to more than a third of the province's endangered and at-risk species. This got our attention, and brought environmental sustainability more prominently into our conversations. Soon we were pondering sustainability in general.

At that time—the early 2000s—not everybody knew what sustainability meant. When trying to describe it, we talked about taking into consideration the health of the environment and the community, as well as finance. We knew that our spiritual awakening was our main priority. What, then, was the relationship between our spiritual path and sustainability?

Doug Sensei grasped it immediately. "Spiritual awakening is the *only* sustainable mind-state!" he declared pragmatically.

In other words, coming from a place of ego or self-centeredness is tiring and actually unpleasant—and ultimately, unprofitable—both for ourselves and others. Unawakening or unwholesome mind-states could be considered pollution of the mind's natural, radiant, awakening state. Since unwholesome mind-states manifest through our actions, the latter become defiled as well. Conversely, an awakening mind-state naturally leads to sustainable actions in the world, considering the karma of our decisions regarding the environment, people, and finances—and anything else. With this in mind, we naturally make the best choices we are aware of, to support the best possible results for everyone and everything that's involved.

In this way, Clear Sky's quadruple bottom line was born: spiritual, ecological, social, and financial sustainability. Though each person had (and has) different interpretations and commitments to each of the bottom lines, these guiding lights provided filters to help us make decisions and plans. And, mercifully, made for shorter, more productive discussions.

Our quadruple bottom line led us to start exploring the budding world of social enterprises and social ventures. Through an organization called the Social Venture Institute and its network, we discovered businesses that measured success by other metrics besides profits, in language that respected the importance of people and the planet. With tremendous relief and anticipation, we could sense our spiritual values and organizational values becoming more aligned.

As we grew into these areas, individually and as an organization, we could share the learning with others. In addition to the all-important practices of meditation, service, and therapy, we embraced cultivating our own financial maturity, beginning with prioritizing healthy revenue generation as part of our decision-making process. We connected with the local community through restoring the native ecosystem, practicing permaculture and holistic land management, growing safe and healthy food, and providing a supportive space and conditions for like-minded individuals and organizations.

Our spiritual practice was branching out to our ecosystem and personal and organizational finances, and growing roots in an expanding community. The quadruple bottom line gave our awakening a delivery system.

STYLES OF GIVING, EAST AND WEST

Relationships with the local community were decidedly positive and our business practices were becoming savvier. At the same time, our culture of undertaking everything on the basis of Karma Yoga and *dāna* (the Sanskrit word for *generosity*) was stalling. When we swapped our little temple in Kyoto for 310 acres in rural Canada, we hadn't planned how we'd scale or translate what we were doing in this new context.

We had excellent support from generous granting organizations, talented consultants, and like-minded organizations in B.C. and Canada. But when these people asked about our staff or operations, we struggled to find language for Karma Yoga and *dāna* that they could easily understand.

Soon, our organization was being described as a non-profit operating entirely with volunteers and donations. We could see people knit their brows as they puzzled over how we could possibly make this work. As the Japanese economy slowed, Wall Street crashed in 2008, and world economics shifted, members of our community wondered, too. Clearly, it was unsustainable for sangha members from Japan to fly back and forth for retreats twice a year.

Though they had similarities, we felt Karma Yoga and volunteerism were quite distinct, as were *dāna* and donations. To us, the English words didn't capture that an act of generosity or contribution of effort and energy were but isolated examples of an ongoing practice of refining our hearts, minds, and bodies in quest of spiritual awakening.

Over time we realized that, if not described well, most North Americans tended to perceive Karma Yoga or service with a glass-half-empty perspective, as though we hadn't embraced modern democracy, or were something of a loser. On a Dharma Trip to the Grand Canyon, for example, one student was glad to serve, of his own accord, morning coffee to Doug Sensei. Typically, students undertake such service to benefit with some extra time to connect with the awakening mindstream and the opportunity to generate merit. After observing this for several days, one of our tour guides advised the student, "Tell him to get his own coffee."

On other occasions people asked whether Karma Yogis felt disempowered, particularly women. The irony was that primarily men had undertaken formal service roles to our teacher Namgyal Rinpoche. As far as we knew, this tradition was based on what Rinpoche experienced with his spiritual teachers in Asia.[75] Catherine had personally dedicated herself to opening this privileged position to women who so aspired, but it became clear that the benefits of serving a spiritual teacher weren't clear if that notion wasn't already embedded in a person's culture. In other words, we realized that we weren't doing a good job of sharing our practice in a way that appealed to modern people, in the U.S. and Canada, anyway.

Closer to home, the allure of the spiritual-awakening-or-bust approach that we'd benefitted from in Kyoto wasn't sustaining itself in the Canadian Rockies. Some Karma Yogis frustratedly grumbled *sotto voce* about free labor, while others complained of burnout. "I need to focus on developing my career," people explained, reducing their time at Clear Sky, or "I need to make more money if I'm going to be able to do retreats." It was hard enough, they added, to maintain a regular meditation practice alongside the demands of modern life.

Naturally, this felt true enough from a North American perspective, which was the culture we were in now. Perhaps because of this, our community was losing touch with the burning determination to pursue ever-greater awakening through a Karma Yoga practice. How could we adapt to our new context while staying true to our core principles?

---

[75] Canadian-born George Dawson was ordained Ananda Bodhi in the Burmese insight meditation tradition by U Thila Wunta Sayadaw in 1958 and recognized as Namgyal Rinpoche in the Tibetan Karma Kagyu lineage by H.H. the 16th Karmapa in 1971. See also http://www.planetdharma.com/lineage.

GROWTH EDGES WITH LOVE

Some of us still had faith in Karma Yoga as a path, feeling it resonated with our interests and aspirations. With varying career and financial situations, a number of us believed that we could use Karma Yoga to stimulate our careers (and incomes) and vice versa. We embraced it as a practice and felt like our spiritual unfoldment was vibrant as a result—and our personal and professional lives, too. One man, a mid-level executive at a Fortune 100 company, epitomized how Karma Yoga could produce career success. Let's call him Dante.

Through Dante's dedicated Karma Yoga work, his growth edges became visible. For example, though he'd developed an excellent skillset, we noticed that it was challenging for him to hold other people accountable and advised that he develop this important skill. Within the year, Dante's seniors complimented him on how well he held his team accountable and gave him a promotion and corresponding salary increase.

Next, we encouraged Dante to relax some mental models about how things at Clear Sky should be. He was very good at what he did. And, he'd be a more integrated human being, we suggested, if he cultivated greater creativity in how he worked and spent more time crafting new possibilities. A year later Dante was offered a major promotion—with a financial raise—to a new department developing innovative products and services.

Using one another's successes and failures as case studies, we exhorted one another to use Karma Yoga to transform one's career into a spiritual practice and vice versa. Nonetheless, we were surprised that one of the most spectacular case studies shone within a very conservative Fortune 100 company. The fruits of the Karma Yoga path were not so overt for most of our community: results could be subtler and took longer to see. So, we knew we had to better describe, organize, and demonstrate the advantages in ways that felt accessible and appealing for contemporary people in the West.

One approach was shaping the Karma Yoga projects and roles to help people build the specific business and life skills they felt they needed. One young woman, let's call her Yuka, wanted better financial management skills. We invited her to work on the budget for a grant application we were writing. Shortly thereafter, Yuka was awarded an administrative role in a prestigious company that she felt passionate about, in part because of her financial and grant-writing skills. A young man who enjoyed playing around with design software began creating maps of accommodation schemas and posters for Clear Sky events. Thereafter, he was hired as a graphic designer.

This was an encouraging direction, and we continued experimenting and refining. We'd garnered enough experience practicing together to perceive how people learned, communicated, and worked in different ways. Gradually, we also observed that having adaptability among the different approaches and styles led to greater success and more enjoyable time together. We asked people to reflect on what worked well for them and their team members, and what didn't. We compared notes and kept tweaking our approach. As time passed, we appreciated one another's disparate styles more, rather than finding them a source of vexation. The reflection in the mirror was a better understanding of our own strengths and weaknesses.

Another harvest was strategizing how to be there for one another as support. For instance, Nora was strong at visioning and creating solutions, but less so with the concrete steps needed to follow through to crystallize the vision. Her colleague Antoine's execution was extremely good, but his creative spark to inspire and further the execution was not as strong. They struggled antagonistically for years, with Antoine urging Nora to be more pragmatic and her entreating him to have more imagination and faith. While our Clear Sky team was putting great efforts effort into cultivating trust and communication skills, it eventually dawned on them that their skills were perfect complements for each other. Their collaboration flowered as a result.

Around this time, Doug Sensei taught from the book, *The Five Love Languages*.[76] We figured out that we'd been trying desperately to communicate that we cared about to one another, but in ways that the other didn't find meaningful—or even register as congenial. One person glowed when commended on a job well done, while another felt awkwardly singled out. Someone else wished their colleague would stop touching their shoulder, while the next person received it as a heartwarming gesture. We wondered how we could have gone all these years without noticing! We asked one another what our love languages were and made a point of expressing friendliness in their preferred modalities, rather than in our favorite, which they might find awkward or otherwise undesirable. The awareness we'd developed on the meditation cushion became more meaningful and more productive with these new applications, like communication skills, love languages, and others.

CONFESSIONS OF A CLINGER

These were happy breakthroughs. But still, successes like these didn't ensure that Clear Sky flourished, or even that people continued with a committed Karma Yoga practice together. Some still felt torn between their spiritual practice and the demands of daily life. Many found independent ways to serve their community in their daily lives, which was wonderful, but didn't nurture our center or the other practitioners who supported it. As we dedicated ourselves to creating more goodness in the world, surely good karma would ripen for us all. Would it ripen in time to assure Clear Sky's sustainability? Did that question entail too much clinging, too much self-interest? Inevitably, the universe was unfolding as it should, but to what extent were we active agents of that unfoldment? What to do, when the benefits

---

[76] Gary Chapman, *The Five Love Languages: How to Express Heartfelt Commitment to Your Mate* (Chicago: Northfield Publishing, 2000).

of Karma Yoga that seem obvious to some people are obscure to others, and our center operates on that basis?

We simply didn't know. Doug kept reminding us to do our best, while dwelling in a wholesome, radiant state. The latter entailed not being attached to results. Fearing that the future of our center might be at stake, this counsel tested our faith and our practice.

Back in Japan, our Karma Yoga had entailed cleaning, cooking, organizing teachings and retreats, interpreting, and the like. By now, our Karma Yoga repertoire had expanded dramatically. As mentioned, we'd been studying up on contemporary business practices. Perhaps Clear Sky's challenges, and that of our Karma Yoga system, were simply a marketing and communications issue? Some suggested we re-brand.

On the one hand, we could read the writing on the wall: there were a lot of other spiritual teachings and retreat centers in North America. People needed to know what made us unique, and that special something needed allure. On the other hand, we longed for simpler days, when liberation from suffering (!) was motivation enough to dramatically change one's lifestyle. Did the Buddha consider the 500 B.C. version of branding? The community of original founders had imagined that whatever a group of awakening beings dedicated to alleviating suffering undertook could only result in good and amazing things. And that surely this would be obvious to anyone. But this felt increasingly elusive.

Spiritual awakening is an inner state, perhaps indiscernible if we aren't looking for it, or when we're caught in our own ego-based turmoil. Yet, it's the gold that alchemists strived to produce, the Holy Grail that knights quested for, the ultimate mode of being as described by all the world's wisdom traditions. It was our privilege to convey its precious value to everyone we met, and deep in our hearts we both longed to do it justice and knew that we could.

People often confuse Karma Yoga with Hatha Yoga, and "the path of service" just doesn't seem to capture people's imagination or attention. We'd often described it as taking what we learn on the meditation cushion into action in our daily life, so we started calling it "Awakening through Action." Just saying it sparked our moxie. Punching up the wording is one thing; we knew we also had to continue to adapt our general approach. Patience is one of the virtues that Buddhist philosophy encourages us to cultivate, and eventually our persistence started to pay off.

Through our ongoing involvement with social ventures and social enterprises, slowly we'd connected with a growing network of business people and organizations who were bringing mindfulness and a more contemplative culture to the workplace. With our strong meditation and awakening through action background, we aimed to meet them in the middle: we were determined to bring more mindful business to our retreat center and awakening through action practices.

We read, trained, shared, and eventually started teaching on organizational development, mindful leadership, change management, money archetypes, and other subjects shared from the likes of *The Fifth Discipline*, Naropa University's Authentic Leadership Center (founded in spiritual practices with similar roots to ours), the Money Coaching Institute, and *Theory U*. In mindful business, these were cutting edge applications of sound business management and leadership practices that drew on spiritual traditions as a foundation to lead to greater effectiveness and productivity. Having previously tried to fit our retreat enter within more traditional business practices, aligning with organizations built on a foundation of mindful practices felt like sliding our foot into the proverbial crystal slipper.

And since these contemporary Western workplace practices were rooted in mindful traditions, they were a perfect match for our Karma Yoga. Moreover, they had a recognizable language and an appeal for Westerners that we'd struggled to find since relocating to North America. Our Karma Yogis were excited to learn how Authentic Leadership could be cultivated through our teamwork together, or how Theory U principles and practices could be applied.

When we went to conferences and other gatherings of progressive organizations or innovation practitioners, we were delighted to realize that we could hold our own. What's more, when we shared what we were doing at Clear Sky, it captured people's attention as something they hadn't seen or heard of elsewhere. Our confidence grew along with our skills, and Clear Sky began to flourish again. This time it was by design, not from beginner's enthusiasm. We'd developed greater financial integrity, improved our social business acumen, grown a stronger and more extensive business network, and continued to develop Clear Sky's ecological health—all based in our spiritual values and practices. Our aspiration to embody a quadruple bottom line was actualizing.

As our exposure increased, we learned that we'd been engaging in something very akin to the emerging field of holistic education, or what the Center for Curriculum Redesign calls four-dimensional education. This includes a combination of knowledge, skills, character, and meta-learning. In the meta-learning dimension, students would practice "reflection, learn about their learning, internalize a growth mindset that encourages them to strive, and learn how to adapt their learning and behavior based on their goals."[77] This makes for flexible individuals nimbly able to harmonize with a changing world.

Our goals had been to grow, as individuals and as a community, based in timeless qualities of loving-kindness, compassion, and wisdom. We'd sought to acclimate to our new environment and conditions so that our spiritual practices were demonstrably relevant. A lifetime's—and planet's-worth—of challenges remain to call upon us to refine our practice. Nonetheless, we came to feel that with our new location, environment, situation, and extended family, and with some birthing pains, we'd come home to ourselves.

---

[77] C.M. Rubin, "The Global Search for Learning: What Meta-Learning?" *Huffington Post*, Dec. 12, 2016, updated Dec. 6, 2017. https://www.huffingtonpost.com/c-m-rubin/the-global-search-for-edu_b_13343564.html.

REFLECTION 7
AWAKENING THROUGH CAREER

Our Work as Our Path

A fine career is built; it's crafted. It's established and developed through the building blocks of skills and character. As we saw in the reflection on Karma Yoga, our spiritual path entails cultivating skills and character to develop awareness as well as careers. It's a rewarding path, and easier said than done. How can we stay motivated?

Throughout our lives, we are always seeking. What we seek, for lack of a better word, is happiness. But happiness is hard to define and can refer to many disparate things. It may refer to sensual pleasure or a temporary escape from loneliness (through relationship, work, or entertainment), or it may point to a feeling of freedom or of meaning. It could refer to a sense of truth, understanding, and wisdom.

In Buddhist philosophy, spiritual awakening or enlightenment is also known as the Great Happiness. This is a more pervasive, sustainable kind of happiness. Given the demands of our day-to-day life, how can we attend to those demands and also attain such a Great Happiness?

Since work is where we spend the majority of our waking hours, using it as a form of meditation makes sense. This transforms our careers into an optimal vehicle to help us move ever closer to the Great Happiness. To do this, we must align our careers with our spiritual aspiration, and then apply the principles of awakening while we are at work. Since interest is key to mindfulness, we have a duty—to ourselves and to our friends and community as well—to develop a career that we find interesting. Then, career becomes an integral part of our spiritual path and vice versa.

What does this mean exactly? First, let's look at the Great Happiness, the awakening, on its own.

Great Happiness = Bliss + Insight

According to Buddhist teachings, Great Happiness has two fundamental aspects: bliss and insight. These break down further into two kinds of bliss and two kinds of insight.

The two kinds of bliss are:

1. the bliss of the senses, which facilitates enjoyment; and

2. the bliss of the mind, which creates fulfillment.

The two kinds of insight are:

1. the insight of knowledge, which leads to understanding; and

2. the insight of wisdom, which supports the shift to the transcendental.

As we can see, when the two blisses and the two insights come together, we enjoy much greater bliss and wisdom. We also enjoy much greater freedom. When we're in a positive mental and emotional space, we think better, our energy is better, and we feel joyful. Being in such a wholesome state ensures we work much more effectively and efficiently than when these qualities are absent. This foundation of bliss and insight is of immense value for developing what we'd call a truly great career, one that helps us cultivate further awakening. And such a feeling of freedom is one of the characteristics of true happiness.

On this path, we should also be aware of potential pitfalls. When either bliss or insight arise on their own, without the other, the energy can stagnate in back eddies. For instance, one potential back eddy of bliss is hedonism. Bliss is impermanent and very easily interrupted. We can chase it forever and occasionally satisfy it, but never sate it. Bliss alone can never fulfill our desire for true freedom. It's also important to note that the bliss of meditative absorption is different in quality than the pleasure of desire. The pleasure of desire (usually based in the senses) requires relatively little focus and yields relatively low energy. In contrast, the bliss of absorption requires greater focus, yields higher energy, and is more pervasive, plus it includes an aspect of mind awareness not found in pleasure rooted solely in desire.

What about back eddies of insight? These include tendencies toward brittle aridity and a lack of passion. Too much emphasis on insight can lead to habitual over-analysis that may be factually accurate but lacking in human feeling. It can manifest as harshness or coldness. Again, the clarity of mind from meditative insight is different in quality from ego-referenced knowledge. Knowledge is localized and particular, based in facts and referencing. In contrast, the radiant insight mind is non-local and universal, and features spaciousness and a strong sense of being in union. As with bliss and desire, the insight mind operates at a much higher energy level.

Still, experiencing either meditative bliss or insight is better than an undersupply of these qualities. In the best case, absence of bliss makes for an emotional flatness, while the absence of insight shows up as thickness, a dull mind. At worst, their absence may manifest as increased suffering and increased ignorance. If bliss and clarity (insight) are absent, we are not in the best space we could be; that in itself is felt as a kind of suffering or at least discontent. It can manifest as anything from a feeling of restlessness to a sense of being disconnected. More intense suffering and ignorance would include classism, nationalism, and selfishness, while more extreme forms include sexism, racism, or speciesism.

And the spiritual path is, among other things, about using bliss and insight to decrease suffering and ignorance. That's why a healthy spiritual path feels so rich, wonder-filled, and generally happy. The Great Happiness arises when bliss and insight come together to manifest through everything we do and are. Focusing these elements inward produces a radiant state of being; channeling them outward produces a fulfilling and engaging career or vocation. The awakening state does not rely on activity to manifest but can be channeled into activity. It's the dialogue between being (resting in peacefulness) and becoming (projects), between resting and doing.

Our Three Brains

In the course of our evolution, our brain developed in three distinct stages for very different reasons. This accounts for the very different ways we process different kinds of information throughout any given day. Another way of looking at a fulfilling career is that it relates well to each of these three brains: the reptilian brain, the limbic brain, and the neocortex.

The reptilian brain relates to our survival, our instincts, and it will let us know whether our career is feeding us or draining us. A satisfying career helps us move beyond a feeling of surviving to one of thriving. The emotional or limbic brain pertains to how we relate to others. Whatever work we do, it communicates something about who we are to others, while others' response to our careers tells us something about who they are. Our careers often feel worthwhile when they're linked to mutually supportive, positive, and healthy relationships with other people. The thinking brain, or neocortex, relates to, among other things, exploration and discovery, and this part of our career keeps each day fresh and alive.

We can easily see that a career that engages healthfully with all three brains will feel far more rewarding than one that only draws on one or two of these brains. A career that concerns itself with both kinds of bliss (sensory and mental) will feel more fulfilling than a career that only includes one. Similarly, a livelihood that engages both types of insight (knowledge and wisdom), will feel more enriching than one that addresses one but not the other. As mentioned, the combo of blisses and insights together lead to supreme happiness. Therefore, the most rewarding career we could craft would engage with all three brains, both kinds of happiness, and both kinds of insight.

So then, what is our dream career? It's not the job per se that matters but how we engage with it, how we feel doing it. When we lived in Japan, a country aiming for full employment, our local organic co-op had an attendant to help customers maneuver in and out of their small parking lot. Every time we saw him, he was upbeat, engaged, and responsible. He seemed to love his job and took pride in each of his body movements directing traffic, his interaction with customers, and the safety and optimal placing of the cars. While this may not work for everyone, it worked well for him, gauging by his consistently cheerful attitude. We all need that same commitment to whatever it is we're doing.

The burning question, then, is: what stands in our way? Just two things. Old habits and a limited self-view. Fortunately, these are within our power to change.

THOSE DARN HABITS

Let's look at old habits first. If we're just focusing on living a more enjoyable and satisfying life, consumption and entertainment probably end up becoming a central focus. These pursuits can start out small and insidiously become habits, because habits are good enough, but not great. If we're honest, consumption and entertainment help pass the time in a typically "good enough" kind of way. Great requires a different kind of involvement.

The term "satisficing"[78] describes settling for an adequate result, rather than going for the optimal one. It's a reasonable approach for things that don't matter all that much, that aren't critical. We don't know whether our dry cleaner is the best, but we know that they're good enough. Habits are fundamentally satisficing. If we want anything great, particularly a rewarding career, we can't rely on habits or satisficing to make it happen.

Generally speaking, life is one attempt after another to distract ourselves from the void, because in the West we're conditioned to often measure it as sadness. This is an emotional void, based on the idea that what we chose in the past no longer works in the present, such as old relationships we've outgrown or left behind. These tend to make us feel melancholy or empty. We build a shell around ourselves to hide from this emptiness, and eventually the shell gets so thick that it limits our freedom, our ability to grow, including our ability to use our careers as a path for spiritual unfoldment.

The good news is that there's a remedy for this troubling emotional void. In Buddhist philosophy, this void is known as *emptiness* or *sunyata.* It's experienced as spacious, full of unlimited possibility, luminescent, clear, and blissful. This radiant emptiness is experienced from *beyond* the ego, in contrast to the dark emotional emptiness experienced from *inside* the ego. It's the same void, looked at from two different perspectives. And we have the power to choose our perspective! A central aim of spiritual practice is to cultivate this new habit: choosing to experience emptiness as radiant, rather than melancholy.

As this example demonstrates, habits aren't all bad. They're important; we developed them to simplify repetitive tasks and ways of being so that we don't have to put so much attention on them.[79] We may have first learned to do this in school, with

---

[78] Coined by Nobel Prize winner Herbert Simon.

[79] For more on this, see Charles Duhigg, *The Power of Habit: Why We Do What We Do in Life and Business* (New York: Random House, 2012).

memorization of the alphabet and multiplication tables, and at home with chores we didn't find engaging or enjoyable. We conditioned ourselves to not pay attention to what we were doing and just zoned out, which can feel pleasant. This began to lay down habits that probably still affect how we work.

One of the challenges with habits is that we are largely unconscious of when they are operating. This may be literal: sleepwalkers can function quite well because of habits.

A transcendental career wakes us up and leads us forward into a future that we mold and create in accordance with our heart's desire. It's challenging and involves risk and pushing the frontiers of our comfort zone. This is sometimes uncomfortable and is why so many of us feel challenged in our careers. We want to grow but we also don't want to be shaken up—we want to be left alone.

But being left alone implies being left in our habits. Our habits feel comfortable because we use them to cover up our conflicting emotions, which are about getting what we want and avoiding what we don't want. When I'm not feeling so good I may compensate with my favorite habit, perhaps getting some exercise, checking social media, or snacking. So when our habits get interrupted—no exercise, no social media, no snack—the conflicting emotions rise to the surface.

Our spiritual path embraces mindfulness or awareness training, which we find is easiest to do off the cushion while in engaged in a Karma Yoga practice. Through Karma Yoga we retrain ourselves to get out of habit, that is, to be more awake. To be awake *while* in habits.

For example, consider Zen monastery gardens where apprentice monks rake gravel into patterns hour after hour, day after day. That's a very repetitive activity, prone to becoming a mindless habit. When undertaken with motivation and purpose, however, it's a training that leads to greater awareness, bliss, and insight. And we can sense the scintillation of their awareness when we visit the garden.

Outside of the monasteries, it may look a little different. The chances are good that you don't rake gravel into patterns every day, but you may drive or bike to work on the same route every day. The activities vary, but the dynamic of habit and awareness are basically the same.

LE SABOTEUR: OUR SELF-IMAGE

The second major obstacle to overcome on our quest for a great, transcendental career is a limited self-view. Our sense of self is built by our conditioning, including parental, tribal, educational, and religious patternings. One function of the tribe is to enforce conformity, which allows it to function smoothly in many ways: it's a good thing that we know to stop at a red traffic light, for example.

But in other ways, this conformity limits our sense of exploration. Can you recall a time when you said something intending to be helpful and other people felt it was outrageous? Or you experimented with some cool new dance moves only to realize they made some people laugh? How did that feel? These kinds of responses often blunt our boldness.

We are social animals after all. Neuroscientific studies of mirror neurons and spindle cells show that our identity is built based on how we interact with others. Consequently, we often feel that our survival depends on support in the form of social approval. This is understandable since not long ago, banishment from our community put our survival at risk. In this fundamental way, a social animal like us perceives the cost of isolation as life-threatening. And while it's less obvious today, it's still true that we only survive thanks to our interdependence with others.

Most of these social functions arise automatically, beneath our conscious awareness. Our need to belong, to fit in and be accepted, is determined first and foremost by the ethos of our family, since from birth our survival depends on them. The family is a microcosm and reflection of the ethos of our tribe. We learn to constrain our behavior first, and later our emotions, and then our views, to fit in with our family and tribe. What kind of family and tribe we come from—of Asian, African, indigenous,

Jewish, etc. descent, with distinctions of course within those too—determines how this shows up in our life.

For example, if our parents were practical and analytical, perhaps they dismissed the arts as something frivolous. Motivated to ensure a secure future for their children, they may have made comments like, "It's impossible to make a living with art." Hearing this in our youth can and often does shape how we perceive the world and the choices we make. In this way, our freedom is constricted, though the cause of the limitations was well intended.

When it comes to developing a career or extending our range of freedom, we must come face to face with what has been driven into the subconscious by our need to fit in. And when it comes to developing a truly enriching career, these subconscious views are some of our best resources: there's a lot of energy and inspiration tied up in them. When these energy blocks are revealed, and we learn how to release them—important functions of any true spiritual practice—our careers become a very satisfying vehicle for our development as a human being.

In my (Catherine's) family, harmony was highly valued and so conflict was avoided. Of course, it didn't mean there wasn't any; the conflicting feelings were repressed, but tended to come out sideways, in outbursts out of proportion and out of context to the trigger. As described so well in *The Five Dysfunctions of a Team*,[80] when we fear conflict, we work to maintain an artificial harmony. Underlying this is a lack of trust, hiding behind invulnerability. At work, this leads to low standards and poor results, issues I used to struggle with in my work organizing retreats with our sangha and within the organization of Clear Sky.

When something inevitably went awry, due to my conditioning, I didn't have the trust or communication skills (which get developed over time with much practice) to work through conflict to resolve challenges together. Instead, I'd often blow up at whomever I perceived to be the responsible party. This eroded

---

[80] Patrick Lencioni, *The Five Dysfunctions of a Team* (San Francisco: Josey-Bass, 2002).

trust even more, leading to more repression of conflicting feelings among the team, perpetuating a vicious cycle. Gradually, I learned to meet conflict by trusting my team's heartfelt desire to work through challenges and conflict for our mutual unfoldment and success. Both our relationships and quality of work improved dramatically.

Also, many Westerners feel they lack self-worth, and this view too has been built by conditioning. It can manifest as self-loathing or feelings of insufficiency ("I'm not smart enough" or substitute your adjective of choice), or be hidden behind an over-specialization, making for a kind of lopsided genius. This is conditioned and perhaps particular to Westerners. When respected dharma teacher Sharon Salzberg asked the Dalai Lama, "What do you think about self-hatred?" because so many of her students experienced it, the Dalai Lama tilted his head and narrowed his eyes in confusion. "Self-hatred?" he repeated in English. "What is that?"[81]

The need to fit in and lack of self-worth constitute common examples of a limiting self-view. Any view we have colors our emotions and affects our behavior. From the point of view of dharma, we are born perfect, with a pure nature. But due to not paying attention, ignore-ance, we fall into error and our essential pure nature becomes obscured. The spiritual practice is about uncovering this original pure nature again. If, however, we deeply believe that we are essentially flawed, it's very difficult to emerge from this ignorance because we don't really believe there's something better to emerge to. The good news is that these beliefs, these views, are conditioned, and we thus have the power to change them to something healthier.

STEPPING OVER OUR EDGE

Amazingly, our ego which can often hinder us can help us here. The ego's an important tool, with two principal jobs. One is to

---

[81] Sharon Salzberg, "Sit," last modified Jul. 28, 2014, reprinted from *O Magazine*, Nov. 1, 2002, https://www.sharonsalzberg.com/sit/.

seek the path back to unity that is called transcendence or awakening (also described previously as greater degrees of freedom). The other is to explore and discover this amazing universe we're in. Okay, the ego has three jobs: it has an additional function of making decisions and planning. The kinds of decisions we make indicate whether we're using our ego to stay in a limited ego position, or whether we're using our ego to become what we're not, and thereby find out who we really are. Our decisions may be to rest in habits that seem safe and comfortable, often with the unintended consequence of stagnation. Or our decisions may lead us to search and reach for new frontiers and understanding; these can feel intimidating and disturbing initially, but result in vitality and richness.

According to master chef Dan Barber, the world's greatest cuisines arose out of scarcity.[82] Japanese and Italian cuisines, for example, make extensive use of anything and everything available, which emerged out of times when there was limited choice for most people. Similarly, most transcendental careers arise out of scarcity, something missing. If we have too much abundance, we have quantity but not quality (fast food!), and we lose the spark of creativity and zest for life expressed through our work.

So, what's missing? Exploring the answer to this question can lead to a career that is both a calling and a mission. This brings all of our being into play, including the parts sleeping in habits, and even parts of ourselves we may not like. The latter represent our shadow, our subconscious urges. When our career is our calling, no stones of our being are left unturned. Thus, a career that supports our spiritual unfoldment draws on all aspects of our psyche and abilities. This yields new resources to develop additional talents.

Consider Carl Sagan, who loved the stars as a kid and was amazed to realize that he could make a living studying them.

---

[82] "Dan Barber," *Chef's Table*, Season 1, Episode 2, 12 Feb. 2015, directed by Clay Jeter, produced by Netflix and Boardwalk Pictures. https://www.netflix.com/title/80007945.

Eventually, it led him into teaching astronomy and hosting a TV show on the subject. In the spiritual world, the Dalai Lama's training as a monk and teacher led him through the labyrinths of the mind to be effective at his job. He's considered to be a manifestation of compassion by Tibetans, and his skill at what he does is so great that even many non-Tibetans would agree.

In other words, our career can either be a prison or a party, depending on how we approach it. As we've said, when the horse of spiritual awakening is in front of the cart of our life and work, then our careers are ever rewarding. Moreover, everything we learn and become is fuel for the next iteration of ourselves.

Our grandparents may have done the same thing their entire lives. As we know, the world is changing constantly and rapidly, and most of us have already moved through several different lines of work, or various manifestations of a theme. When our career is our vehicle of discovery, this is a natural and exhilarating process.

For instance, let's take a middle-aged dancer, who can no longer move as he or she did as a youth. New manifestations await, such as choreography, teaching, and writing about movement, or perhaps teaching movement therapy, dance therapy, or meditation in form: observing the mind and its emotions arising as we move through space. This is only possible if he is not overly identified with the actual physical movement and performing that he can no longer do. If he were to cling to that, frustration and bitterness would naturally follow.

In essence, these options are second or third careers. As these demonstrate, a successful career is not a fixed thing; it is always transcending itself, pushing its own boundaries. To become more than we are, we explore what we are not.

Yet.

REFLECTION 8
AWAKENING THROUGH CREATIVITY

Becoming a Work of Art

Whoosh! Bang! Creativity arises from nothing. According to physicists, mostly men, the universe started with the Big Bang. What would the beginning of the universe have looked like had it been discovered by women? The Big Birth (whoosh) maybe. Theravadin Buddhists seemed to have a sense of this, since they call our universe *Tathāgatagarbha. Garbha* means "womb" or "embryo;" *tathāgata* is one of the names of the Buddha, and literally means "one who has thus arrived." In this way, it seems that Buddhist thought considers the universe a tremendous womb to birth awakening beings.

Of course, truly inquiring minds may ask: what was before the Big Bang/Big Womb? Along these lines, we could also ask, what was I before I showed up in this body? When we trace our self all the way back, we end up with the same question about what was before the Big Bang. In fact, every phenomenon we try to trace leads us back to this question: what was before the Big Womb Birth?

The Buddhist response would be: what came before was *emptiness*. The Old Testament seems in accord, describing, "Now the earth was formless and empty."[83] Emptiness, or its Sanskrit equivalent *sunyata,* are other words for *no-thing*, not to be confused with "nothing."[84] No thing is a very hard "something" to discover and even more difficult to describe. It must be experienced. Even then, with words it cannot be described, but without words it cannot be expressed, to paraphrase Lao Tsu.[85] As far as we've seen and heard in our study of world cultures, it comes down to the same statement in almost every spiritual tradition: everything began from no-thing.

This is not very satisfying for our egos. It wreaks havoc with economics, politics, the arts and other important pursuits like horseback riding and golf.

Nonetheless sunyata, emptiness or no-thing remains the *source* of everything, including the wellspring of all major insights and creative impulses. While some of these insights or impulses feel like they come out of nothing and nowhere, out of spaciousness, they must still be triggered by something, like a question. By posing a question, we await an answer in a state of no answer, or emptiness. We rest in emptiness, along with our question. And then, spontaneously, from this no-thing comes something, which we call an insight or a realization. From there, we bring it into the world, in some form or another, as creativity.

---

[83] Genesis 1:2 (NIV).

[84] "Nothing" usually implies absence (nothing in the drawer) or a destruction (nothing was left standing). "No-thing" implies a potential, spaciousness, or lack of inherent objectiveness (the table is empty of solidity at the quantum level).

[85] Lao Tsu, *Tao Te Ching,* trans. Gia-Fu Feng & Jane English (New York: Vintage Books, 1972), Ch. 1.
The Tao that can be told is not the eternal Tao;
The name that can be named is not the eternal name.
The nameless is the beginning of heaven and earth.
The named is the mother of ten thousand things.
Ever desireless, one can see the mystery.
Ever desiring, one can see the manifestations.
These two spring from the same source but differ in name;
this appears as darkness.
Darkness within darkness.
The gate to all mystery.

This is what we would call quantum creativity: brand new insights, ideas, or forms emerging from emptiness or spaciousness. Quantum creativity embodies bold responses to big questions. These often take us completely out of ourselves as we make leaps into new understanding, paradigm shifts. We've seen the fruits of quantum creativity with Einstein and relativity, the invention of the wheel, the discovery of zero, as well as innovations like radio, solar panels, biomimicry, the electric car, and ice cream.

This is distinct from what we call adaptive creativity. Rather than a paradigm shift, this type of creativity is an important new iteration or re-molding of what has gone before into new shapes and forms. Most of our day-to-day improvements or small changes are of this type. These two types of creativity are more different in scope and impact than essence. We'll take a closer look at both of them.

Creativity, Sex, and Diversity

Perhaps one of the most popular forms of adaptive creativity is sex or procreation. Historically, asexual reproduction arose first as cells and organisms reproduced through fission, budding, or some other kind of division to create new cells or organisms that are basically identical. The problem with this kind of creativity is that if one thing goes wrong, the whole family may be wiped out: a virus infecting one cell could infect all of them, or other environmental changes could make them more susceptible to extinction.

So, the creative drive evolved toward mixing things up, taking half of this and half of that, leading to divergence through sexual reproduction. While this system provides a much better chance of survival on the one hand, on the other it also opens to a greater chance of errors creeping into the coding though mistakes in the copying of genetic material. Every time a cell divides, its DNA replicates, meaning it has to copy exactly a sequence of three billion nucleotides to its daughter cells. On occasion, inaccuracies creep in. These mutations introduce a kind of genetic gamble:

they may affect nothing, lead to a major illness like cancer, or make for survival advantages.

Sexual reproduction and the new life it brings are accompanied with other costs as well, responsibility for one. With many species, the new life has to be looked after, at least for a time. What could possibly motivate us to undertake such a commitment? To start with, obligations like this usually come with some self-identification: this new creature is half me, and in preserving this creature, I preserve me. Long before that, however, comes motivation in the form of intense pleasure. Sex floods us with endorphins that make us dizzy and hungry for more. Post-sex cuddling releases oxytocin, which makes the would-be parents feel bonded. These are some of the deep instincts and chemistry that help the parents want to stay around and take care of the young together. Sex is just one example of how creativity can deliver a big endorphin reward. In this sense, creativity is not really under our control. We're wired or built to seek the high instinctively rather than intellectually.

This is an example of how creativity makes us smarter. Since the creative urge (in this case, a sexual drive) seems to come from nowhere and is thus out of our control, it forces us to adapt and integrate whatever it brings—like babies. Similarly, creative divergence has made for a dance between viruses and our bodies, one that makes both dance partners more adaptive and more sophisticated. A study from Sweden's Lund University indicates that inherited viruses play an important role in building up the complex networks that characterize the human brain.[86] In this way, viruses make our bodies and minds smarter.

---

[86] "We have been able to observe that these viruses are activated specifically in the brain cells and have an important regulatory role. We believe that the role of retroviruses can contribute to explaining why brain cells in particular are so dynamic and multifaceted in their function," says Johan Jakobsson, head of Lund University's research team for molecular neurogenetics. *"Do viruses make us smarter?"* Lund University, Jan 12, 2015, https://phys.org/news/2015-01-viruses-smarter.html.

Similarly, being deceived requires our faculties to evolve in new ways. Being able to see through a lie demands questioning, observation, investigation, and comparison, all means to hone our minds' powers of perception. For instance, if we fall for a bait and switch scheme once, we learn to spot them and are unlikely to make the same mistake again.

These are some examples of how sex, viruses, and lies may usher in greater creativity through adaptation. Similarly, our biggest challenges and questions can steer us toward creativity of a quantum kind.

QUANTUM CREATIVITY AND PARADIGM SHIFTS

As mentioned, quantum creativity represents a paradigm shift. An example would be when Galileo proposed that the earth goes around the sun rather than the other way around. Or the idea of quantum entanglement:[87] a particle light years away can sense when its partner particle has been modified and instantaneously change its state to match. What makes these prime examples of quantum creativity? Both these observations have defied our concurrent perceptions of space and time.

While fascinating, few people really like such paradigm shifts. From our ego-centered point of view, they don't make any sense. It can feel very upsetting at first, with potentially dire consequences: Galileo was jailed for blasphemy by the Vatican for sharing his discoveries, Socrates was sentenced to commit suicide for refusing to maintain the status quo, and Jesus' wisdom met with crucifixion. The discoverers themselves may not like the paradigm shift. More recently, quantum mechanics proponent Erwin Schrödinger commented, "I do not like [quantum mechanics], and I am sorry I ever had anything to do with it." Whether or not the deliverers of the message are persecuted by

---

[87] In 1935, Einstein and his coworkers discovered quantum entanglement lurking in the equations of quantum mechanics and realized its utter strangeness. This led to the EPR paradox introduced by Einstein, Poldolsky, and Rosen.

their contemporaries, paradigm shifts force us to re-orient ourselves in ways we often find uncomfortable.

With quantum creativity, we inevitably need to be ready for the applecart of our daily life to be upset. It messes with everything we already know and are accustomed to. As described, there may be mainstream backlash toward the message or the messenger. According to innovation diffusion theory, this may be because only 2.5% of any population are innovators and only another 13.5% are early adopters, with 84% of the population waiting for majority concurrence.[88] However, eventually quantum breakthroughs become the norm—a heliocentric view of the solar system and Christianity have become the establishment—and in retrospect, the revelation and revelator are celebrated.

By taking what's currently known and flipping it on its head, quantum creativity presents a whole new way of seeing, except that we often can't see what we're not prepared to see. Our attention can be so focused on what we think we know that we miss what is directly in front of us,[89] even to the point of insisting it's not there, despite evidence to the contrary. Our selective attention can blind us to new ways of seeing or experiencing: we simply can't see what we don't believe. After all, the nature of a blind spot is that it's blind. This is why a great question is so important for quantum creativity. Our questions have to be bigger than our current life.

Galileo must have asked something like, "How do the planets and sun interact?" For a meditator, a big question might be, "What is the nature of consciousness?" Or, more pragmatically, "How do these thought and emotional patterns I'm observing in meditation affect my actions in day-to-day life?" For every breath there is an emotion, a sensation, and usually a thought. When we change one, we change the others, even if only slightly. Slight shifts, we know, can lead to big changes; so accumulating small

---

[88] Everett M. Rogers, *Diffusion of Innovations* (New York: Free Press, 2003).

[89] See, for example, Daniel Simons' famous *The Monkey Business Illusion*, published Apr. 8, 2010. https://www.youtube.com/watch?v=MFBrCM_WYXw.

adaptive shifts in our consciousness can, and eventually does, lead to a quantum jump.

In the spiritual context, this quantum jump is called *awakening*. From our perspective, the realization of the awakened mind is the ultimate quantum creativity breakthrough. It is a paradigm shift of the first order. Our teacher Namgyal Rinpoche, for example, was born Leslie George Dawson with modest origins in Toronto, Canada, but later in life was recognized by the 16th Karmapa as an accomplished master.

Namgyal Rinpoche compared the shift from pre-awakened to fully awakened consciousness to the difference between apes and humans, a truly quantum leap to make in one lifetime. How's that for upsetting the applecart of the ego? Take note that this quantum leap is possible for each of us to realize this state in this very lifetime. For every human, spiritual awakening is a whole new ballgame. And like all quantum creativity shifts, we can't quite get what it all means until we actually experience it. And once we've experienced it, we can't ignore it.

For the vast majority of beings, the awakened mind must be chosen.[90] We have to want it, and we have to want it a lot. And we have to *know* we want it: at depth, every human being longs for the state of blissful unity and wisdom that comes with spiritual awakening. To actualize it, this longing needs to be conscious and acted upon.

The great value of a quantum creativity shift is that it changes life for everyone. Upsetting or not, we're all included in this new expansion of knowledge and awareness, which is a good thing. When the first being awakened spiritually, life irrevocably took a new turn for all of humanity. Just as Galileo's discoveries have eventually affected all of us, so does another person's spiritual awakening. This is because once something is experienced by

---

[90] It is possible to awaken unintentionally, but it's not recommended. It's like finding yourself in an unidentifiable foreign land, without a map, currency, place to stay, language dictionary, or way to get home. But more disorienting.

one of us, over time, it spreads to all of us. We can see how the realizations of awakened human beings has transformed and continues to transform the world, through such figures as Fatima of Cordoba, Christ, Buddha, and numerous others. They presented their insights as a kind of quantum creativity, and we have been drawing on their wisdom to improve our understanding, lives and world ever since.

Our teacher Namgyal Rinpoche taught that, sooner or later, the future of humanity includes everyone experiencing spiritual awakening (we vote for sooner). When that comes to pass, another huge quantum leap will occur. A growing cadre of awakened beings on the planet could help reverse our current unsustainable/self-destructive inclinations, healing the planet for the very reason that its chief polluters—us—do less harm when we're freer of greed, hatred, and confusion. Additionally, one day we might take the planet out of orbit by creating a mind field around it to travel through space. Although we are traveling through space now, we are going in circles. Imagine if we could go anywhere! Whatever we can imagine, we can eventually make happen.

ADAPTIVE CREATIVITY

As described earlier, in addition to quantum creativity, we observe another kind: adaptive creativity. This kind is much more common and builds on what has come before. With the invention of the wheel came carts, then carriages, then trains and cars; finally, planes and rockets transcended the wheel that spawned them. When the Book of Ecclesiastes proclaims, "There is nothing new under the sun," it indicates how adaptations of what came before can be barely perceptible. Even so, minor changes slowly accumulate over time, gradually leading to much bigger quantum changes, such as a cart eventually evolving into a rocket, or Darwin's study of how finches' different conditions on various Galapagos Islands led to their evolution into distinct species.

To do something different, we need what came before as a point of reference. In terms of world religions, Buddhism is an offshoot of Hinduism, and similarly Christianity draws on metaphors and symbols of the religions that predated it, such as Judaism, Roman, and Celtic mythology in Europe, and Mayan spirituality in Latin America. In classical music, each period (Baroque, Romantic, and so on) was built on what had come before. Classical architecture formed the basis for the Renaissance style. Chemistry emerged from alchemy. Thus, the new is built upon what came before, and what came before is integrated into the new.

Though not as extreme a change as quantum creativity, nonetheless, new forms of adaptive creativity may also upset the proverbial apple cart of the general public. For example, consider Igor Stravinsky and Vaslav Nijinsky's *The Rite of Spring*, which debuted in Paris in 1913: "The notorious premiere . . . elicited such a volume of abuse that the music itself was frequently inaudible."[91] And yet, "Since 1913 generation after generation of composers—from Varèse to Boulez, Bartók to Ligeti—has felt impelled to face the challenges set by this seminal masterwork."[92]

The ego likes what it knows already, and we draw on this with most adaptive creativity, building on the foundation of what we already know. By its nature, the ego doesn't like to *not* know; it feels like an insecure state of being. But exceptional creativity, quantum creativity, only arises from the unknown. So, to be creative we need to step over our limiting ego views and what we think we know. This means getting comfortable with not knowing, embracing the unknown, and welcoming the emerging person we're becoming.

---

[91] George Benjamin, "How Stravinsky's Rite of Spring has shaped 100 years of music," *The Guardian* online, May 20, 2013, https://www.theguardian.com/music/2013/may/29/stravinsky-rite-of-spring.
[92] Ibid.

LEARNING AS A CREATIVE ACT

We can get more creative about learning. Learning from what's been said, discussed, or demonstrated has been called single loop learning.[93] From there, we would create from what's been shared. However, we can look more closely at our assumptions, the views and values that underlie what is being shared in a learning environment, to take our exploration deeper; this is referred to as double loop learning.[94] In this scenario, we examine the framework in which we are learning, and perhaps adjust or otherwise reshape it. This comprises learning about learning, meta-learning.[95] This empowers us to take our understanding to another level, to work consciously with how we learn, the learning schemata we're using, and how those interface.

For example, to be good at what she does, a businesswoman learns about the values and mission of the business, supply and demand, finance, strategy, regulations, metrics, and so on. This is, of course, essential, and it's single-loop learning. For double-loop learning, she and her teams would look at the assumptions or beliefs that the business was based on; for example, that being socially or environmentally responsible is costly. In these cases, double-loop learning would entail asking questions like: Is this actually true? Does it have to be? How are we measuring, and are there other ways to measure? How could such approaches be more generative? Could the business be more efficient with existing resources?

To engage in meta-learning of the awakening kind, the business woman might, for instance, reexamine her firm to see how its practices could further foster social justice, ecological

---

[93] Chris Argyris and Donald Schon, *Organizational Learning: A Theory of Action Perspective.* (Boston: Addison-Wesley, 1978).

[94] Ibid.

[95] For more on meta-learning see: C.M. Rubin, "The Global Search for Learning: What Meta-Learning?" *Huffington Post,* Dec 12, 2016. https://www.huffingtonpost.com/c-m-rubin/the-global-search-for-edu_b_13343564.html.

health, and/or community well-being.[96] She might look at finances as one component of corporate engagement, and at other factors too, perhaps including joy, creativity, and a feeling of connection or freedom among staff, clients and the broader community. She could examine how business could support beings to grow and unfold, including undertaking the same kind of meta-learning. With an ongoing practice of double-loop learning or meta-learning, we continually transcend our previous levels of creativity.

Even highly creative people can get stuck in single-loop creativity, at which point endeavors or interests can begin to plateau. Spiritual awakening through creativity entails double-loop learning or meta-learning. While awareness is good, it's a single loop; awareness of awareness is double loop.

Another approach to achieve greater creativity is to reshape our attitudes about perceived challenges. Focusing on obstacles or potential obstacles,[97] for example, can dampen our creativity if we fixate on all the reasons why our ideas won't work. Or it can be a tremendous asset to strengthen a plan so that potential hindrances are creatively circumnavigated. An outstanding example of this is NASA's Apollo 13 mission. When things went wrong, members of the NASA team at Mission Control didn't spend time on the potentially disastrous nature of the predicament. Instead, they concentrated on how to use articles on the spaceship (including a cardboard box, duct tape, plastic bag, and a hose) to keep the astronauts alive and get them back to earth safely on less oxygen and power than the mission was designed

---

[96] The Greyston Bakery mentioned in Reflection 2, under the subhead *Adapting to the Now*, is an outstanding example of an organization that undertook meta-learning of the awakening kind. Bhutan's Gross National Happiness metrics would be another.

[97] Using the lens of astrology, this is one of the functions of Capricorn and Saturn. See more about the application of astrology to spiritual awakening and personal transformation in Reflection 16, AstroDharma: Because We're Made of Stardust.

for.[98] They used profound creativity to meet and surmount tremendous risks.

Note that risk—and the personal transformation that's forged when we meet risk—lies at the heart of true creativity. Real creativity is a wild ride. So, playing it safe is very deleterious for rich creativity. Spiritual awakening, too, requires that we push the limits of our courage and trust that the universe is unfolding as it should. This is why Asian wisdom traditions refer to spiritual awakening as "riding the dragon."

SPECIAL SECTION: QUANTUM CREATIVITY TOOLKIT

How do we apply quantum creativity in our daily lives? To unleash this creativity, we need to look where we tend to avoid looking, and for this, we need some tools and approaches. Here are some we recommend:

1) **Study what's come before.** As Goethe said, "A person who does not know the last 3,000 years wanders in the darkness of ignorance, unable to make sense of the reality around him." When we understand the history and development of our own profession—say, music or science—we can better explore and situate ourselves within the conversation we're part of. Going back helps us go forward.

2) **Quality listening.** Although rebellion, opinion, and ideas allow us to step out of the confines of the status quo, they can also hold us prisoner. Being stuck in any viewpoint means we're not listening; we're arguing, and not really hearing anything. When we drop our concepts and just listen, deeply, we give unimaginable new ideas space to emerge. This is as true when listening to other people as to our own minds and ideas.

---

[98] James A. Lovell, "Houston, We've Had a Problem," *Apollo Expeditions to the Moon*, chapter 13.4, accessed Jan. 6, 2018, https://www.hq.nasa.gov/pao/History/SP-350/ch-13-4.html.

3) **Passionate learning.** Absorb, observe, inquire. The more engaged we are with learning, the more insights we can gain into what's currently unknown. This is the path to new paradigms. Get the best education possible in your field (e.g. economics, art, psychology, etc.). And remember, education isn't the exclusive domain of academic institutions. Apprenticing with a master is another time-honored approach.

4) **Be curious**. Every new insight derives from a good question. In fact, we don't really need answers, we need better questions; a better question tends to answer the previous question. For example, instead of asking, "How can I write a bestselling book?" we could ask of every book we admire, "What makes this book so good?" Keep notes. Apply what you learn to your own work. Repeat.

5) **Take risks.** A.k.a. willingness to go all the way. History is full of stories about people who risked disrupting the status quo to embrace a higher calling. St. Francis was on the way to becoming a businessman and war hero before he took up his calling to become the patron saint of animals! Push your boundaries: travel to new places, eat unusual foods, try new sexual positions, study something you have no interest in (and get interested), or wear or do something outrageous. This opens our minds and makes us more empathic and interesting people. It also provides input that opens up our imagination to new ideas and ways of working and being.

6) **Confidence.** It's important to feel confident that we'll succeed, and what's more, that we'll move forward. It doesn't always look that way, but whether or not we do succeed is not so relevant. While success is externally encouraging, it's effort itself that generates creativity. *Confidence* comes from the Latin meaning "firmly trusting, bold," "reliance on one's own powers, resources, or circumstances" and even "a secret, a private communication" (15th C). Bold belief in oneself is a vital tool in the quantum toolkit, along with the understanding that almost no one gets it right the first time. How we deal with failure and adapt is what makes (or breaks) most successes, while the learning process builds confidence and inner strength.

7) **Integrity**. In relationship to creativity, integrity means being honest with ourselves about when we are or aren't really pushing the edges of our comfort zone. It's pleasant enough to look good and feel comfortable, but true creativity lies on the other side of those things. This means we also need . . .

8) . . . **Courage.** In particular we need to be willing to test an unpopular position. It might even be unpopular with our self! Such courage can stimulate our creativity: since social and cultural harmony rest on consensus of opinion, an unpopular opinion may lead to some discomfort but also greater insight and knowledge—both necessary for pushing our creative edges. Imagine how much courage Galileo needed to propose that the earth revolved around the sun, the opposite of what everyone believed at the time.

9) **Integration of our psychological shadow.** From a Buddhist philosophical perspective, human suffering arises from three poisons: greed, hatred, and delusion. Greed is about resources or survival; hatred is about control and independence; and delusion is about the view of oneself and what others think. Much of our energy gets bound up in protecting ourselves from the terrors associated with these poisons—of a lack of support, defensive control, and trying to please everyone. In learning to let go of these, a tremendous amount of energy is released and becomes fuel for exceptional creativity.

10) **A creativity-based lifestyle.** The best way to practice creativity is to make our lives a work of art. How creative we get with our lifestyle is limited only by our imaginations. On our own and in community, this means experimenting however we are drawn—perhaps with housing or familial arrangements, fashion, energy generation, cuisine, architecture, design—the sky's the limit.

On the other hand, we also need good habits to support our creativity, because it takes discipline to do anything well. Paradoxically, the greatest freedom lies within the greatest discipline. Resolving the paradox means transcending the frame of reference so that both sides—spontaneity and discipline—become integrated.

There is always a gravitational pull toward seemingly safe territory that we're familiar with. But creativity ushers in new alignments and cross-pollination that enriches our future with untold possibilities. And to become more than we are—more creative and more spiritually awake—we step into becoming what we didn't used to be.

REFLECTION 9
SECRETS FROM OURSELVES

Exploring our Edges

While a "secret" is usually regarded as something that's hidden or kept from knowledge, the word also means: discretion; unacknowledged; remote from notice; secluded; designed to elude observation; and revealed only to the initiated. When we're talking about keeping secrets or secret teachings, it's important to consider all these definitions and to be cognizant of which one we mean when.

From the point of view of the ego, there are always secrets of every sort. The nature of the ego is that there are things it doesn't want known, and more importantly, doesn't want to know. So with the ego much remains hidden, and therefore secret, even to ourselves—similar to the 90 percent of an iceberg that is underwater.

Interestingly, when we are keeping things hidden from others, it is usually a conscious choice, but when we are keeping things from ourselves, it is usually unconscious. The tricky thing is that when we are keeping things hidden from others, we may be hiding other aspects of these same secrets from ourselves as well. In other words, aspects of ourselves that are unresolved because they're hidden from ourselves *also* get played out in our lives as secrets we keep from others.

From the point of view of the transcendental, or a fully awakened being, there are no secrets, in that nothing is kept hidden from oneself. There are still mysteries of the universe that await exploration, and more knowledge and experience remain to be gained. But through the process of moving to full spiritual enlightenment, no stone has been left unturned, and thus there remain no hidden aspects of the psyche. It doesn't mean that everything we know is shared. It also doesn't mean everything is known. The fundamental nature of the awakening consciousness is resting in the unknown and discovering. The act of discovery raises the question of what do I want or need to know that I don't know already?

Thus there are two avenues of discovery: one is to ask questions, and the other is to go experience for oneself. To this end, one purpose of the spiritual path is revelation through direct experience, to go explore. We can study Mayan history and culture extensively, but only by going to Latin America and experiencing it do the wonders of Mayan civilization truly begin to be a part of us. Once there, do we spend most of our time drinking limonadas by the pool of our hacienda hotel with the other gringos? Or do we visit archaeological sites, museums, and the towns and jungle in between, and listen to locals, guides, and anthropologists? Nothing against limonadas and pools, but much of Mayan culture (or anything else) remains secret if we don't explore. Whatever the exploration, revelation depends on our own will, choices, actions, and questions we ask. Or don't.

Life is about desire! We humans use two methods to manifest our desires: we either manipulate or we control. Depending on our awareness, skill, and intensity, this is not necessarily a bad thing, but no matter the desire, these are the tools that we use to get the object of our desires. For instance, Josephine would like to see a certain movie together with her partner, Liliana. If Josephine says, "I want to see this movie; please come with me," she's being somewhat controlling. If she says, "I hear there is this great movie, and everyone says it's wonderful. Do you want to go?" she's manipulating.

We use these same approaches to fulfill any desire, whether it's a desire for an object, for more knowledge, for love, attention, and so on. How we use these strategies to achieve our ends reflects our degree of awareness and emotional and psychological maturity. This is what we call developmental maturity, in that it demonstrates how much we've developed ourselves in terms of our potential for human evolution.

Let's look at another example. Say we feel upset if we don't get our way. Getting upset is one form of the human instinct to manipulate and control situations to try to get what we want. However, upset often results in some kind of conflict, and maybe hard feelings, which are unpleasant. To avoid this, we hide our upset, and overlay them with more subtle strategies of manipulation and control. When others challenge us on these semi-hidden impulses—"Are you being a little controlling?"—we often try to evade such labels, even when they're accurate, because it's embarrassing or otherwise uncomfortable.

The problem is that, over time, we end up believing our own strategies. Eventually, our more primitive drives become secret, hidden even to ourselves. When it is hidden in our psyche it's called "the shadow,"[99] first coined by Carl Jung.[100]

ME AND MY SHADOW; US AND OURS

As individuals, we compensate for our feelings of loneliness by clinging to our self-image, and by association to our tribe and its image. The aspects of our psyches that the group finds unacceptable get repressed and become the shadow, unconscious forces that drive our behavior.

The shadow hides our fears, anxieties, and insecurities underneath a cloak of compensatory propriety and correctness. Over time, they become our secrets. This largely unconscious process

---

[99] For more on this topic, see Reflection 15: Only the Shadow Knows.

[100] Carl Jung, *Aion: Researches into the Phenomenology of the Self* (Collected Works of C.G. Jung Vol. 9 Part 2, 1951).

ensures that we can fit in and belong, and that we're valued by (or at least get along with) our family, friends, and neighbors. To grow and unfold as people, we must come to terms with this personal and collective shadow element. We each have our own shadow, and we—as families, groups, tribes, and nations—also have a shared shadow.

A collective shadow usually involves a group cover-up of something we find shameful or otherwise reprehensible, or that we fear others will judge us for. Interestingly, the hiding causes us another—sometimes thicker—layer of distress, on top of the troubling thing itself. For example, a student of ours was in his 20s before he found out that his father had committed suicide; the family story was that he'd died of a heart attack. While, of course, finding out about the suicide itself was distressing, he said he found it more disturbing that he hadn't known for so many years.

While the secret about his father's suicide was maintained in the family's collective shadow, in part because the rest of the family didn't reveal that information, it's also true that he hadn't inquired very deeply, a hallmark of the personal shadow. There are things that part of us doesn't really want to know because bringing them into awareness makes us feel so uncomfortable. It is only by getting to the edge of our comfort zone that we can start to see exactly what kinds of things we're keeping secret from ourselves.

The most secret parts of our own personal development are revealed in the ways we respond to the unknown, or anything that deeply tests our mettle. Such challenges push the limits of our usual frame of mind, and even more viscerally, our emotional and psychological identity. These challenges and unknowns add another dimension to the definition of "secret:" *that which is unacknowledged.* We could say that when we aren't reaching for greater developmental maturity we're living a kind of lie, hiding among secrets kept from ourselves.

These tests can be distressing, so part of us tries to avoid or otherwise protect ourselves against them. Doing this in a customized fashion throughout our day could be a full-time occupation, so we learn to systematize. How do we do this? Fundamentally, the ego is alone, and ironically, it's this sense of separation that drives us to form bonds with individuals and groups, mostly with people who somehow seem like us, so we feel safer and less lonely. We then protect our tribe from attack by keeping others—anyone or anything perceived as too different from us—out.

Protecting our clan or group is an extension of protecting our ego identity. If we feel that others are very different from us, we may fall into seeing them as the enemy. Racism, sexism, and nationalism are some obvious and unfortunate examples of how this dynamic works. In these cases, our secret is what we keep from others. If you're not one of us, we won't tell you the secret you need to know to become one of us. Professions and socio-economic classes often function on this basis, too. It's a way of keeping others out, because the group in question would like to avoid the unknown or prevent potential challenges. This indicates another aspect of the definition of "secret:" *what is remote or secluded.* By keeping people out, a kind of secrecy is maintained. Others don't get to understand who we really are as human beings: our cares, our fears, our loves, and our deepest aspirations. Who they really are remains unknown, a secret to us, too. It's a lose-lose situation.

All of this begs the question of who gets to decide what or who is too different. The short answer is "I do." That is, the ego's nature is to always think that my way—or by extension the way of my group or tribe—is best. This is an ego-based form of con-sensual reality, and in the negative, collective blindness. What's actually happening is that we aren't looking at other ways of being, other perspectives. Or we aren't looking honestly, to see whether other people's ways of being may have strengths and benefits that ours do not. We reinforce this act of not looking by mostly engaging with people who have more or less the same level of questioning that we do.

We can imagine, hear, and read about higher levels of devel-opmental maturity, but knowing them takes firsthand experience.

When we do look, when we do consider others' points of view, the benefits are immediate and valuable: greater understanding and compassion, plus more feelings of interconnection. In other words, bliss and insight. Now we've moved to a win-win scenario.

We all would like to be more developed, and it seems that part of being human is to ripen over time, in stages. Ken Wilber has well described how stages of development indicate our maturity in various spheres of life (which he calls "lines of development"), such as the cognitive, values, orders of consciousness, world views, faith, and self-identity.[101] These can be developed in steps respective to the particular area of development. In the case of self-identity, for example, Wilber[102] describes it in ten steps or levels. We start as symbiotic at birth (that amazing feeling of union with mother) and progress through stages he calls the impulsive, self-protective, conformist, conscientious, individualistic, autonomous, integrated, ego-aware, and finally the transpersonal stage.

Each of the other lines of development follows a similar sequence progressing through various stages. Wilber's is the best map of humans' developmental maturity that we've seen, and a brilliant illustration of why meditation alone can't make us effective as awakening beings. Meditation addresses our mind and heart-states, but we need to actively explore our growth edges to develop our stages.

ALL THE WORLD'S A STAGE

From a higher level of maturity, we may perceive differences in levels, but acknowledging that difference may seem discriminatory or elitist or both. This would be a medium level of maturity. The highest level of maturity comes when we recognize that the differences in level are there and acknowledge their relevance. In other words, every person on a spiritual path is also cultivating

---

[101] Ken Wilber, *Integral Spirituality* (Boston: Shambhala Publications, 2006), 50–70.

[102] (following on the work of Jane Loevinger and Susanne Cook-Greuter)

their own *skillful* use of one of the definitions of "secret:" *revealed only to the initiated.*

We'd like to emphasize that higher levels of maturity bring their own special bonus: our fears and insecurities lessen (huzzah!). However, for the ego, anything outside our range of comfort is seen as a threat and is therefore rejected. When we get comfortable with our growth edge, we can muster the courage to begin exploring the subsequent stage. Thus we could say that our comfort zone delimits our developmental maturity.

This implies that anything above our current level or stage of maturity is, by definition, a secret. It's either one that others (perhaps wisely) keep from us, or that we keep from ourselves by simply not going there. Again, here "secret" has the sense of *revealed only to the initiated.* Each of us gets to decide whether we would like to be initiated or not, but we have to commit the blood, sweat, and tears to do so. It takes education, training, courage, and old-fashioned grit to learn to integrate things outside our comfort zone and to extend our development.

For example, someone who is more sexually conservative might be aghast at, say, the graphic nature of sex on prime time TV. Someone who's very liberal may find such a response uptight or anachronistic. Both of these are ego-based reactions, and both parties are limited by their belief that their own values are best. But the latter is a bit more mature than the former, not because it's more correct, per se, but because it includes a quality of open-mindedness or acceptance. Someone who was even more developmentally mature about sexuality might feel that all the debate around sexuality is overwrought and that, among consenting adults, choices of sexual behavior is the concern of the individuals involved. And again, each higher level is "secret" to the one below it in terms of not being able to perceive the validity of the view.

WHY KEEP SECRETS AT ALL?

We can trace the roots of every secret back to a deep ego-based fear.[103] As previously mentioned, the ego is, was, and always will be alone. While we can transcend the ego in states of meditative and concentrative absorption and eventually integrate these meditative states into our daily life, our ego fears may still remain and get acted out while interacting with another ego. Transcending ego fears and navigating life with other egos is more about stages of development, not states.

Long before we embark on a spiritual path, our level of developmental maturity is firstly determined by our conditioning. Conditioning—from our parents and family, our communities, our religions, our culture, and even the times in which we live—tell us who and what to be and how to behave. But ultimately—through education, experience, reflection, and meeting challenges—our level of developmental and spiritual maturity is our own responsibility.

In other words, our conditioning shapes our values and views, which then determine our emotions and actions. The limiting factor for developmental maturity is how conscious we are of the conditioning—the secrets—that have shaped us, and how much we have freed ourselves from those aspects that limit us. And this is determined, essentially, by how much we want to be free of it, and what we're willing to do to achieve this liberation.

It's worth noting that there are good aspects to our conditioning: all those positive things we absorb from others as we grow up, like being encouraged to talk and walk, our education, the many wholesome aspects of our family, and societal culture. Those are gifts to be celebrated. Here, however, we're addressing the problematic aspects that limit our growth and potential to be more awake and caring human beings, such as tribal conditioning to be prejudiced against other groups or tribes.

---

[103] See more on this in the section on the *Four Deep Ego Fears* in Reflection 3.

If we have secrets that we don't want others to know, it's likely because we are protecting our self-image. We may be afraid we'll lose something—like a friendship, social acceptance, a certain reputation, opportunities, or property—or get into trouble. Maybe, ultimately, we fear being abandoned. Presenting a particular persona to others is necessary; we have to show up somehow. When done with awareness, it can be skillful. This is another definition of "secret:" *discretion or to elude observation.* However, if we believe our self-image is "real," or present it solely for self-centered ends, then it becomes a kind of falsehood.

As egos, we are self-seeking. While we try to consider others, we want what we want. The shadow aspect emerges when we can't meet the conflict of the competing desires: what I want vs. what you want. One ego-based option is to indulge our own desire at the expense of the other person's. We may try to pretend that's not what really happened, or that we didn't know, or that we don't care, all of which entail presenting a self-image that serves our own ends. Again, these are untruths.

Another option is to shut down our desire and pretend we don't have it or that it doesn't matter. This is another kind of fallacy. In extreme cases, we go unconscious to our own desire. Nevertheless, the desire is still there and surfaces in some form or another that might look like greed (for example extreme wealth) or hatred (such as an extreme skin condition). The shadow becomes our own secret from ourselves.

A classic example would be choosing to not address an issue with our partner, or to keep it a secret. This is a choice we make. Perhaps we think we don't want to get in an argument, hurt them, or damage our relationship. Behind this may be a much deeper issue—the fear of being abandoned. This may be something we haven't chosen to see yet, so we keep it secret from ourselves.

Experiencing these fears is part of being human. And the spiritual path is about learning when and how they are in play, and how to transcend them. We can feel these fears arise in us, but we don't have to live, react, or make our choices from them. The degree to which we can be present with such fears and discomfort, but still choose to live from courage and love (versus fear), defines our level of developmental maturity. This, combined with our inner state as developed through practices such as meditation and Karma Yoga, helps us keep growing the edges of our spiritual development, our birthright.

REFLECTION 10

WHY THE "SECRET" TEACHINGS ARE SECRET

Growing from Secrets to Understanding

Secrets also serve an important function, to protect people from what we are not ready to know. This is what's meant by "secret teachings" in some spiritual traditions. Secret teachings manifest in two ways. First, it's said that teachings are self-secret in that we are only able to know things when we are ready. We may hear the same teachings tens or even hundreds of times, and then one day the lightbulb goes on: "Wow! That is really profound!" Before that moment, we'd heard the words but somehow they didn't hold so much meaning.

Second, it's more skillful to share certain teachings when we've shown we're ready to integrate them. Just as we get good at doing fifty sit-ups before attempting one hundred so we don't get discouraged or strain a muscle, spiritual teachings are designed to be shared and practiced in a particular order. It's like building a house; first, a solid foundation is built, then the basic frame, then the details. We are only ready to know certain things as our loving-kindness, compassion, and wisdom develop enough to embrace and integrate them. The key to what is shared or not, what's "secret," is determined by our level of developmental maturity.

The same holds true in relationships and the rest of our lives. For instance, after my (Doug's) father died, my mother confided in me that she had never really loved him. This was a secret she kept not only from him and us—their children—but perhaps from herself, since they were married for sixty years! She had loved someone else, she confessed, but this other man couldn't provide her the security that was important to her. This didn't really come as a surprise, as she'd often expressed frustration about her life with my father. But it would have been inappropriate to share this background story with my siblings and I when we were children. By keeping it secret, she was protecting us from knowledge that we weren't ready to integrate. When the child—in this case me—grows older and more independent, they have the ego strength to better integrate this. When my mother finally told me, I was in my fifties, and I had as much compassion for her frustrations and failure as I had empathy for my dad's unfulfilling marriage.

Each of us has found ourselves in experiences that are far enough outside of our social and cultural conditioning that we weren't prepared—developmentally mature enough—to handle very well. It's not until after we mature that we see our ignorance. Think of the censorship of Elvis' dance moves on 1950s television, or the oppression that LGBTQ people still face in many cultures. To facilitate our own and others' ongoing maturity, it may be helpful to keep in mind that most of the people who were upset about Elvis' immorality or who stigmatize queer folk probably believe themselves to be developmentally mature. They may be offended at the suggestion that they aren't. They also probably see themselves as compassionate and wise—don't we all?

As we indicated, Tibetan Buddhism describes some teachings as *self-secret*: when the student is ready, the understanding opens like a flower of its own accord. Until such a time, the understanding is not available even if the teaching itself has been received. Buddhist philosophy holds that there is a kind of protection—safeguarding both the teachings and the practitioner—inherently built in. Each stage includes all the ones before it, but the subsequent ones are as though invisible.

Not everything is self-secret all of the time, however, and practitioners on a spiritual path learn how to practice skillful communication and action together with truth, which Buddhist philosophy describes as being of both the relative and absolute varieties. For example, it may not be compassionate to tell an ill person that they look terrible. It may be more compassionate to share that their scarf is beautiful, or that their smile is radiant.

APPLES AND ORANGES; STATES AND STAGES

According to Ken Wilber, a state is an internal type of consciousness (waking, dreaming, meditative, altered, peak experience) that comes and goes. Stages are permanent: they represent levels of growth and development that are integrated into the daily operational level of a being. With the earlier example of stages of self-identity, we start out at the symbiotic stage as infants, and with effort, develop later into the conformist stage, then (again, if we apply our intent) individualistic, autonomous, ego-aware, and finally transpersonal.

It's important to be clear on the difference between states and stages. As an example, a racist would be in a lower stage of development compared to a humanitarian. Even when the racist is having a good day and feeling his or her best (a higher state), he or she won't attain a higher stage. We must work for stages over time. By comparison, when a humanitarian is having a bad day and feeling their worst (a crummy state), she or he won't fall to a lower stage. Once earned, stages cannot be lost. Hooray!

It's vitally important that we move forward into actualizing our own better states and stages. Spending energy to try to hasten our own or others' evolution before we or they are ready, or spending too much time in victim[104] or martyr roles, hobbles our human endeavor to explore, learn, and unfold as more compassionate

---

[104] Arthur C. Brooks, "The Real Victims of Victimhood," *The New York Times*, Dec. 26, 2015, https://www.nytimes.com/2015/12/27/opinion/sunday/the-real-victims-of-victimhood.html, accessed Jan. 22, 2017.

and caring human beings. While everyone benefits from the generation of great love and compassion toward all beings, it is incumbent on us to move forward in our individual development as a greater act of compassion toward this and future generations. The best way to ensure that others join us on this journey is to lead by example. As Walt Whitman says in "Song of the Open Road:"

> *I and mine do not convince by arguments, similes, rhymes,*
> *We convince by our presence.*

Lofty states can at times occur spontaneously as manifestations of grace—such as feeling an amazing sense of union with all of creation while watching a spectacular sunrise. And while we honor and appreciate anyone's good state, we'd do well to recognize that, for the average person, a good state is temporary, but we live in our stage of development.

One of the purposes of a good state is to apply it to growing our current level of developmental maturity, our stage. We use the good state as a positive place from which to take a look at our current stage, and bring it higher. Being in a great state and ignoring the ongoing development of our stage is a dereliction of duty, a failure in compassion, and an illusion of ego aggrandizement. It's far more compassionate, wise, and generally beneficial to ourselves and others when we leverage a good state to become more aware, more awake. In a sense, we take the light of a good state and shine it on the shadow of our current stage, to bring that darkness into ever greater light.

Combining a good state with ongoing development of stages could be one way to describe how we evolve as individuals and as a collective. Improved stages make accessing increasingly better states more likely. Perhaps more importantly, they herald a clearer, more compassionate, and more spiritually, socially, economically, and environmentally sustainable planet.

It's key to note that the secret of higher stages is not actually secret, per se. These secrets are open to anyone willing to do the work to attain the developmental maturity needed to receive them, anyone ready to initiate themselves (with a little help from our friends, such as teachers and mentors) into the higher stages. Wilber's lines of development that identify different stages are not, from our perspective, designed as a system of ranking. Rather they're an invitation to explore potential for growth and to look at that in what may be new ways.[105]

Our motivation to cultivate developmental maturity lies in the understanding that lesser stages are less sustainable, less free, and more prone to greater suffering. Meanwhile, greater stages yield greater degrees of freedom, wider prospects, and a more loving, joyful experience of life. The purpose of spiritual teachings is to help people learn precisely how to use clear meditative states to transform stages, thereby helping us become ever more compassionate, enlightened, and life embracing. This makes for a life worth living!

FOREWARNED IS FOREARMED

There are a few predictable areas where our societal and familial conditioning are most likely to limit our developmental maturity. Not surprisingly, these three major areas are where our ego identities are most rooted:

1. Our sense of ego survival, grounded in a feeling of belonging;

2. Sexuality as a defining element of our sense of self; and

3. Power, that sense of being in control of our own lives and not subject to being controlled by others.[106]

You'll notice that these issues originate in the lowest three chakras: the root chakra is about survival; the second chakra at

---

[105] To explore further, we recommend Wilber's *Integral Spirituality*.

[106] We address these three areas further in Reflection 17 on Money, Sex, and Power.

the abdomen/reproductive organs is about sexuality; and the third chakra around the navel (sometimes the solar plexus) pertains to power.

Traditional religions are in a thorny spot on these three spheres of the human experience. Mainstream religions tend to enshrine a status quo-based view of morality, which helps society function and offers a collective feeling of belonging and fitting in. But religions are challenged to keep pace with the rapid change of modern times regarding our views on wealth and resources, sexuality, and personal power. Some religions' views on birth control, women's rights, gay marriage, open relationships, etc. are in stark contrast with many people's daily lives, which causes considerable inner turmoil and flight from religious institutions (often without a better alternative). It's an unfortunate situation for the people involved as well as for religion.

An unintended consequence is that these primary energies of our lowest three chakras populate our personal and collective shadows. The exposure of religious institutions' cover ups (abuse of power, sexuality, wealth, etc.) over decades, centuries, or even millennia then come back around and terribly upset our feelings of trust and belonging. This is an example of secrets kept for the wrong reasons. In such cases, compassion, kindness, and wisdom have been sidelined for unwholesomeness to persist. The Catholic church's sexual abuse cases and avoidance of accountability related to them, or the Rajneesh organization's misuse of power through criminal activities, are just two examples. When such situations come to light, those affected feel not just alone, but also betrayed.

To benefit ourselves and others on this journey of growth and unfoldment as enlightening beings, our spiritual path must foster developmental maturity. And this process has to include addressing and integrating the shadow, the lies we tell (sometimes unbeknownst to ourselves), and secrets we keep from ourselves and each other out of self-interest.

It's not possible any time soon to eradicate the shadows of this world, but we can embark on the path to integrate our own shadow and choose to be with people doing the same. By starting with ourselves, we shrink our familial, societal, and global shadows in a very powerful way. This practice requires courage and awareness.

Any path of true liberation addresses all of our issues around survival (with money as its most obvious symbol), sexuality, and power, to grow our developmental maturity. Yes, these are explosive topics, mostly because we are so unaccustomed to addressing them honestly and maturely.

There are, of course, different ways to skillfully address them, appropriate for different people and varying situations. This may be why, over the millennia, Buddhists developed what are called three different vehicles: Theravadin, Mahayana, and Vajrayana. Theravadin Buddhism adheres to the original teachings of the Buddha and teaches how to cultivate good states by avoiding bad ones. It's a teaching of renunciation. With fewer temptations (few belongings, no personal adornments, no special treatment), it's much easier to get into good states and stay in them. However, it also means all that troublesome secret stuff tied up in all those enticements—no sex or intoxicants either—get sidestepped. Since they don't come up, their complexities don't need to be worked through and integrated with daily life experience.

Mahayana Buddhism takes a more engaged approach. It added the bodhisattva vow to Buddhist philosophy and practice, addressing the fact that we're all in this together. This is the version we use:

> However innumerable beings are
> I vow to meet them with kindness and interest.
> However inexhaustible the states of suffering are,
> I vow to touch them with patience and love.
> However immeasurable the Dharmas are,
> I vow to explore them deeply.
> However incomparable the mystery of being is,
> I vow to experience it fully.
> From this moment forth,

With wisdom and compassion as my lamp and staff,
I dedicate all my life energy to the welfare of all beings.[107]

In other words, if you're suffering, I'm suffering too, and so is
everyone else. So I make an effort to help you to alleviate your suffering, recognizing that I and all of us benefit thereby. Mahayana
steps into our worldly lives, rather than stepping out of them.
It embraces considerate behavior as the vehicle to transform our
lives and teaches loving-kindness and compassion meditations
as the methodologies by which we can bring our behavior in the
world in sync with our hearts and minds.

Finally, Vajrayana Buddhism approaches temptations directly,
upcycling them as grist for the spiritual mill. Literally illustrating
this, Vajrayana iconography is full of "monsters:" some deities
and saints have the heads of animals, bulging eyes, sharp teeth,
genitalia, startling arsenals of sharp weapons, and saintly figures
having sex, sometimes *en groupe.*

Due to their potentially provocative nature, these are the
more "secret" teachings, in that traditionally they were "revealed
only to the initiated." Before the Internet and other global media
made these available to just about anyone (alas, unskillfully and
inappropriately so), such teachings were only shared when a
practitioner had demonstrated their readiness. They did this by
undertaking enough practice to establish a solid, abiding foundation of calm, concentration, loving-kindness, and compassion.
Only at this relatively advanced stage of developmental maturity
would Vajrayana teachers share these practices, which take the
"monsters" hiding in the closet of our psyches—our fears and
desires—and bring them into the light.

When we're living in the light, nothing is very scary; there are
no secrets left in dark corners that might catch us unawares and
strike fear into our hearts. And bringing our shadow elements
into the light frees up an enormous amount of energy. We're no

[107] There are numerous versions; this one is based on one from Thich Nhat
Hanh via Lama Tarchin Hearn.

longer limited by dread of what ifs, what we might do, or who we might be, so we're not simultaneously braking and hitting the gas as we're living. Our energy is now available and naturally inclined toward a life of exploration and discovery, rooted in friendliness and compassion.

To help us get there from here, Vajrayana Buddhism includes four levels of Tantra[108] to foster deeper meditative states, and also to promote developmental maturity. Each level reveals more of the so-called secret nature of the teachings. Each level requires an increasing commitment to the practice, more intimate communication between self and other (initially the teacher and then the community of practitioners), and deeper journeys into oneself, including exploring the shadow elements. Unveiling our secrets requires not only reading/hearing about them but also experiencing them somatically, emotionally, and psychologically. Thus Tantra requires that we get up close and personal with our practice. In essence, the core of the practice is the experience of union with other, sometimes called non-duality.

As we become more developmentally mature, the clear sky mind[109] that manifests as clarity, bliss, wisdom, and compassion reveals more and more of its secrets. We experience directly how many secrets are self-concealing and self-revealing, from and to ourselves. The secrets remain so until we open our hearts and minds beyond the mere rules and regulations of social convention and let go of attachments and fears rooted in ego clinging.

Maintaining the secrecy of secret teachings serves a valuable purpose, particularly for the uninitiated. If we aren't yet in a position of developmental maturity to be able to respond compassionately to the information and experience, this functions as our own protection. However, as our spiritual maturity and wisdom grow, we're able to perceive and understand these former

---

[108] See Reflection 13 for more on tantric stages.

[109] We first define clear sky mind—after which we named our Clear Sky Retreat Center—in Reflection 3: If You Want The Present You Have To Open The Box, under the subhead *The Ego is a House on Fire*.

secrets, and further deepen our realization. Until such a time, the secrecy also helps protect the integrity of the teachings, so they're there for us, profoundly, when we're ready and able to integrate them.

There is one ultimate secret that few of us—though perhaps an increasing number—perceive: the secret of *universal* compassion. Compassion is not just for people close to us but also for those far away, for those we don't get along with, for those we dislike, for the environment, other species, social institutions, the global economy, for everyone and everything. Wisdom dawns when we apply this compassion and understanding to both our own and others' development. This is when we realize the clear sky mind, the spacious, luminescent, awake radiance of non-clinging awareness.

REFLECTION 11
SPIRITUAL AWAKENING THROUGH RELATIONSHIPS

The Breath of Life

The word "spiritual" may mean different things to different people, so what do we mean when we use it? It's derived from the Latin *spiritus*, meaning breathing, breath, or breath of god. For us, this implies something that is flowing and life-giving.

As spiritually awakening beings, we're learning to relink the relationships between the spiritual and material realms, between our sensing bodies, thinking minds and breath of spirit. As we conjoin these aspects, we deepen our relationship with ourselves. This yields a being—us—who explores and discovers in an ever-growing state of awareness.

And, somewhat paradoxically, *self*-awareness requires *other*: we must see outside of our self to see our self, to have a mirror and a context for our thoughts and feelings. This growing relationship with our self makes us more aware of others, their thoughts, feelings, and breath.

While we may not have direct access to others' minds, since we are all human, we can intuit that others' bodies, actions, thoughts, and feelings are similar to ours, or that they are quite different.

We can intuit their similar intentions, or their very different ones, and enjoy the familiarity of the likenesses or the richness of the variances. Our fundamental instinct is to feel good, and to be social; we are drawn to share and learn from each other. And this sharing is a major component of relationship.

So relationship denotes connection, how we interact with ourselves and each other, as well as how we relate to nature or objects. The influence of Zen on traditional Japanese arts illustrates the latter beautifully. How we relate to a flower arrangement, a cup of tea, the interconnection between brush, ink, and paper—all reflect how we relate to ourselves and others. The presence with which tea is served, or the indelible lines and telling splashes from brushstrokes, all mirror the state of our being in those moments, our relationship to each object, and to the viewer of stroke or flower, or recipient of tea. When we are out of sync, with ourselves or others, we have one kind of relationship; when we are in harmony, a different kind of relationship can emerge.

The word "relationship" first appeared in the 1640s to mean "the sense or state of being related," but was not applied specifically to romantic or sexual relationships until 1944.[110] Our ideas of relationships today, particularly romantic ones, are very modern. Historically, around the globe (and still in some parts of the world), marriages were often practical and strategic arrangements between families involving an exchange of property, all or part of which may have consisted of the bride and/or groom. Their feelings toward each other or spiritual inclinations were not usually taken into consideration.

OUR PRIMARY RELATIONSHIPS

The universe as we know it can only exist because everything is in relationship with everything else. That said, for a harmonious coexistence, we must first and foremost have a healthy connection

---

[110] "Relationship," Online Etymology Dictionary, accessed June 16, 2018, http://www.etymonline.com/index.php?term=relationship.

with ourselves. But we don't live and relate in a vacuum. When we use relationships for awakening, we use all these connections—with our self, with other people, with objects—to become more aware, to explore, and discover our interconnections with life.

Our original relationship is with our mother, dating back to the womb, when we experienced our self and our mother as one organism. When we were in our mother's womb, we couldn't distinguish between me, her, and us together, and this feeling of union was generally blissful. Earlier, we addressed the shock of the original realization of our physical separation with mother and the survival fears that follow, around age two.[111] We could say that our most intimate relationships are, in part, an attempt to return to the contented state of union in our mother's womb, which seems preferable to the shock of separation and accompanying vulnerability. In a sense, before that separation, mother was our universe, or at least the safe mothership of our universe.

Falling in love feels blissful in this same union kind of way: everything feels just right. And, as anyone who's been in love knows, it's not possible (nor even desirable) to stay in this undifferentiated state, in such a small womb-sized universe, forever. After the first relationship with our mother, all the others are a different ballgame. There are diverse rules, agendas, desires, interests, and so on that sooner or later distract us from the bliss of being in love.

Some relationships are intimate, some are romantic, and some are both or neither. A relationship with a colleague with whom we work closely all day, every day for years, for example, may be intimate but not romantic. Similarly, some romantic or sexual relationships can be, in some ways, not intimate. Other times, we can share space with someone for years and hardly get to know them at all. Or maybe we do but don't realize it. Even when we feel we don't especially like a person, familiarity often brings some kind of fondness.

---

[111] See the Four Deep Ego Fears in Reflection 3, as well as Reflection 14.

IT's EASIER WITH OTHERS

Relationships and familiarity grow in the context of time and place. Throughout most of human history we lived in communities. Whether in a town, a neighborhood, at a workplace, or on an estate, we lived and worked with a relatively tight-knit group of people whom we saw every day for many consecutive years.

Due to modern mobility and the wonders of technology, nowadays many of us live and work in numerous different places, with regularly changing social circles, teams, and clientele. Naturally, both local community and the global village have their pros and cons. Local communities consist of a resilient fabric woven of interrelationships. And it can feel constraining if there's a sense that everyone knows everything about everybody all the time. Working in the global village provides a sense of possibilities, freedom, and the stimulation of diversity and change. Lack of awareness about people's histories can feel light, the opposite of heavy. And it can also feel risky, lonely, and alienating.

Trust takes time to build and earn. Working with people we don't know that well can, at best, lead to increased communication problems and at worst major conflict. This is why in smaller communities and some countries (like Japan) it can take years to establish relations that people trust and rely on. In addition to our own direct experience, our mutual acquaintances, friends, and colleagues inform us about the others' reliability and character, forever weaving the fabric of interrelationships.

In terms of relationship, nowadays the most pervasive models in the developed world are the nuclear family, within which we also include the nuclear relationship. By "nuclear relationship" we mean an exclusive pair bond between two people who, beyond the legal benefits, generally don't have a sustainable and mutual support network as a couple and as individuals. As mentioned, historically, we lived in neighborhoods or villages with our extended family or close acquaintances for most of our lives. When challenges arose, community was there to provide support as needed, and this was part of daily life.

With nuclear families and relationships, generally speaking, such a community is not part of the picture. That is, they're in it, for the most part, alone. All difficulties must be self-resolved within the family or relationship unit, without easy access to a variety of role models and perspectives, or input from numerous people who know all the parties involved well. Recourses like counselling are helpful, but still out of context from day-to-day interactions.

Living in community, on the other hand, means there are people nearby who naturally care about, and are involved and invested in, our well-being, as individuals, couples, or as families. Visually, imagine the difference between two people facing each other, compared to five people or more in a circle. Two people can easily polarize, while by comparison, diversity of perspectives and input can both smooth out the rough bits and enhance the discussion. In spite of our egos' isolationist tendencies, life is easier with others. We can see this on a larger scale with two-party politics (U.S.A.) compared to multiple-party systems (Canada, Germany), where forming coalitions is both necessary and constructive.

Without such a community context, one of the unintended consequences is serial monogamy: I'll be in an exclusive relationship with you, and if it doesn't work out, we'll quit and be in an exclusive relationship with someone else, over and over. This means that the relationship isn't exclusive after all, but that the group of people involved is organized in a binary linear trajectory.

Again, egos think they are independent, single, and permanent, and therefore, when they meet another such ego, anything that threatens that sense leads to conflict. Since living with others implies different desires, conflict is unavoidable, but the pressure gets diffused if it's not just binary. More on this to follow.

Whoever came up with the adage, "It takes a village to raise a child" (thought to be an African proverb) knew what they were talking about. Raising a child is not something we'd wish on people who don't have the support of an extended family or its equivalent. Child-rearing can be relatively easily and joyfully shared among numerous willing people accustomed and able to do so. But for just one or two people (a single parent or a couple), raising a child alone can be a daunting responsibility, as any parent knows. Hats off to the people who are making it work the best they can.

For the majority of human history, we had a diversity of role models around us to help us make relationships work. Each of us has different preponderances, and if one person didn't happen to play a particular role that felt important to us—say, being good with children, or numbers, or mechanics, or enjoying the arts or the outdoors—chances were good that someone else around us did, and the communal needs could all balance out.

Often in today's workaday world of the nuclear family, the day-to-day concerns can take up all of our energy. Getting things done, looking after the kids, keeping track of all our passwords, and holding everything together can eclipse our spiritual aspirations. We may one day wake up to find ourselves in a situation that seems to be in disharmony with the dreams we once shared with our partner, or we may not resonate with why we first got together. Perhaps it wasn't originally for spiritual reasons, but we hoped that eventually it might become so, and it hasn't.

It's challenging to stay in a relationship under these conditions. How then can we grow spiritually in relationships in the conditions we find ourselves in?

RELATIONSHIPS IN COMMUNITY

We believe one of the purposes of a spiritual community is to foster relationships that orient around our spiritual practice and development. When facing discord, it's easy for two people to drift into ego positions and polarize into a sparring match. Spiritual community serves to take out the oppositional nature of conflict in relationship. By adding other people into the dialogue, the dynamic can get triangulated and spread out. Conflict can thereby be transformed into a generative force, supporting inquiry and the search for optimal resolution for all concerned through the group. This fuels the liberating potential of relationship.

Consider a situation that arose at Clear Sky. Felix asked Marquetta a question she thought he should know. She felt he was passing off his responsibility on to her because of laziness, and according to Felix, Marquetta responded in a surly tone, angry but not directly addressing what was going on. Later, she criticized Felix to Richard. Richard brought the conflict to a group meeting and the team suggested that Felix and Marquetta mirror each other's position. Marquetta mirrored Felix accurately reflecting back what he had said in the conflict, but Felix gave his own opinion—not a true reflection—of what Marquetta had expressed in their dialogue. Richard asked Marquetta if she felt heard, and she said no. The group encouraged Felix to mirror more objectively, which he did. At that point, each saw the polarization and could let it go, even with hugs of appreciation.

In sum, trust is the big issue, and without it, conflict cannot be successfully met. Marquetta and Felix grew the trust between them *through* resolving conflict. They also grew confidence in themselves, that they could address conflict skillfully and come out the better for it. The group provided a safe container in which they could do it. More conflicts are sure to arise—it's part of being human—but everyone involved now had more tools to transform the conflict into growth together.

In spiritual community, everyone becomes our partner, everyone becomes our teacher, and we learn that there is more than one way to have intimate relationships. This doesn't mean one has sex with everybody (or anybody), though for a small number of people this may be their path. But it does mean that we learn to have multiple special relationships with varying types of people, not necessarily of our choosing, and with fluctuating degrees of intimacy. We see the benefits of learning to get along with different kinds of people, and even to enjoy it. We learn that there is no one special person or group of people with whom our ego can rest in the delusion of a pseudo-freedom for long, covering up our own unconscious habits and inner conflicts.

Living and working together in such a way is a central part of the path of Karma Yoga, or what we call awakening in action. It's the meditation of working together as individuals and as teams to become more spiritual, more integrated human beings, while still undertaking the day-to-day activities that must be done.

We consider this process of learning a kind of training. Most of us haven't been trained to be intimate in group situations, nor even with our significant other. When things get intense, many of us have been conditioned to leave, to go back to our room, apartment, or gadget as a way to step out of what's happening until it blows over. With Karma Yoga, we learn and continue to re-learn how to stay present and work through it together.

Of course, this doesn't exclude being in romantic relationships and/or having families. The key is that we learn how *not* to use these relationships as a place to escape to avoid something else. We can be in them to grow, not to hide. For most people, this makes our romantic and family relationships healthier and lighter: we choose them from a place of strength and love, rather than cling to them from a feeling of deficiency.

In relationships where we get close with another—maybe even in an antagonistic way—we often use the other person (and vice versa) as a mirror, to help us see what we may miss or ignore when we get too self-focused. We cannot see our own face unless we have a mirror. This is, in part, the function the other person serves: they are a reflection of how we're connecting with life.

For instance, let's say Raj is angry at Malini because she didn't ask him about his day. In other words, Raj is hurt because Malini ignored him. Raj let Malini know, and then Malini felt upset because she felt attacked. Now, both parties are in reactions to hurt, most likely replicating how they were conditioned through witnessing their parents' reactions to hurt. Raj might think, "Why is Malini so upset? I'm the hurt party here," and he might have the wherewithal to see that she's hurting because of how he expressed his anger. Then Raj has the option to see how the way he communicated with her was a hurt reaction as well and see the vicious hurt cycle they'd fallen into. Then he can transform it into a virtuous cycle by addressing his own hurt, sharing with

Malini what he observes happening between them, rather than trying to get her to be a particular way to suit him.

In contrast, if Raj and Malini were work colleagues, Raj might go home at the end of the day and just feel irritated by Malini. He might let the dynamic carry on, and have it affect their ongoing relationship while he dealt with it by going home and stewing on his own. Raj could, of course, work it out with Malini at the office, but this takes an exceptional amount of trust and courage. Commonly, we save these qualities for our significant other.[112]

THE UNION OF LOVE

When we're in love and flooded with endorphins, our attention is biased and blissful. We project our desire for complete union onto this particular person. On the one hand, the urge is regressive: we have fond longings for that unitive state with our mother's womb and would like to return to that. On the other hand, the longing is transcendental: we have an instinctual desire to reconnect with the cosmos, the blissful spacious energy that permeates the entire universe.[113]

Either way, a mere mortal can't fulfill these urges for us. We'd need to stay oblivious to their idiosyncrasies and bad habits, which gets harder and harder over time. Seeing these more clearly tends to knock us out of our endorphin rush. If unexpected, it can be a painful crash.

To put it another way, when in love, we contact the unitive state. From the point of view of spiritual practice, the beloved can become a meditation object to help us reconnect with the unitive experience, the universe itself. Rumi, a 13th-century Sufi mystic, expresses this in his poetry to tremendous effect:

---

[112] This is one of the reasons we are such fans of Karma Yoga: it provides the space and the means to address whatever is coming up with our teams, training us to bring these skills into the workplace and other relationships, including romantic. See Reflections 5 and 6.

[113] In terms of AstroDharma (see Reflection 16), this urge for transformation through dissolution of boundaries is the realm of the planet Neptune.

If anyone wonders how Jesus raised the dead,
don't try to explain the miracle.
Kiss me on the lips.[114]

As we've seen, different traditions call this experience various things, including cosmic consciousness, God, spiritual ecstasy, etc. When one realizes that the "I" that is perceived has *never* been separate, it is a fully embodied experience that Buddhism calls the Great Awakening. The "I" is only one facet of the totality of the unitive. It is totality flowing through the mind and senses. It is one manifestation of the universe observing and expressing itself.

A sense of separateness drops away when the unitive is experienced. This means there is no perception of self and no other, so linking self and other—how we usually think of relationship—is moot.

Ironically, to know that we are in union, we have to take a step back from the union to observe it. Upon this stepping back, separation returns, and so do relationships. Whenever we step back, look away from, or ignore the unitive experience, the dynamic of relationship comes into play.

When we focus too much on self, "other" emerges more strongly, and we move further away from a feeling of union. When we can perceive the interconnectedness of self and other—love—we move toward union.

And it feels better.

SACRED INTERCONNECTION

We can see this sentiment narrated throughout the world's wisdom traditions. The Bible, for example, holds that, "In the resurrection, people neither marry nor are given in marriage but are like the angels in heaven."[115] The idea here is that if one is in the flow,

---

[114] *Like This*, from Coleman Barks and John Moyne, *The Essential Rumi*, (New York: Harper Collins, 2010).
[115] Matthew 22:30 (ISV).

the spirit, of exploration and discovery, if one is aware, and feels connected (resurrected, reborn), there is no need for "other," for someone else, to make that happen. Again, Rumi described it so well:

> If I love myself
> I love you.
> If I love you
> I love myself.[116]

Roots of this belief extend deep into human history, before sexuality was so strongly linked to property rights, ownership, and, hence, exclusivity. According to cultural anthropologist Barbara Walker, "'Holy Virgin' was the title of harlot-priestesses of Ishtar, Sherah, or Aphrodite. The title didn't mean physical virginity, it meant simply 'unmarried.' The function of such 'holy virgins' was to dispense the Mother's grace through sexual worship: to heal, to prophesy, to perform sacred dances, to wail for the dead, and to become Brides of God."[117]

We can sense that such a person may not have been destined for or desirous of typical married life with another man or woman. That is, they lived in a different kind of unitive experience; they were "self-wed," or wed to spirit, with a commitment to an ongoing experience of unity.

Regardless of gender, married to or together with another person or not, each of us has the capacity to be in connection and interdependent with awareness of the flow or spirit of the universe. As the Book of Galatians puts it: "There is neither Jew nor Gentile, neither slave nor free, nor is there male and female, for you are all one in Christ Jesus."[118] This implies that

---

[116] From the poem, *Do You Love Me?*

[117] Barbara G. Walker, *Women's Encyclopedia of Myths and Secrets,* (San Francisco: Harper & Row, 1994), 1047–1048.

[118] Galatians 3:28 (NIV).

our primary relationship is with spirit or god, however we define that. We call it spiritual awakening.

If we're in ongoing relationship with spirit, are relationships with other people part of the picture? It may be easy to think that being single or celibate is more holy, and makes it easier to be connected to spirit. Not necessarily. In fact, one of the major challenges for single people is feeling separate, a.k.a. loneliness. Unitive experience, love, is all about *not* feeling separate, whether we are in relationship or alone.

That said, if you've never been intentionally celibate, we highly recommend it for a specific timeframe—say, a year minimum—as a practice to become more aware of one's patterns of relating with others and oneself. And it has to be *intentional*: the intentionality brings an added dimension of how and why we make choices in relationship, or out of them.

From the perspective of deepest mind essence, there is no gender, and there is no "other." In relative terms, however, we need to be able to enter comfortably into a state of mutual inter-penetration for an experience to be unitive. This is the purpose of relationships: to embrace the unitive through exploring the nature of self and other.

Sounds potentially wonderful, so what stops us? We often experience others as threatening due to two things: insecurities about ourselves, and misplaced belief in an inherent and inviolable separation between "me" and "other." That's the relative domain.

In the absolute realm, union is experienced as a flow between union and non-union. In other words, in a state of union, our sense of self dissolves into the bliss-ocean of oneness. But we cannot remain there idly. As humans, we live in the relative world, too, where we need to interact with form, feelings, ideas, and other people. In this interactive relative realm, there is give and take, an ebb and flow of relating that can seem unitive at times, distinct and separate at others.

But in the absolute sense, this apparent dichotomy may also still be experienced as union. Whether the tide is ebbing or flowing, it is all still one ocean.

At its most fundamental, spiritual awakening is the experience and understanding of non-separateness, a perception that gets totally obscured by self-focus. Relationships—romantic or otherwise—demand of us that we focus on someone other than just ourselves. Love requires that we focus on them as much as we focus on ourselves. Love blurs the sense of distinction between us, and healthy love does so in beautiful ways. This doesn't necessarily come easily. Through the process, relationships help us realize how obsessed we are with our own thoughts, feelings, and sensations. What's more, relationships reveal that others have *their* own thoughts, feelings, and sensations, which are as equally important to them as ours are to us.

Not dissimilar from Galileo's predecessors who believed the sun travelled around the earth, our ego remains convinced that the sun and solar system—maybe even the whole universe—revolves around *me*. It takes a certain amount of intimacy with another person for us to come to the somewhat shocking realization that they believe the universe revolves around *them*. It sounds comical, but it's true, isn't it?

Through sincere spiritual practice, we can cultivate the developmental maturity to individuate from our conditioned upbringing—also known as the ego—that's shaped our life to date, and the self-centeredness that the untamed ego brings. It takes relationships to show us that, to come into union, we have to be able to let go of the self. By transcending our self-orientation and putting our focus on others, we can begin to see the underlying union.

With spiritual practices, we come to experience that beyond the union *between* me and the object of my affections there is simply union itself. We learn that the universe simply is, and we are but a few sentient beings on a planet revolving around one of millions of stars.

And that—gloriously—small is indeed beautiful, and even small, beautiful things make for tremendous reverberations through our beings.

DESTINATION: WOMB OR COSMOS?

Sometimes relationship may be used as an escape from being more awake, and ironically, from our imperative to be in union. In our attempt to alleviate the ego's loneliness, the boundaries between two people may become blurred, in a co-dependent rather than interdependent way. This suboptimal connection has been referred to as "fusion."[119] It could be seen as more of an attempt to return to being one with mother in her womb—an impossible feat, as among other things we're too large to fit—rather than moving out to be one with all of creation.

As children, mother comforted us, and it's human to seek that feeling of reassurance. The irony is that greater comfort awaits us as we push the envelope of our comfort zones, to become comfortable with what used to be uncomfortable. Our fears and challenges can serve to flag where our growth awaits us, or as catalytic messengers to help us wake up.

Kiara disliked making budgets and spreadsheets, but her partner enjoyed such work and so took care of their finances. Eventually, though, a promotion at work required Kiara to oversee budgets. While excited about the promotion, responsibility for budgets filled her with dread, paralysis, and even nausea; she'd go blank and stare at the spreadsheets without comprehension. She wondered if she could find a way to do this part of the work at home with her partner's support. Deep down, Kiara may have wistfully hoped she could avoid the nausea if her partner helped quite a lot. It's human to be tempted toward fusion, when we misuse each other to keep our egos in place, to distract ourselves from the growth calling to us from our fears.

Kiara's partner, however, was well aware of Kiara's abilities and encouraged her to persevere to overcome her aversion. It was mostly about the decision. With a bit of time and patience, Kiara got the hang of budgets and wasn't sure herself what the

---

[119] David Schnarch, *Passionate Marriage* (New York: W. W. Norton & Company, 2009), 67-68.

big deal was. She felt empowered, more independent, and more self-assured, not just about budgets but also about meeting challenges in general. The household finances became a joint undertaking with her partner. Eventually other people asked Kiara for help with budgeting.

Before meeting the challenge, Kiara's relationship had an aspect of fusion. Though the example here is around finance, we might rely on another for anything, including nurturing or even making our lives meaningful. With greater integration and interdependence, our relationships are celebrations of togetherness and synergistic strength, rather than an escape from loneliness or arrangements where we outsource our weaker functions.

Our goal is integration, which means using one another in relationship to become ever more aware. This serves to help us grow and learn how to support others to do the same, all to be of greater benefit to all beings, and to the planet and cosmos as a whole. After all, we're one big union. The unitive state of spiritual awakening is a supremely healthy and worthy goal that is accessible to all of us.

One reason relationships have so much potential for transformation is they are very difficult to rest in comfortably, as every person in a long-term relationship will attest. Using relationships for mutual growth and unfoldment, leading us back to unity, is in fact reliably uncomfortable. Preferences and habits *seem* comfortable but tend to keep us right where we are. That is, stuck. And stuck isn't comfortable either.

As always, there's a gravitational pull to habit, and to relate through habits. Namgyal Rinpoche once called relationships "business as usual." We enjoy having someone to eat with, talk to, sleep with, and with whom to share the demands of daily life. While functional, this arrangement isn't usually satisfying on a deep level. Accommodation of both daily necessities and emotional fusion are rooted in unconscious habit. Spiritual integration through relationship challenges, exhilarates, and gratifies.

How do we apply this in our relationships? A consistent meditation practice under qualified guidance is invaluable to help us learn to be content when alone with ourselves. Then we bring our whole being to our relationships, rather than looking for an escape from loneliness, from not feeling whole. From the perspective of spiritual awakening, our teachings include this important topic of awakening through relationships, as we've described throughout this reflection.

In some ways, a relationship founded primarily on attraction cannot avoid fusion, but when that strategy is no longer enough, integration or awakening is the only door that will keep the relationship vital. One couple we knew had passionate sex regularly, but also fought passionately just as much. The sex fed their self-identities (for example, as a lover or sexual being) but was not enough to carry the relationship. They used the fusion of sex to avoid the fear of aloneness behind it. Through meditation, plus exercises such as mirroring, weekly meetings to air points of contention (rather than bringing them up in the heat of the moment), and undertaking some counseling with third parties for perspective, their relationship has improved. They've gradually learned to be more harmonious, both together and alone. (In case you're wondering, they say the sex is still good, too.)

From an awakening perspective, the dance between self and other reveals how the body, mind, and ego are all tools to rediscover and manifest human potential. This then gets channeled back through our egos to explore and discover, to share and to love all manifestations of life. Our partner becomes our meditation object, a representation of all of creation.

The great magic of this journey is that, as we stumble back to our source, the stumbling is part of the journey. A sense of humor is a priceless asset. Paradoxically, it is the discontent of the struggle, portrayed here in terms of relationship, that leads us inexorably to the unitive state. The discontent is the trumpet call, summoning our attention and indicating our path forward.

From the perspective of the unitive state, we are one being in billions of bodies. As such, our power for growth and unfoldment as conscious beings in a conscious universe is immense. The journey is inevitable and unavoidable, and filled with joy and wonder.

PART 3

CRAZY WISDOM

Taking a Walk on the Wild Side

REFLECTION 12

THE DANCE OF TANTRA

Transformation Through Sense Impressions

T he esoteric teachings of tantra have become more mainstream nowadays, at least in name. A quick Internet search
turns up numerous results related to sexuality, many of
which feature scantily-clad people. Tantra does include sex (and
hooray for healthy sex as part of integrative spiritual practices)
but is much more than that.

In tantra, we use deities as objects of meditation; they epit-
omize the qualities, concepts, and behaviors that lead to clear,
radiant states of being. Each one represents a theme or understanding. For example, in Himalayan-style Vajrayana Buddhism
(known as Shingon in Japan), Chenrezi[120] is an image, archetype,
or deity that has formed around the theme of compassion. By
practicing this archetype in meditation—more on how this works
later—we learn to resonate with this quality of compassion,
cultivate it, and gradually learn to actualize it in our daily lives.

How do we practice an archetype? With tantra, our intent
determines the result: what we reap is what we sow; the mind finds

---

[120] Interestingly, in the Himalayas, this archetype is depicted as male,
whereas in China and Japan, Chenrezi manifests in female form: Guan Yin
and Kannon, respectively.

what it seeks. If we put fantasy in, we get fantasy out, garbage in means garbage out, and if we put compassion in, we get compassion out. Tantric practice is an ancient immersion experience that helps us grow into archetypal qualities we admire, for the benefit of all beings. Does it work? It's been practiced for at least a few millennia, so it has certainly withstood the test of time.

Tantra derives indirectly from the Pali word *sutta* (*sutra* in Sanskrit), which means "thread." It shows up in English (an Indo-European language) as the root for words like "suture." Suttas were the lectures that the Buddha gave to his disciples. We can think of these lectures as threads of ideas on various subjects, similar to the format of this book. Buddhist philosophy, on the other hand, is more like a weaving, a tapestry, and this is one meaning of the Sanskrit word *tantra*. Literally, the Sanskrit word *tantra* means "loom, warp, the string of a lute, a sinew of the body, a framework or doctrine." Complex teachings which involve ideas, practices, and more broadly, approaches to how we engage in the world evolved and became known as *tantras*.

Similar to the way atoms combine to form molecules and eventually the basis of the rich texture of life, suttas evolved to form tantras to reflect the rich and layered nature of spiritual life. And just as there are millions of molecules in nature, there could be millions of tantras. Typically, however, the traditional list of tantras in Vajrayana Buddhism contains 100. Of these, 42 are considered peaceful or calming, while 58 are considered wrathful. With our modern sensibilities, we'd prefer to call the latter energizing.

The message of these tantras is represented visually (traditionally in paintings), to make them easier to relate to. These depictions are archetypal, though naturally Buddhism is not the only teaching to use archetypes. We find them in the Kabala, shamanism, Western psychology (Jungian archetypes), and in myths from around the world.[121]

---

[121] Joseph Campbell described this so beautifully in *The Hero with a Thousand Faces* (Princeton: Princeton University Press, 1973).

While Western archetypes tend to be more idealistic and theoretical, Tantric Buddhist archetypes are meant to be embodied or engaged with somatically, in practical living terms. This is why there are 58 energetic (wrathful) deities or archetypes: life can be so challenging sometimes. While a peaceful way of living and serene deities may be our option of choice, life has a way of delivering problems that require more verve. Sometimes we need a turbo charge or some fire to break through major obstacles, usually the ones inside ourselves.

For example, Demchog is the archetype of bliss in Tantric Buddhism. We all like bliss. However, if we cling to bliss, it can become the source of tremendous suffering; everything in form is impermanent, so clinging can't ever really work. Therefore Demchog is also wrathful to remind us: have bliss, enjoy it, but no clinging. A different kind of breakthrough is represented by the deity archetype known as Mahakala. He addresses anger and also embodies protection, as in keeping us, our practice, and the teachings safe. With Mahakala practice, we come to perceive more clearly that anger is a powerful mirror: we are what we hate when we hate it. The skillful and appropriate use of anger (as a protection or as a tool for cutting through ignorance) is one of the most challenging qualities to cultivate, so this practice is not for the faint of heart.

Another reason for having both peaceful and wrathful categories of tantra is that it's sometimes difficult to see the situation we're in. In other words, the nature of a blind spot is that it's blind. It often takes someone or something outside of ourselves to show us what we're missing. That's the role of the energetic archetype—to wake us up. This dynamic mirrors the two roles of a spiritual teacher. The first role of a spiritual teacher is to help us calm down (as represented by peaceful practices), while their second role is to help us wake up (with energizing ones).

For this reason, in tantra the teacher and our relationship with them are of prime importance. The teacher's job is to be a trainer, and one way that happens in Buddhism is by having an excellent grasp of all the various archetypes. As previously noted, in addition to being a teacher, the Buddha was renowned as a trainer; the *Recollection of the Buddha* prayer calls him "the unsurpassed trainer of people fit for training."[122] As a result, we feel that Buddhism could be better considered as a training system than as a religion.

Tantric deities (a.k.a. archetypes) are not gods in the usual sense; they are more like manifestations of principles that we can utilize in our day-to-day lives for practical use. (More on how this works later in this reflection.) The word "deity" comes from the Sanskrit root *dev*, meaning "to shine." We could think of deities as beings of light. When visualizing them in meditation, they are created by the mind.

Curiously, the Sanskrit root *dev* gave rise to both the English words "devil" and "divine." Divine refers to how we feel when we rest in peaceful clarity, and devil refers to what we need to wake up from. Living is about shining, radiance, and light. "Devil" is also "lived" spelled backward: the antithesis of being alive. If we aren't having ongoing contact with radiant emptiness, then we aren't truly living—we're bedeviled, overlooking the luminous qualities of life.

Whether we refer to them as deities or archetypes, we're referring to principles rather than entities. In other words, they are empty of inherent existence. This emptiness is akin to spaciousness or energy in potential. Because Westerners tend to be materialists, we often see the embodied forms of objects and then take these forms to be real in an absolute sense. Meanwhile, due to millennia of Buddhist, Hindu, and Taoist (etc.) thought and practice in the East, more people there understand the arising and passing away of form as emerging out of and returning to emptiness or spaciousness.

For instance, when I look at you, I see you, and tend not to notice the space *between* us as being important. Taking this one step further, spaciousness is seeing not only the space *between*

---

[122] In the Pali language (spoken by the Buddha): *Anuttaro purisadammasarathi.*

things but also the space *within* things. Ultimately, of course, as quantum probability tells us, no thing exists.

The West's material bent has given the world very useful things, such as electricity, telephones, automobiles, and computers. But the corresponding lack of cultural connection with spaciousness may be the reason that Westerners usually perceive "emptiness" as a deficit, a kind of emotional vacuity with painful qualities. In contrast, in Asia, emptiness is seen as the source of everything, and therefore as both peaceful and blissful.

A Door to Spaciousness and Radiance

If we're trying to get something or somewhere with tantra, ultimately it's this peaceful, blissful clarity, grounded in an all-pervasive non-clinging. This mind state of spaciousness and radiance emerges of its own accord. It's the mind's natural state. This state comes about when the mind is freed from its ongoing identification with the thoughts, feelings, and sensations that arise as part of our daily life.

With tantric practice, we learn that things arise out of, and return to, emptiness. Non-clinging is the principle result. This view and understanding includes everything from atoms to galaxies; in between, only our timeline changes.

If we rest in—but don't cling to—the experience of spaciousness, a state of contentment and joy grows and expands, flooding our consciousness with bliss and light. Bliss is the midwife of insight, and with greater insight comes greater freedom.

A word of caution, however: this spacious bliss is easily interrupted by our habitual thoughts and feelings. This is why it is so important to understand our habits, and to know how to transcend them when they are getting in the way of our joy and freedom. Imagine sitting on your deck enjoying a beautiful sunset in a relaxed and blissful state. Then, you check your email on your smartphone and see an email from your accountant about taxes. Have we cultivated the habit to maintain a bliss state during this process? Or do we fall into a habitual mind state of agitation around taxes? It is possible—essential!—to remain in spacious bliss even when it comes to challenging topics or events.

Tantra helps us with this transformation, particularly around what we desire and what we don't. Life is all about desire. It's the driving force of our lives. We are drawn toward whatever it is we desire, whether it's sunlight, good coffee, adrenaline rushes, time with loved ones, porn, or a trip to see the Egyptian pyramids.

Through tantra, we learn to transform desire from the mistake of trying to hang onto fleeting experiences, in favor of letting them pass through our experience. Tantra is neither about indulging nor slaying desire, but about using its great force to liberate us from the mistake of thinking that we can nail it down and permanently get or hang on to that which we desire.

Another word for this process is purification. We purify our attachments, which are rooted in ego fears. We do this by surrendering into the so-called here and now. It is only the here and now we can ever live in anyway:[123] attachment and clinging are all in the past or future.

This may sound rather complicated. In fact, tantra keeps things simple by summing up all desire into one form: the union of male and female energies, or the Tao of yin and yang. Traditional tantra visually represents this desire with the image of a male and female in sexual union. Heterosexuality or pair bonding need not be your style, but the principle holds: in the world of form, we communicate in terms of self and other and an eternal quest for balance.

Communication, then, is at the heart of tantra: how I perceive myself, how I see others, and how we interrelate are all negotiations of desire. Tantra's job is to show us the mechanics of this desire. Awakening, the "goal" of tantra, is to live life large: *total* desire, total bliss, total clarity, and total non-clinging awareness. How we get there, how we transform whatever it is that stands in our way, is the path of tantra.

---

[123] To be technically accurate, in spaciousness there is no here and no now: it is beyond time and space.

THE TANTRIC PATH

As mentioned, the mind's natural state is one of blissful, clear non-clinging. But in the process of living in the sensorial realm of objects or forms, we tend to adhere to them. Why? Since our ego suffers from its feeling of separateness, it is always seeking to reunite with the totality. We cling to our objects as a child clings to its mother.

Through meditation, yoga, tai chi, prayer, and other unitive practices—and sometimes through grace, such as a beautiful moment with a loved one or in nature—we may reside in the natural radiant state. However, habitual thoughts and feelings inevitably arise, and we may get distracted and move toward them, abandoning the divine. These habitual patterns (thoughts, feelings and sensations) contain conflicting emotions and limiting self-views.

Tantra is one way to transform these limitations to bliss and insight, which are the foundation for wisdom. Wisdom then yields increasing degrees of freedom. This allows us to explore our inner and outer worlds without being bogged down by the unnecessary fears, worries, and other self-limiting habit patterns that typify a narrow view of oneself.

Tantra consists of meditating on archetypes or deities (including Buddhas, bodhisattvas, saints, and other exemplary beings) to transform these habits of conflicting emotions and limited self-views. Using these particular meditation methodologies—traditionally called deity practice or Arising Yoga—we create visualizations. The visualization process helps us learn how to transform conflicting, troublesome states into bliss and insight.

How so? First, we set our intention to do so, and then we follow through with action. Depending on our inclinations, we may create the visualization in a material way: we may paint it, dance it, or create a devotional shrine to a visual image. From Tibetan deity dances and sand mandalas, to the earliest Theravadin Buddhism meditations on radiant deva beings, and back into early human history with divine mother worship rituals and so on, humans have been embodying our spiritual inclinations for thousands of years, developing substantial cultures along the way. These activities are designed to prepare for and support what is traditionally the main practice: visualization through meditation.

Spiritual awakening is a receptive state, but it's actualized through the application of our will, which is active. This is the basis for the transformation. We focus our will on creating a particular change by inculcating it first in meditation. Gradually, we then apply what we've learned in meditation to our daily actions, transforming our overall state of being.

For instance, since I (Doug) was a serious type of person, our teacher Namgyal Rinpoche suggested I bring more joy into my practice. I meditated on the Tibetan archetype for joy—Milarepa—who curiously had a lot of suffering in his life. I repeated his mantra ("I am the great happiness") countless times, which did indeed increase my joy level. But more importantly it taught me to look for—and see more—joy more in daily activities. We also engage in joyous activities—among others, golf for me and horseback riding for Catherine—as another kind of bliss practice. While it's true we still tend to be serious types, we've cultivated joy as a central component to our lives. Humor, salsa, and East Coast Swing also help!

Through tantra, in a sense, we're creating a new view of ourselves. We are remodeling the ego. By its nature, the ego is rooted in a fundamentally insatiable desire, and therefore in greed and fear, which yield clinging and dissatisfaction. Tantra empowers us to use the incredible and largely untapped power of our minds to transform these into something beyond the ego's understanding: spaciousness and transcendental union.

Through the meditation's visualization practices, we imagine ourselves to be loving and compassionate, blissful and clear. We abide where there is no abiding: in spacious emptiness. We use our senses to embody this mind-feeling in form and then imagine we *are* that form. We then pay homage to the form as manifested by the deity image, the visualization, and the emerging embodiment we are becoming. If we can imagine it, it can happen. And so then, gradually, we act accordingly in daily life.

In line with the meaning of the word *tantra* (loom or framework), the process of tantra makes connections that produce something greater than its parts. We use our sense doors (sight, hearing, taste, smell, touch, and our cognizant mind) as a framework, the loom, so to speak. We see the image of the archetype, we may speak and hear mantras, taste ritual food and drink, smell the fragrance of incense, feel the beads of our rosary on our fingertips, or create a beautiful shrine with offerings to this symbol of our own aspiration to become a source of compassion. And all this while our mind is weaving these components together into a comprehensive, radiant, archetypal experience.

The tantric deities typically resemble humans and therefore express human qualities, such as wisdom, healing abilities, kindness, bliss, joy, and so on. Sometimes, the images resemble animals and their archetypal qualities, such as a bull's strength or determination, or a horse's freedom. Whatever the image, it helps train our mind in diverse ways.

For example, the bodhisattva Chenrezi—as mentioned, an archetype of compassion—is visualized as white, representing purity. Additionally, the fact that white reflects light implies that the compassion is reflected back on everyone and everything. In two of his hands he holds a crystal rosary and a lotus, indicating the release of clinging (each bead continually passing through our fingers) and our connection with the vast wisdom of nature (lotus). His other two hands hold a wish-fulfilling gem, implying that we can get what we wish for: in this case, compassion.

The image of Chenrezi is adorned with various ornaments representing different qualities. For instance, he wears large, golden earrings to represent generosity (*dāna*), a long necklace symbolizing patience, and a sash around his waist referring to energy. As we repeat his mantra, it helps us engage our voice and hearing sense. The mantra means "Praise to the jewel in the lotus." The lotus represents the ground of being and the jewel represents appearances, that is, any phenomenon in our life, including emotional and mental as well.

Similarly, other deities employ our senses and minds to connect with other virtues, concepts, and understandings and to bring them into our lives in a variety of ways. Everything a deity holds, wears, or embodies has particular significance and power, which we learn to perceive gradually, or in a flash, through meditation. Though greater understanding can be helpful (especially to help us focus the mind), we don't need to know all the symbolism or meanings for them to act on us.

The tantric approach empowers us to see that our mental and emotional states are our creations. It also teaches us new ways of relating. For example, how we manifest toward imagined beings—such as archetypal deities—can be the same or similar to how we relate to actual living beings, in this case, with an orientation of compassion.

In tantra, the inclusion of animal and other nature elements in the creation of archetypal images helps us focus our minds beyond the ego-centered constructions of our day-to-day lives where only other people count. Nature also needs our compassion. To be more precise, our very existence depends on our ability to be compassionate toward nature, since it provides the foundation for the survival of humans as a species.

PRACTICING THE JOY OF NON-ATTACHMENT

Our ego's fundamental desire is the same as that of Narcissus, who was so enamored with his own image reflected in water that he drowned: our ego is totally preoccupied with its sense of self or self-image. We feel the need to promote and defend our beloved self-image, revealing our attachment and clinging to seeing our self (and others seeing our self) in particular ways. This is the source of all our suffering.

The ego, living solely for the satisfaction of its desires, has no vested interest in the archetypal objects of our meditation. When meditating on a tantric deity, the ego isn't likely to feel attached to what it knows is a creative visualization. There's no way we can cling to visualizations, and through this experience we learn about non-attachment, how to let things go. Over time, the mind learns to relax into its natural state of spacious radiance.

We build the visualization step by step, and at the end, our mind dissolves it step by step. With practice, we begin to understand that everything in our lives builds, arises, and passes away in similar fashion. The "halfway house" of creative visualizations of the tantric archetypes helps train us in non-clinging. We learn to not take things so personally, to not get obsessed with things we believe to be real while dismissing others as imagination. Our minds determine the quality of all our experiences, and tantric visualizations help us learn this. More to the point, we experience it for ourselves as truth.[124]

Tantra gives us tools to learn to love without attachment, engage without clinging to agendas, and experience without trying to hang on. We learn to live with spontaneity and joy, without regret or sorrow, and in the end, we learn to die smiling.

Because everything arises out of emptiness, has duration in form, and then passes away, the tantric practices are designed to follow this truth, that of the flow of all existence. As we practice this with the archetypes, we train the ego to recognize and acknowledge that we can never really hang on to anything, that all objects are passing through, and that bliss arises when we learn to let go into the arising of the moment.

The ego tends to fixate, and when it tries to hang on, we unintentionally start to smother the vibrancy of the ephemeral moment. That's why falling in love is so powerful: the ego has not yet fixated. And that's why we tend to fall out of love: the fixation sets in, and the joy and spontaneity of being in love wither.

By using the senses in tantric practice—such as through visualization, mantra, and shrine offerings—we learn that just as we build and dissolve them in turn, we must also learn to build and

---

[124] We share some resources on such visualization techniques at planet-dharma.com/pureland/learn.

dissolve appropriately in our daily lives. So even a relationship that has endured for many years is seen as arising, lasting, and dissolving. In this way, we learn not to cling in each moment.

Practicing tantric meditation is believed to purify each of the sensing functions because we use them in the meditation—saying mantras, touching beads, smelling incense, etc.—to help us learn to drop all of the personal dialogue focused around ourselves. For example, staying present with the mantra is impossible if we're following an interior monologue, so we have to choose. We learn through personal experience that it feels better to focus on the mantra (or the fragrance of incense, or the sensation of the beads on our fingertips, etc.), so gradually we learn not to choose the interior monologue.

Through this practice, we bring our consciousness out of its history, out of its stories, and into the present moment of experience. Then, in the moment of seeing, there is just seeing. In the moment of hearing, there is just hearing. This is living in the moment.

Part of the purpose of practicing meditation with the deity archetypes is to train ourselves to, in a sense, lay a transparency of the deity archetype over whatever people or activities we engage with outside of the practice. We can then encounter everyone and everything as beings of radiant light, as devas. In this way, we can stay in a clear blissful state throughout our daily life. With practice, we can maintain our good state even when things get tough.

MEETING BLACK TARA

We've been discussing creative visualization through tantric meditation and also how tantra can manifest in daily life. Both may occur in surprising ways; perhaps a personal example will help demonstrate how.

As a young man, I (Doug) had been traveling around Nepal with some friends and one day ended up feeling very ill with a stomach ailment. My fellow travelers went out shopping for thangkas—sacred paintings of deities—and I stayed back in the hotel, lying in bed, probably feverish.

At some point, I glanced over at the next bed, and there was a complete, total manifestation of what I later understood to be Black Tara sitting there, as real as any person is to me now. She was female in form, intensely beautiful, black as ink, sitting nude and at ease but alert,[125] with a beneficent smile. The depth of her eyes was bottomless, and when I looked in them, I felt that I disappeared into a blissful void. The entire universe as I knew it dissolved into vast spaciousness.

Then my awareness came back, and I was again primarily cognizant of feeling poorly and lying in bed. I looked over once more, and there was Black Tara. Now, I was so sick that it didn't strike me as being odd that this very beautiful, inviting, warm, nourishing—for the young male consciousness, everything desirable—female was sitting there smiling at me. I didn't say, "Whoa, who are you? What's your name? Where did you come from?" I just thought, "Oh, wow," looked into her eyes and disappeared into the void. I'm not sure how long that lasted. Maybe thirty seconds, maybe ten minutes. When I returned to my sense of self in bed, I looked again, and she was still there.

Then, since I wasn't feeling well physically, I rolled over and faced the other way. At this point, it struck me that this being sitting on the next bed was out of the ordinary, and I rolled back over to take another look.

But she was gone.

It wasn't until it dawned on me that she wasn't supposed to be there, and I rolled back over to look again, that she disappeared. A different function of the mind, a different kind of intelligence—more rational, perhaps, more empirical—had come to the fore. Part of my mind asserted, *There can't be a naked goddess the color of deep space sitting on the next bed smiling at me.* And then it was

---

[125] Later, I understood this to be Tara's standard posture: seated, left leg drawn in, right leg outstretched, simultaneously relaxed and ready to act.

so. She had manifested out of nowhere, and then she disappeared back into the void.

These are the kind of things that may transpire when we "encounter" a deity. Much later, I learned that Black Tara is the manifestation of the infinity of space; I was also told that she's the patroness of Nepal. This kind of Tara experience addresses a fear of oblivion or the void, of disappearance, our fear of anni-hilation, or even our fear of insanity.

With such an experience, one realizes that there is nothing to fear, that the experience of spaciousness (manifesting through the form of Black Tara) is incredibly peaceful and indescribably blissful. This first-hand, experience-based knowledge has stayed with me ever since.

MEDITATUS INTERRUPTUS

As we've noted, our unconscious habitual states are rooted in our ego's desire for self-protection and identity, and they manifest as greed, aversion, and confusion. Tantric practices are about transforming these into radiant energy forms of light, bliss, and clarity, which we can put on like a magic cloak to greet the world. Through our practice, we weave different kinds of mantles to represent varying arrays of tools that help us navigate our lives. We may weave cloaks of compassion (Chenrezi), discerning clarity (Manjushri), health and relationship with nature (Green Tara), effective multitasking (Yamantaka), artistry (Sarasvati), and so on.

Putting a cloak on, taking it off, and exchanging it for another— it sounds so easy. In fact, we often find ourselves unintentionally disrobed at inopportune times. So, it might be helpful to understand how we lose track of our power cloaks to preempt such interruptions.

What happens is that the ego makes the error of what we call false refuge. In other words, we try to find satisfaction where it simply can't be found: by clinging to objects. The object may be a partner, a job, a new car, or simply a good cup of espresso. It might also be an abstract "object," such as a general notion of love, security, success, or happiness.

The unintentional interruption of wholesome states of being is a phenomenon we become familiar with as infants. In fact, we're conditioned to have our bliss and concentration interrupted during our earliest training as a human being. This necessary training teaches us how to live in the world; nevertheless, it disturbs our bliss union and makes us self-conscious and defensive. We then start to internalize the interruption and do it to ourselves, often unnecessarily. The tantric path teaches us how to act appropriately in our daily life—not just in the sense of good behavior, but in terms of living from a clear state—while also maintaining a feeling of bliss and union.

One formative experience of interruption occurs in the womb. For most of the nine months that we're in the womb, we tend to dwell in a tremendous state of bliss: we're bathing in complete union with our mother, who is often delighted about our existence, and supplies all of our needs as they arise.

But there are interruptions ranging from mild to intense. They include when our mother's stomach gets upset, when contractions start, and finally, when we get squeezed and pushed out through the birth canal.

Once we're born, well-intended but unpleasant interruptions may take place when our mothers become especially concerned about our welfare. As babies, we can get very blissful. For example, we get absorbed into shapes, colors, or sounds around us. As a result, we may become very quiet and still. This can be worrisome for a parent, who may wonder why their baby has stopped moving. They may interrupt the state—maybe they gave us a little shake—to make sure we're okay. When this takes place repeatedly over time, we learn not to relax too much into the bliss because we anticipate the interruption may come at any moment.

We probably all have early memories of how this same phenomenon occurred when we were young children. I (Doug) have one such memory that I'm rather fond of. Around the time I was a toddler, my father's career matured, our economics improved, and my parents bought a newly constructed house in the suburbs. You can imagine my mother's delight as we moved from an older home—where the walls didn't meet squarely, the floors weren't even, and the plumbing dripped—into a brand-new house.

In the process of bringing household items into the new place, my mother gave me some oil-based crayons to keep me pleasantly occupied. Even today, I remember the exhilarating feeling of possibility when I saw the blank canvas of a bare white wall before me with these beautiful multi-colored crayons in my hand. I crayoned my way across the length of the wall, from the picture window in the front, to the dining room in the back. I was in a state of ecstatic absorption.

My mother, of course, had a different orientation toward this event, and was, not surprisingly, somewhat upset. I still remember feeling it was terribly unreasonable of her.

Because of experiences like these, when we do get into bliss states, we usually have the expectation that they're going to be interrupted. As a result, over time, we learn to preempt this unpleasant interruption by interrupting the bliss state ourselves. We do this to lessen the shock. Part of us feels that by being in control of the interruption it makes the loss of the bliss and radiance less devastating.

Of course, we can practice with methodologies such as meditation to re-learn how to extend these bliss states for longer periods of time and in more depth. But there will always be this element of anticipated interruption. This expectation gradually pulls us out of a bliss state, at least temporarily. In any case, we can settle back into a bliss state by once more returning to the sense bases—the body—and meditation practice, re-contacting the bliss and light.

One of the main ways we interrupt our bliss state as adults is by thinking or feeling that we have things to do. We are sitting there in a nice bliss state, and then think, *I've got to get the laundry in* or *I've got to send one last email* or *Is it time to start supper?* We interrupt our bliss state because we have a sense of a required task which we may not even want to do, but somehow, we feel that we'd better. It's a pattern based on the external interruption we couldn't ignore, such as mommy's tickling and cooing at us to see if we were still responsive.

As adults, we'd probably prefer to sit in the garden and watch the flowers blossom rather than get up and take the garbage out. The best way to extend the bliss state is, curiously, to incorporate the garbage into it. It's much more difficult (and less efficient) to try to remain in the bliss state and keep the garbage out of our mind. In other words, we can carry the bliss state with us while taking out the garbage, responding to an inbox of emails, and during any other day-to-day activities. To do that, we need to stay in the present moment as best as we can.

Here's how this works. We are in the here and now with the flowers in the garden, so we need to remain here in this present moment while standing up, getting the garbage, and walking it to the curb. We need to remain here in this moment while sitting down at our desk, opening our email, and reading and responding to various communications. We need to keep this presence while a text comes in (whether or not we read it or reply), or when someone calls us from the next room.

In this way, we can extend the bliss state into more and more parts of life, and experience fewer interruptions, even when interruptions happen. The bliss states in the garden are based on our senses, which can easily be disturbed as our attention shifts from stillness to activity. We need meditative practices that also embrace activity and the transitions between. Tantra can be helpful here.

The wonderful thing about tantric yoga practice is that it takes all of our senses and related activities—visual, smell, touch, hearing, taste, plus the mind—and combines them into one meditation. Some meditations, such as breathing practice, are powerful precisely because they are so simple that they invite our most subtle attention. In contrast, tantric meditations involve many different sensory functions, and moving between them. This helps train our minds to stay with the blissful, radiant states as we inevitably shift from "sitting" meditation practices to "doing" meditation practices.[126]

---

[126] This is also the aim of Karma Yoga practice, the training of remaining in states of bliss and clarity while going about our daily activities. See Reflections 5 and 6 for more on Karma Yoga.

REFLECTION 13
THE WEAVING OF TANTRA

The Art and Science of Arising Yoga

Around the world, no matter which tradition we look at, there are basically two categories of meditation. There are Samatha meditations, which develop calm and concentration. If these are held for a period of time (quite short actually), bliss is the natural result. The second category are Vipassana (insight) meditations that develop clarity and discernment, which lead to wisdom. Samatha and Vipassana break down further into seven kinds of meditation, which we describe shortly.

These two meditation categories are like the two feet that carry us forward. One without the other leads to an imbalance in our body/mind system. Together, they balance one another and help us to really move. Meanwhile, their result—bliss and wisdom—are enough to get us through even the worst kind of day. Put in a more positive way, they make for a life worth living. Let's take a closer look at both.

Samatha meditations can be broken down into six types:

1. Visualizations (anything done with the eye, inner or outer)

2. Mudra (anything done with the body, mostly externally)

3. Mantra (anything done with the voice or sound, inner and outer)

4. Chakra (energy movements in the body, mostly inner)

5. Breathing meditation (anything done with the breath, which covers pretty much all inner and outer practices mentioned here) and

6. Devotional meditations (anything done with a sense of devotion, including both spiritual and mundane rituals, inner and outer).

Devotion can feel a bit uncomfortable for contemporary Westerners to engage with, but we love seeing other cultures who still embrace this practice: people giving flowers, incense, and other offerings at temples in Asia, for example, are popular images, and therefore, this approach is somehow attractive to us. This kind of practice shows up in the West if we create a shrine for our meditation practice. We may adorn the shrine with the traditional offerings of water, candles, incense, food, scented water, or a chime. Our meditation practice may include these offerings as part of our devotion and dāna practice: generosity to one's own aspiration, to the deity, to ourselves, or simply practicing the act of giving for giving's sake.

Devotion can also manifest in more mundane ways, such as how we organize our room or desk, interior decor, how we dress, how we share food, or even how we eat. Many secular people are particularly devoted to their first hot drink in the morning. In other words, our habitual behaviors are forms of devotion, consciously or not.

As noted above, the second category (and also the seventh type) of meditation is insight meditation or *Vipassana*, which in the Pali language means "to see again and again." Insight meditation is a form of witnessing: the mind observes whatever arises, without getting caught up in it. We sometimes describe it as being aware of being aware.

With insight meditation, we practice witnessing the nature of the arisings in our body-mind from a sense of spaciousness. Witnessing the sense of spaciousness is what allows us to recognize the insight connection. We see the connection between this and that, how phenomena connect to and interpenetrate each other. A thought may trigger a subtle change in the breath, which then shifts to an emotion, for example. Or perhaps it's the other way around. It all arises in milliseconds. With insight, we are not absorbed in this, or that; we're observing the nature of the interplay between things that appear in our mind's eye.

There are many elaborations on the six types of samatha meditation, but fundamentally there's only one type of insight meditation. Whether we call it insight, Vipassana, Zen (Ch'an in China), Mahamudra, or Dzogchen, they're all different names for what is essentially the same meditation: dwelling in spaciousness and witnessing what arises there.

In the Arising Yoga (deity practice) style of meditation, or tantra, all six forms of samatha practice are included as well as the insight style. When we meditate on a particular deity or archetype, we are doing all of the different meditations. The standard *sadhana* (tantra meditation text) starts with emptiness (basic insight) and progresses through different stages of creating the archetype invoked, incorporating the deity's qualities. We use visualization, mantra, movement, devotion, and the energies that ride on the breath to magnetize our senses and attention so that our absorption allows the values that we're calling forth (such as compassion) to materialize. Finally, we dissolve the archetype in stages, returning back into emptiness.

For instance, the Chenrezi meditation on compassion starts from a space of emptiness. Then, slowly, using the various aspects of samatha (visualization, mantra, and so on) we build up the image. Starting with the primordial sound of a sacred syllable, light coalesces and metamorphoses into the figure of Chenrezi. We meditate on this as long as we like, and then, to close, dissolve the figure back into emptiness.

Over time, this practice nurtures ever-increasing bliss and insight. The process seems almost magical, because our aspiration and applied efforts summon these qualities to emerge from the depths of our minds and hearts. At first, it may be difficult to understand how a visualized image can produce such wondrous states of joy and clarity. But it works, because our aspiration and determination to embody compassion, backed up by our actions (the meditation), produces the results we have set our minds and hearts to.

Let us share an example of what this looks like. Once I (Catherine) was sick in bed with the flu. I was lying on my back, meditating on the nature of illness, reflecting on how exactly I felt, what sensations, and where in the body. It was kind of interesting to map the overall ache, the mildly throbbing sinuses, the dynamic between heat in the head and chill in the body. In short, it was a meditation on the nature of misery, and while a bit fascinating, I still felt poorly.

Serendipitously, at the foot of my bed, there was a *thangka* or ritual painting of Medicine Buddha, a deity of healing. It seemed like it might be a good idea to say his mantras. On saying his mantra—Om Bekanze Bekanze Maha Bekanze Raja Samugate Svaha—relief came so quickly and abundantly that I felt embarrassed for not having "taken the medicine" sooner.

Our minds determine our reality, and this is mind training. Himalayan or Vajrayana Buddhism specifically dedicates this training to the benefit of all beings, also known as the *bodhisattva vow*.[127] A bodhisattva is a being on the verge of Buddhahood who intentionally delays it to roll up his or her sleeves and dive into the illusory rounds of metaphorical mud wrestling known as *samsara* or daily existence. This is done to help all other sentient beings also move closer to Buddhahood. We highly

---

[127] We share the bodhisattva vow we use and love in Reflection 10, under the subhead, *Forewarned is Forearmed*.

recommend this as a vocation. In fact, we challenge you to find a better one.[128]

Spaciousness is a key element of this mind training, and of tantra. We journey into emptiness to open the space necessary for the bliss, radiance, clarity, and insights to arise, channeled through the imagined meditational deity of tantra.

To be able to dwell in this spaciousness, we must also dwell in the here and now. Interestingly, this places us outside the standard space and time constructs as we know them. Time and space are markers: they cut totality into sections by positing duration and location. If we let go of the marking, or measuring, we return to totality, and thus time and space, as such, disappear.

This is the beauty of arising yoga (tantra): we experience directly how something can arise from nothing, last for a while, and then dissolve. What's more, we make it happen ourselves. When troubles arise in life, we can see how we brought them into being, how we cling to them, and most importantly, how we can let go of them.

The ego is a kind of a management tool for decisions that are made based on our needs and desires. Desires, by definition, are tied to clinging and attachment, which cannot sustain bliss and clarity (insight). The purpose of the tantric meditations, the deva (deity, light) meditations, is to bring our consciousness back into a radiant place very much in the here and now, while also leaving the ego the room it needs to take care of business.

It's possible for the ego to reflect the bliss and clarity of our depth mind, the mind of blissful radiance, peace, and stillness undisturbed at the bottom of the psyche. To do so, we must orient from the depth mind of bliss and clarity. In other words, depth must precede apparent desires. We must put the horse in front of the cart. There are versions of this in many religious traditions. Indeed, this is the origin of the exhortation to "Seek

---

[128] If you do, let us know. We like this path because we believe it to be the best there is (and we have tried a lot of other ones, bad and good, along the way). If there's a better one, we're there.

the Kingdom of God above all else, and live righteously, and he will give you everything you need."[129]

Then, the ego, too, becomes shiny.

HOW DEITY PRACTICE WORKS

How do we practice this meditation? First, we visualize the deity, using all the senses to make the experience as real or as multi-dimensional as possible. We try to smell the deity as a perfume, taste the deity as nectar, touch the deity as a lover, hear the deity as a guide and teacher, and see the energy body of the deity. All of this we present to consciousness as a multi-dimensional entity in front of us and eventually we try to bring it inside us, to integrate and embody it.

In addition, we offer gifts to the deity to express our gratitude and as a request to stay present with us as we go about our daily life. This is a devotional way of setting our intention to remember the practice, to recall that we're aspiring to be a manifestation of—in the case of Chenrezi—compassion, and to see all other beings as the same.

As mentioned, Chenrezi is considered to be the Tibetan embodiment of compassion. He's visualized as white in color, very calm, quiet, non-threatening, the epitome of safety and purity. The idea that the compassion aspect may be considered male (as Chenrezi in Tibet) or female (as Kwan Yin in China and Kannon in Japan) is somewhat arbitrary, and also introduces the idea of flexibility regarding characteristics and gender. But the idea is that we are reflecting upon a human-looking being with human-like characteristics acting in archetypally pure ways.

As part of the tantric practice, we imagine ourselves, everyone we know, and everyone we meet as an embodiment of Chenrezi, full of compassion. In this way, tantric practice provides a meditation framework that can transform our interpersonal connections.

---

[129] Matthew 6:33 (NLT).

This makes tantra unique compared to all the other (six types of samatha plus insight) meditations.

To describe it another way, with tantric practice, we throw ourselves wholeheartedly into the deity manifestation. It's safe and comfortable, because we're creating it ourselves. It's okay because it isn't a real, live, walking, talking human being. We're not going to have to worry about the deity taking advantage of us, taking all our money, challenging our sexuality, or gaining control over our psyche, because it's an archetypal energy being that we're generating ourselves. It's the ultimate imaginary friend!

By throwing ourselves into Chenrezi, or throwing Chenrezi into ourselves, we are getting ready to relate with other, "real" people, who may not always be manifesting as purely as Chenrezi, and who may, in fact, have ulterior motives. To develop our capacity to be compassionate with human beings, we practice with a seemingly unreal archetypal figure. This helps us get accustomed to the idea that we can be compassionate to imperfect, "real" people, with less than completely pure consciousnesses.

As we develop compassion with a human-like figure of our own creation, human-like stories are going to arise in our mind. We'll remember past hurts and joys, both difficult and pleasant moments with various people we know. Because we're focused on compassion, some of this compassion will start to drift into any internal rants we might be having. Since we start the meditation from emptiness and dissolve the meditation back into emptiness at the end, we eventually start to see that our rants also arise out of nowhere, and dissolve to the same place. Over time, the practice allows us to let go of our rants more and more, leaving what was there before the rants arose: compassion and emptiness. We also start to perceive how much better the compassion and emptiness feel, so we become more aware about choosing mind-states and heart-states. We start to let the compassionate energy of Chenrezi in more than before.

In other words, we are getting comfortable with the notion that we can live and survive, even thrive, when our consciousness seems to be dominated or possessed by another consciousness.

Chenrezi and his compassionate energy can move in, and it's okay. It's better than okay since compassion is beneficial to our and others' well-being, especially compared to other energies that sometimes move in without our conscious choice. For instance, if Anapan is furious with his wife Janjira, we could say he's possessed by the demon of anger because he didn't get what he wanted, or he got what he didn't want. But if he can see that it is not Janjira's job to always tend to his needs, he can let the anger go, and it won't possess his consciousness. Practicing tantric meditation can give Anapan space between his anger and his hurt, helping him to not identify with the anger so much, and to let it go.

How else can the different deity practices contribute to our current life situation or our character makeup? Let's look at some examples. If our astuteness is a little weak, we'd benefit from some practice with Manjusri, the Buddhist deity of wisdom. If the dexterity of our mind—our ability to manipulate and handle objects or concepts in an integrated way—could use strengthening, Yamantaka practice would be helpful. For healing, Medicine Buddha.

For depressive or clinging tendencies, it'd be salubrious to practice with Vajra Yogini: she helps us to learn to bring the bliss up, and then let it go. If we tend to be a little too critical, too narrowly focused, or too caught up in things, we could develop more liberative bliss by practicing with Demchog. Demchog represents the ability to manifest spacious consciousness and bliss energy, to cut through different types of attachment.

There are twenty-one forms of the savioress Tara, each serving different transcendental functions. Green Tara is for freedom from fear as well as healing. White Tara practice is optimal when our life is a little confused or we're feeling lost. She helps us develop a stronger sense of contact with the spiritual aspect of mind, the wisdom of true life purpose. If, on the other hand, we fear chaos, the void, and dissolution, Black Tara practice balances out our mandala.

Consciousness itself is empty and spacious, so no real possession or domination by another energy—deity, archetype, or person—is in fact possible. What's more, we practice creating and dissolving the deity archetype, and so when we meet an archetypal energy in our daily life, we have the experience of knowing how to dissolve the energy when it's time to move on.

STAGES OF TANTRA: OLD-FASHIONED DATING

We live most of our lives in the relative world (compared to the absolute one of radiant spacious emptiness), which manifests as duality. The most basic duality is male and female. Whether literal or energetic, this dynamic is the source of life that drives us to seek partners and relationships. Tantric Buddhists use this core drive and appetite to represent all of life's relativities. By mapping the dialogue, the desire, between male and female (or yin and yang) energy, and the attachments that ensue, we map all desire and all attachment. By liberating this attachment, we liberate all attachment.

Before we go further, let's note that the higher levels of tantra are intense, profound, and powerful. This is why tantra is considered dangerous if undertaken without proper training or with an impure intent. It was considered a secret teaching for many centuries for this reason. It's best undertaken gradually under the guidance of someone who has experienced and integrated these stages themselves.

Traditionally, tantric practitioners (known as *Tantrikas*) demarcated four stages in the process of desire represented by the male/female dance. Mapping these helps liberate practitioners from attachment, even while engaging with desire. Note that when we refer to men and women, we mean archetypal masculine and feminine energies, not biological sex, as gender itself is fluid. Practitioners of tantra work with the range of sexual/gender energies.

The first stage of tantra, *kriya* or action tantra, is symbolized by a smile. Woman looks at man, man looks at woman, and they smile. A smile is an invitation, and an invitation is the momentous opening of the door of desire. Every woman knows a smile is an invitation, and every man hopes his smile will be returned. In this context, a smile is very powerful. However, a smile is still distant, with a lot of room remaining between them.

The second stage of tantra is called *carya*, relating or performance tantra. It's traditionally depicted as a couple holding hands. The stakes have risen. It takes more commitment, more trust, and greater investment to touch one another, particularly with our hands, which are so sensitive and dexterous, and our main points of interfacing with the world. Thus there is more at risk, more to lose at this stage: the prospect of some sort of relationship is now on the table, so we have hopes and fears. Our hopes and fears are rooted in habits and habits are rooted in attachments, so the stakes are high.

Tantra's third stage is *yoga* or *joining* tantra, traditionally represented by kissing. Typically, this is quite intimate: we don't do this with strangers, or the person who was a stranger isn't anymore. Intimacy opens us to greater vulnerability. This degree of relating gets under our skin. Our core attachments start to reveal themselves, and therefore we can be more easily hurt. Consequently, not clinging at this stage represents a far greater challenge than it does at the stages of kriya and carya tantra.

Lastly, with the fourth stage, *anuttara* or *union* tantra, we are in full and complete contact, symbolically depicted as sexual union. It's a highly vulnerable, sensitive, and powerful state where we're wide open to the experience. We're not trying to hold on to it even for an instant, because we instinctively know that this will cause its passing away. We're also fully committed to and fully engaged with the experience, which means with the union itself.

Before it gets too fiery, let's back up for a moment. Tantra's four stages illustrate how the path of tantra involves gradually revealing and uncovering ever deeper layers of attachment and clinging, and then letting go of them. In any state of union, the distinctions of self and other disappear. We enter a liminal bliss and clarity, awareness untrammeled by separation and self-protection. In a sense, "we" are no longer there—we directly perceive what Buddhists call no-self.

Once more, tantra is an extremely powerful practice, which is why it was considered a secret teaching for most of its history. If it interests you, we highly recommend finding a qualified teacher with whom to train. As this practice works with the organism's energy system, it takes time to be able to undertake it well and safely.

Let's recall that tantra's male/female dialogue is also a metaphor. Tantric stages indicate deepening degrees of non-attachment or non-clinging, as well as simultaneously deeper levels of surrender and release into trust and love. Typically, the standard love affair quickly roots itself in either ego positioning around self-determination and independence, or a fused codependence. From the tantric perspective, interdependence and integration are experienced as union, not as a refuge from loneliness and an attempt to escape it.[130] An ordinary love affair is not likely to produce the experience of the highest tantric level of union, because the egos involved have not been trained to get past the agenda of the conditioned ego. Instead, our conditioned reactions determine the nature of the relating, perhaps making for an indifferent hook-up or a default attempt at pair bonding.

We must have a very strong sense of self to be able to let go into the experience of union, or no-self. All of this takes time and training. The sense-based samatha meditations of tantric practice help us to get from here to there.

Sensing meditations feel very accessible to us because they take out the most difficult aspect of being human, which is the interpersonal. When we have another ego in front of us, when there's another person present, we position ourselves; then our personal stories start to take over. Among the many different types of traditional sense meditations, none address interpersonal relationships. In fact, in the forty classical meditations of the

---

[130] For an interesting discussion of this topic, see Emmanuel Ghent, M.D., *"Masochism, Submission and Surrender: Masochism As a Perversion of Surrender,"* *W.A.W. Institute, New York, 1990,* www.wawhite.org/uploads/PDF/E1f_9%20 Ghent_E_Masochism.pdf.

fifth-century *Visuddhimagga*, one of the oldest meditation manuals in the world, interpersonal relationships aren't mentioned.[131] And yet, most of our modern lives take place in the interpersonal world of the day-to-day. Tantra helps us to bridge this gap. The beauty of the tantric system lies in the practice of visualizing a deity, which is fundamentally, archetypally, another person.

But "real" people tend to be so difficult! And imaginary people are easy. When we were small, we had imaginary friends. We didn't have any real problems with our imaginary friends because we could do what we wanted, and they would do what we wanted. They would behave in any way we chose. In this sense, our imaginary friend is a vehicle for us to practice positioning our ego in relationship with another ego, and yet isn't as challenging as a real live human being. We practice relating to real people by exploring our relationship with "other" in our imaginary world.

In this way, we imagine a semblance of a human being as an archetype of compassion and interface with him or her or them. Over time, we learn how to interface via the archetype of compassion when we return to the so-called "real" world of ego-oriented beings.

Besides human qualities, the deity images may incorporate animal-like elements, which help us to integrate characteristics of our instinctual natures. Yamantaka (the lord of death and also creation) has the head of a bull; Hayagriva has the head of a horse and represents the freedom and triumph of pure knowledge over the dark forces of unwholesome passion and darkness. Including animal elements is vitally important because our instinctual natures may represent parts of our suppressed shadow. It's an excellent approach since the deities are imagined rather than "real." Even if we start exploring the previously murky areas of

---

[131] One exception might be the Brahma Viharas, or Divine Abidings: the feelings of loving-kindness, compassion, empathetic joy, and equanimity. As you can see, however, these are more about states of being than about interpersonal relationships dynamics.

our shadow, we don't take the experience as personally. It helps make shadow work more accessible and less intimidating.

In addition, through practicing with the deity images, creating them and dissolving them, meditating on their component parts, we slowly get used to the idea that we're not quite so "real," either. We begin to see that our bodies, our feelings, and our thoughts have also been imagined or created out of spaciousness, like the deities. Before our life began, we were no more than a twinkle in our parents' eyes, and after we die, we hope to be a fond memory. In between, are we as substantial as we think? We begin to perceive how we have imagined ourselves into being every bit as much as we imagine the archetypes into being. We decide we want to become more intellectual, caring, or fit, and we gradually try on this new "me" just as we try on a deity of healing or discerning wisdom. Since we imitate who we admire, deity practice suggests we imitate compassion, healing, wisdom, and other qualities embodied by tantric deities.

Perhaps you are worn down by life, feel joyless, and have a lack of passion. Demchog might be just the thing. He is visualized as calm, sapphire-like blue color, in union with his female consort, Vajrayogini, who is passionate red in color. These represent the red color of our blood going out from the heart and its blue appearance as it returns. He holds implements that represent determination and wisdom, while she holds implements representing passion and non-clinging. They're imagined dancing in sexual union, indicating our ability to find passion and joy in every moment. If we meditate on Demchog with the aspiration to feel more bliss, sooner or later more energy and delight will emerge.

Because the archetypal figures whose qualities we are trying to integrate into our daily lives aren't personal, gradually we learn not to take other people in our lives, their idiosyncrasies and habits, so personally either. Since the tantric archetypes are imagined and created, they're temporary and impermanent. Nonetheless, over time, we experience how helpful it is for us to spend time with them, and so we learn to cherish them even though they are not so real. By extension, as part of our tantric practice, we learn to treat people in our lives with similar appreciation and respect.

BEYOND CONDITIONING: TANTRA AS HALFWAY HOUSE

We've shared a lot about using spiritual practice to free ourselves from the confines of our conditioning. We are not going to suddenly stop being the person we have been our whole life, but we develop the capacity to go beyond being unconsciously imprisoned by our conditioning. The deity in tantric meditation acts as a halfway house.

What does this look like? Let's meet Armand, who was born and raised in France. For all his wonderful open-mindedness and adaptability, he does not look and act like an American woman. Nor does he act like someone from Indonesia. By and large, he acts, talks, moves, and functions like a Frenchman. The conditioning is there. If we know France and French culture well, we may be able to tell which part of the country he's from, or various things about his background.

We are culturally conditioned, that's fine. There's no problem with that. The conditioning is the conditioning. And why not? After all, we've got to be *something*.

But because Armand's conscious mind is being dominated by unconscious factors (in this case of the French kind), Armand needs a halfway house to transcend the unconscious aspects of his conditioning. The tantric deity meditation provides him with a halfway house, a place where he can see the unconscious aspects free from the identification with his conscious persona as a Frenchman.

In the process of allowing ourselves to contact and merge with or *into* a deity, we allow ourselves to step out of the peculiar qualities of our particular conditioning and into the purified aspects of the deities' consciousness. This is a transformation of our consciousness.

Please take note that we don't step beyond ourselves because there's something wrong with us. There isn't, really. But a sense of "me" limits our degrees of freedom. It does this by maintaining limited or restrictive self-views, due to the inescapable labyrinth of conflicting emotions that arise from interruptions to our habitual conditioning.[132]

After all, other people have an amazing talent for interrupting our habitual conditioning. This fundamentally compassionate—if perhaps at times unskillful—act is commonly called "pushing our buttons." If Jayden is particularly fastidious and his sister Olivia tends to be messy, we can see how they could get on each other's nerves and become very reactive toward each other. In their case, both Jayden and Olivia's tendencies interrupt one another's preferences. They have a good opportunity to learn something from each other. But will they? Do we? The journey of spiritual awakening is a journey toward having no more buttons left to push.

Let's take a look at how this typically works, in the case of Aja and Francisco. While interacting with all other beings in the world, how many other Ajas is Aja going to meet? Zero. And how many other Franciscos is Francisco going to meet out there in the world? Also zero. So how is Aja going to relate to Francisco? If Aja is *doing* Aja, completely immersed in her identity as Aja, and Francisco is *doing* Francisco, totally identified with his personality, how are they going to communicate with each other? How are they going to find that place between them where something is shared? From this orientation, it's not possible.

This is where the deity practice proves so important.

Because they've practiced tantric meditation for years, Aja naturally becomes (or chooses to become) Chenrezi. Francisco becomes Chenrezi. And then, in the embodiment of compassion—because that's the defining characteristic of Chenrezi—they can communicate. And that communication can be a beautiful, compassionate exchange. Aja is not threatened by the fear of

---

[132] Read more about habits, our conditioning, and the spiritual path in Reflection 7: Awakening through Career.

being taken over by Francisco. And Francisco isn't afraid of being consumed by Aja. Instead, they have common ground where they can meet and interrelate.

As Aja and Francisco start to see that they can each manifest this Chenrezi, gradually there are ripple effects. The compassion starts to ripple into the depths of their being. They both realize they can relax into being themselves as an embodiment of compassion.

In the psyche or ego structure of Aja and Francisco, impurities may still remain regarding intent and traces of greed, hatred, and delusion, based on fears, attachments, unwholesome conditions, etc. But due to the power of compassion, they each recognize that any impurities that may linger don't have the power to affect him or her adversely. The power of compassion overpowers any impure effects that a consciousness might otherwise have when we allow another into our hearts.

The power of compassion gives us the strength to not keep others out due to perceived imperfections, but rather to allow them in as they are. If we can let them in just as they are—along with the impurities in their consciousness—while maintaining our heart of compassion, *this transforms their consciousness as well as ours*. It is freedom.

In this same way, Francisco's feelings of jealousy can be transmuted in Aja by her compassion, or vice versa. If both can maintain the strength of their practice and thereby avoid falling into a reactive pattern, the power of compassion becomes what is known as the Great Healing or transcendence.

Let's get more specific, since things in our daily lives can feel so tricky. As an example, let's say that Aja has some degree of attachment to Francisco in her heart.[133] She wants him for herself. Francisco, meanwhile, is doing the full manifestation of the meditation on compassion. He's contacted Chenrezi, and he's dwelling in that space. He knows that Aja is relating to him

---

[133] It could, of course, be the other way around. Feel free to swap the names and use any gender orientation that works for you.

together with the defilements of her conditioning—in this case, clinging. Yet he's letting her—as an embodiment of Chenrezi—into his heart.

Now, it turns out that Aja also has a little bit of attachment to Francisco's house (as a representation of security). She's hoping that by being with Francisco that she'll also get his house as part of the arrangement. So, there's the impurity of a vested interest involved. But because the power of Francisco's compassion practice—and the power of compassion itself—is so much greater than that of this relatively minor impurity in Aja's being, Francisco holds her, as a manifestation of Chenrezi, in his heart, but does not get fooled by the pollution.

Francisco may say something like, "Of course you can come and visit me, but no, you can't live here. I love you, I love you, I love you. Now go home." He's rejecting the pollution aspect of it, but he's not rejecting Aja, nor does he lose sight of the fact that, at her core, there's compassion, too. And he recognizes that the only reason she wants his house is because some confusion remains—due to the conditioning of Aja's upbringing—around the fact that neither a house nor another person can guarantee love or security. Both have to come from inside, not an external agent.

The power of the Chenrezi that Francisco is manifesting helps Aja see the attachment to the house as an impure manifestation of a deeper underlying love. She starts to realize through her own efforts, practice, and contact with the embodiment of compassion that the house is not the thing. Compassion is the thing, love is the thing.

As this sinks in, she also overcomes the fear of allowing another person into her heart. With that barrier removed, she can fully experience other—in this case, Francisco.

And then they'll find, through compassionate meeting in Chenrezi, that Aja is Francisco and Francisco is Aja. Through that tuning fork principle, she has dropped the attachment to the house and security, entered into compassion, and now she's back in her own heart and mind, contentedly living her own life. They may even live together in their house. Or not. At this point, it doesn't matter, because both know that the house and the other person are not something to get and keep, but are something to appreciate, love, and share.

A GEM WITH MANY FACETS

Compassion is one manifestation. But life contains many facets of experience, so there are many, many different deities to reflect these. We could say there are an infinite number of deities because, of course, in human experience, there are an infinite number of manifestations. I may have known Joon for thirty years, but there may still be situations where I discover a Joon I've never seen before. In fact, it's a certainty. Actually, I don't know Joon at all. I only know Joon in this moment. Chances are good, though, that on an overall, day-to-day basis, we'll interact fairly consistently, and therefore practice the same ways of showing up and deities with each other.

But there may be a moment where he appears differently—or I may. A new mandala of being could arise, which might require a brand-new deity for this fresh relationship between us. It will be a new meeting ground. The integrity of Joon and the integrity of myself meet or manifest under new conditions. The integrity of each is recognized, and yet we're unified in the common space of the deva practice.

Naturally, for any given mandala, there are related archetypes, and each is suitable for cultivating different qualities.

Formal meditations are designed to allow us to bring our self into appropriate manifestations at suitable times. Perhaps Jefferson is going through security at an airport and feels he is being unfairly hassled. Rather than getting upset, he could practice, say, Green Tara, and see the situation as a stroll through a garden (perhaps with buzzing insects). Or if Leticia and Agnes were nervous about their upcoming wedding, they might imagine being the Great Umbrella Mother, who protects everyone under her loving care.

In a sense, practicing one deity or archetype helps us develop the capacity to master them all. Some people just practice the same one over and over again. This allows the meditator to experience one kind of manifestation truly profoundly.

On the other hand, some people practice with numerous deities to develop contact with diverse energies. The advantage of this approach is that the practitioner becomes adroit with a variety of manifestations. People who are going to teach are encouraged to practice many different deities to skillfully meet the many different ways life and people can show up.

Perhaps some examples could illustrate this. We already shared about my (Catherine's) transformational experience practicing Medicine Buddha when I was ill. Another time, I was with my grandfather as he was dying, and I stayed with him all night, saying mantras for White Tara, who links us with the transcendental, to support his transition. From time to time, he would cry out in the night, or moan, and I would vocalize the mantra a little more. Each time he quieted down.

Once, we made a pilgrimage with a group of thirty students to Bhutan's Tiger's Nest Monastery, where two of the founders of Buddhism in Tibet—Guru Rinpoche and Yeshe Tsogyal—are known to have practiced in the 8th century. We journeyed hours by bus then hiked up the mountain for several hours to visit the sacred site, saying their mantras the entire way. When we arrived, a security guard told us that the monastery was closed, and we couldn't enter. We stood there saying Guru Rinpoche mantras while our guide asked him to make an exception. It seemed he sensed our commitment, because he did let us in, probably risking his livelihood.

We can, of course, apply these archetypes when we don't have a particular problem, when we're feeling healthy and content. As with anything, an ounce of prevention is worth a pound of cure. Practicing when we feel good helps keep us well-balanced. It helps prevent us from falling prey to illusions about our own ego-oriented magnificence or believing that the current heaven will last forever. Due to the fact that everything is impermanent, we can be sure that it won't.

Practicing when we're feeling poorly helps improve our state, our view, and thus, our situation. Practicing when we're feeling great helps us stay grounded. While our overall state improves, bringing more clarity and joy, we can also see that over time, in the daily ups and downs, the troughs get shallower, and the highs get lower. Our new low is higher than our previous highs. But, the best part is that the highs and lows become less and less distinct; the waveform balances out more and more. This is one of the Holy Grails of any spiritual practice—the very pleasant feeling known as equanimity.

REFLECTION 14
SPIRITUAL ENERGY TRADERS

On Giving and Receiving

We know that we live in a society that's pervasively capitalistic. Merriam-Webster defines capitalism as an "economic system characterized by *private or corporate ownership* of *capital* goods, by *investments* that are determined by *private* decision, and by prices, production, and the distribution of goods that are determined mainly by competition in a *free market*." (italics ours)

This gives rise to all sorts of questions, such as who defines the parameters of "ownership?" Why are economic decisions that affect everyone private? How do resources get privatized? And what exactly does "free" mean in this context?

The answers are complex, but one way or another, it's all about boundaries. Boundaries are what separates mine from yours, and thus, me from you. It brings us back to that feeling of separation that we spend so much energy trying to avoid.

It's no wonder that we feel alone and lonely.[134] Since we are social animals, and our success as a species has come from

---

[134] Elizabeth Renzetti, *Life of Solitude: A loneliness crisis is looming,* Nov. 23, 2013 and updated March 25, 2017, https://www.theglobeandmail.com/life/life-of-solitude-a-loneliness-crisis-is-looming/article15573187/.

working together, being alone is perceived as not only terrifying but also dangerous: when we're alone, we're more vulnerable. So we create backup plans to try to ensure some feeling of safety. A common form this takes in the modern age is money. We need enough to see us through any difficulties that might arise or for when we are no longer earning a living. We can't know how long these periods might last, plus we're living longer, and the global economy is becoming more volatile. It's natural then to expect we might need more than anticipated, so we may feel the need to store up as much as we can get our hands on. As would everyone else.

In other words, fear causes us to get greedy. Capitalism has proven to be the most effective system to date for accumulating wealth. A consequence is that it's also a system that isolates us from each other. The overarching result is a greedy society rooted in insecurity, but nevertheless with a sense of entitlement. This could be a definition for consumerism. Both insecurity and entitlement make for a lack of sustainability, marked by extreme challenges in producing cooperative and responsible management of our environment and resources.

Is it any wonder we feel vulnerable and anxious, and have a pessimistic view of the future?

This sense of vulnerability is accompanied, in our deepest fears, by the fear of abandonment and annihilation. These fears can drive us crazy, and if that happens, who knows what we might do. Earlier in the book, we discuss these four ego fears—abandonment, annihilation, madness, and being "evil" (what I might do if threatened)—as the four core fears deep within all of us.[135] All of our other troubles—such as worry, anxiety, tension, and insecurity—ride on the coattails of these four. And they all stem from feeling unsupported, unprotected, and uncared for.

Another unintended consequence of the capitalist system is that it reinforces precisely these fears. Even the stock market

---

[135] For more on this topic, refer to Reflection 3, under The Four Deep Ego Fears.

industry describes itself is as driven by greed and fear.[136] Given that we live in such a system, the cycle perpetually reinforces itself: greed causes fear, which then causes more greed. Such a cycle drives all of us crazy, even so-called "successful" people.

The good news is this cycle is neither inevitable nor predictive. There is a better way to organize ourselves that is both practicable and enriching for everyone. It will, however, require a revolutionary change in our mentality, and that will probably take some time. Social ventures, social enterprises, co-determined board structures, and co-operatives are a few examples of improved, more sustainable ways that business can be undertaken. These are models that may include social and environmental health as well as financial profits as part of decision-making, to contribute to collective well-being. Additionally, organic agriculture, fair trade, and local businesses support sustainability as well as local communities and economies. As nature is incredibly efficient, we'd benefit from increased use of biomimicry—sustainability-oriented innovation based on natural patterns—as a global model.

Where to start? To cure a disease, it is first necessary to understand its pathology. The pathology of the dysfunctional side of capitalism is greed. How did this system begin?

CAPITALISM AND THE MOTHER-CHILD DYNAMIC

Perhaps capitalism arises from our upbringing. If mother is the resource (*capital*) from which a child draws support or energy (*resources*) to pursue his or her own (*private*) goals (*investments*), then the roots of capitalism start with mother and child. The child, backed with the parent's resources, goes into the world and competes in school and on the playground *freely*. But "free" implies all things are equal and coming from wealth and privilege cannot be equated with coming from hardship. At the very least, it is unequal opportunity.

---

[136] See, for instance, the *Fear and Greed Index, CNN Money, accessed June 22, 2018,* http://money.cnn.com/data/fear-and-greed/.

Within the family, it's true that the child must provide some compensation for this support, in the sense of conforming to the demands of the parents. But by and large—in our society in any case—when measuring in terms of resources, the child receives far more than he or she gives. When the child considers the mother's energy to be its own (*ownership*), and rarely considers the (re)source (mother), then the child will also be unlikely to offer any return on mother's investment. Mothers accept their child's love as payment enough. The child, meanwhile, may or may not have any idea what that means. And the child's love may be as much about securing resources—including protection and connection—as about emotional identification with mother.

In this way, mother is the ultimate good creditor. In all likelihood, she may hope for—but not demand and perhaps not even expect—a return on her investment. As we grow up, it's natural that this becomes the basis for how we believe things should work: I should get what I need for free and use it to get other things I want. Along with this, we also come to believe that what I get is mine. It may be impossible to fully value everything that a loving mother does for her child, but generally these things can be taken for granted, and all that she does doesn't have a recognized value in and of itself, at least not economically. What is the worth of cooking supper, doing a load of laundry, or simply caring about us? We may appreciate her doing these things, but when it comes to valuing them in terms of our resources, how much would we pay? Once we're adults, do we send thousands of dollars her way for her years of support? Or do we spend that money on ourselves (or our families, an extension of me) instead?

Moreover, most of our parents—since they were probably raised in a similar system—are role modeling the adult version. We see our parents accumulate goods or cultivate a lifestyle, and thereby learn to function the same way.

In other words, "free market" means learning how to maximize my accumulation of goods with as little interference or reference to others as possible, without getting socially, emotionally, or otherwise isolated.

The free market implies that I'm empowered by the system to maximize my welfare, as are you. Sharing is often ignored in this process of accumulation. Sharing is a learned skill when it comes to wealth: it needs to be taught (shared!) and practiced. When *competition* sets in instead, its inventions—like electricity and the car—can be channeled to raising our standard of living to hedge against the possibility of scarcity. As mentioned, research has shown that people fear loss twice as much as we desire gain,[137] meaning that I need a good likelihood of getting two dollars to be willing to risk my one. This is one of the driving forces of capitalism: our risk aversion drives us to get as much as we can to insure against loss.

Of course, most parents encourage their children to learn to share. But most parents will also inadvertently teach our children to hang on to more than they give away, because parents are often driven by these fears. Whether we actually need to worry about them or not doesn't matter: the capitalist system itself promotes the anxiety, even among the wealthy.

Not convinced? Generally speaking, the modern, capitalist sense of "community" has largely been replaced by the nuclear family. Consider what percentage of our net income is used for the welfare of beings outside our immediate families, and we see how this operates. This strategy of more for me meaning less for someone else is the thin edge of the wedge in our slide into isolation, self-protection, and therefore insecurity. In other words, we live private lives. It's the status quo model, especially in North America, so it's challenging not to.

We've dedicated a lot of our time and energy over the last two decades to cultivating community. We've been surprised to realize that truly living and working in community requires skills that we no longer have; we didn't learn them growing up. Well-rounded communication, group decision-making, balanced

---

[137] Kahneman, *Thinking, Fast and Slow*, 28. See also the beginning of Reflection 3.

mutual support, etc. are very important talents that we've had to re-discover, learn, and grow.

One of the ways that we've come to define community is the group of people we can't afford–or refuse–to leave. This can show up in an economic sense, perhaps indicating the community of our workplace or our clients and professional support system. Or it may show up in an emotional sense. Either could manifest in healthy or unhealthy ways. Using this definition, in modern society, many of us don't really have community. We use the word to mean people who we work, live, and share with, come what may. Tribal communities live and work in the same kind of paradigm. If we go home to our own house or apartment, have jobs that are unconnected to our friends and neighbors, with social lives with another distinct group of people, then we're moving between three communities, which means we don't really have one.

A recent example brought this home for us. Two of our students had been teaching together in a collegial way, and eventually they ran into some areas of contention. They struggled to resolve them, and one communicated to us that, unfortunately, the "divorce" seemed irrevocable and permanent. We've all had these kinds of feelings and experiences, and our relationships naturally wax and wane, but excising people from our lives does fly in the face of true community. If we extrapolate their relationship dynamic to society at large, then the fabric of that society is likely to experience intense challenges holding together. If we're not truly part of a viable community, then loneliness will be a major struggle.

Thus, we've become conditioned in society, directly or indirectly, to each look out for ourselves. The natural consequences are problems such as environmental degradation, overpopulation, rampant consumerism, corporate malfeasance, and social isolation. With over seven billion people, it becomes harder and harder for the haves to remain haves. *Eight* of the world's richest *individuals* own more wealth than the poorest *half* of the world's population,[138] and this inequality gap is increasing rapidly.[139] EIGHT individuals! As human society slides back into a kind of global feudalistic system, what can those of us in democratic populations do? What might true economic freedom look like, outside of the capitalist model?

With capitalism, the default is to pacify ourselves with consumer goods, settling for nice meals, cars, or flat screen TVs rather than true economic freedom. One alternative is to learn how to co-create communities and organizations where we can rely on and share with one another in ways that allow each of us to have some flexibility. We can take a trip, visit someone, have extra time with the kids, get ill, or explore something outside the standard day-to-day, without the intense stress of needing to constantly generate income or otherwise maintain external responsibilities. Such a system supports *interdependence* rather than independence. This could mean between communities as well as within them. Ultimately, economic freedom begins to emerge when we see ourselves as one planet, one people, and fundamentally, one being. Then we naturally start to act in accordance with innovations in biomimicry and other forms of sustainability.

WHY CAPITALISM?

Historically, capitalism flourished to fund large projects that were deemed to serve important national and economic interests but were too big for individuals or small groups to fund. The classic example is joint-stock chartered companies that undertook

---

[138] Ben Hirschler, *World's eight richest as wealthy as half humanity, Oxfam tells Davos*, Reuters, Jan. 15, 2017, https://www.reuters.com/article/us-davos-meeting-inequality/worlds-eight-richest-as-wealthy-as-half-humanity-oxfam-tells-davos-idUSKBN150009.

[139] Tami Luhby, *The 62 richest people have as much as half the world*, CNN *Money*, Jan. 18, 2016, http://money.cnn.com/2016/01/17/news/economy/oxfam-wealth/index.html.

sixteenth-century trans-oceanic trade voyages, often multi-tasking for scientific exploration and imperial expansion.[140]

Capitalism continued to evolve with societal and commercial needs. "With the invention of the railroad, you needed a great deal of capital to exploit its purpose," says Columbia University professor John Coffee, an authority on corporate law. "And only the corporate form offered limited liability, easy transferability of shares, and continued, perpetual existence."[141] In other words, "corporations provide a mechanism for society to make long-term, intergenerational investments that are not linked to government or a specific family."[142]

When the corporation acquired some of the rights of an individual, including limited liability, the accountability of its officers became seriously compromised. For example, when subprime loans collapsed in the early 2000s, millions of private homes were "subject to foreclosure actions,"[143] which translated to millions of people losing their homes. Meanwhile, Wall Street firms trading in mortgage securities were injected with trillions of dollars of taxpayers' money to prevent their collapse.[144] While execs from

---

[140] Bamber Gascoigne, "History of Capitalism," HistoryWorld, accessed June 22, 2018, http://www.historyworld.net/wrldhis/PlainTextHistories. asp?historyid=aa49.

[141] Nina Totenberg, *When Did Companies Become People? Excavating the Legal Evolution*, July 28, 2014, Morning Edition, https://www.npr. org/2014/07/28/335288388/when-did-companies-become-people-excavating-the-legal-evolution.

[142] According to the legal scholar Lynn Stout, in Kent Greenfield's *If Corporations Are People, They Should Act Like It*, Feb 1, 2015, https://www. theatlantic.com/politics/archive/2015/02/if-corporations-are-people-they-should-act-like-it/385034/.

[143] "Subprime mortgage crisis," Department of Statistics and Operations Research, University of North Carolina at Chapel Hill, accessed July 1, 2018, http://www.stat.unc.edu/faculty/cji/fys/2012/Subprime%20mortgage%20 crisis.pdf.

[144] Neil Irwin, "This is a complete list of Wall Street CEOs prosecuted for their role in the financial crisis," *The Washington Post, Sept. 12, 2013,* https://www.washingtonpost.com/news/wonk/wp/2013/09/12/ this-is-a-complete-list-of-wall-street-ceos-prosecuted-for-their-role-in-the-financial-crisis.

smaller banks and private lenders were prosecuted for mortgage fraud, in the end, only one top Wall Street banker went to jail for his role in the crisis and its effects on millions of people.[145]

Opportunity (such as business opportunities) needs to be commensurate with responsibility and accountability, or exploitation is sure to follow. Aside from the important question of ethics, it is about karma: we reap what we sow. Wouldn't it be best if we were all reaping good crops that are healthy for people and the soil? We've seen what happens when crops are abundant but leave the soil in deteriorating condition: it's a vicious cycle that degenerates for everyone and everything concerned, karmically as well as practically. Some of us may try to walk away from inherited woes, leaving them for someone else to deal with, but this is only possible for so long on a finite planet.

We can see this dynamic play out in many aspects of life. For example, a businessman may generate profits from the labor of those who work for him, while not giving fair compensation. A spouse may work all the time and generally ignore their partner, but expect attention from them on demand. Or a housemate may leave his or her dishes for other residents to clean up. This is very human. In other words, we are all capitalists in so far as we'd like maximum returns for minimal investment.

The reason capitalism has done so well as an economic system is because it's smart. Wanting the best outcome for the least effort is intelligent.[146] The problem we face is that most of us often haven't really thought through what the best outcome is. Economic dominance, resource depletion, environmental degradation, and social anxiety may produce capital, but do not constitute healthy, sustainable, and compassionate goals. These are clearly not the best outcomes. As H.H. the Dalai Lama observed, "It is important that when pursuing our own self-interest we should be

---

[145] Jesse Elsinger, "Why Only One Top Banker Went to Jail for the Financial Crisis," *The New York Times Magazine*, April 30, 2014, https://www.nytimes.com/2014/05/04/magazine/only-one-top-banker-jail-financial-crisis.html.

[146] In fact, we promote this approach, too. See Reflection 1: The Vision, for more on getting the most beautiful for the least effort.

'wise selfish' and not 'foolish selfish.' Being foolish selfish means pursuing our own interests in a narrow, shortsighted way. Being wise selfish means taking a broader view and recognizing that our own long-term individual interest lies in the welfare of everyone. Being wise selfish means being compassionate."

On a grander scale, we'd be wise to include our planet and its systems in this approach. Especially in developed countries, we've long taken for granted the fact that the earth provides us with fresh air, clean water, and other primary resources for free or at very accessible prices. The corresponding responsibility to balance that presumption would be a sustainable human population with lifestyles that respect the environment and endeavor to maintain ecological balance. Just as our egos tend to be blind to the demands we expect our mothers and mother substitutes to dutifully meet, so too capitalism tends to have an opportunistic relationship with the environment and planet.

Both the ego and capitalism tend to ignore the balance required for holistic health, until the reality of the current situation starts giving us increasingly louder wake up calls. Fortunately, a growing number of people are moving into greater balance, together with governments, corporations, and other organizations.

SPIRITUAL GUIDES AND SACRED ECONOMICS

Part of the spiritual path is learning to become our own mother, to nurture and care for ourselves so that we don't try to place that responsibility indefinitely on another person or entity such as money. It's at this beautiful turning point that we can also truly—willingly, consciously, healthfully—care for others.

Along the way, it's natural to use our spiritual mentors and guides as a halfway house. We've learned not to rely on our mother to take care of us, we're learning not to outsource this function to our significant other, but we're not quite able to entirely take care of ourselves emotionally, psychologically, and physically. Our spiritual teachers, meanwhile, are providing us with a lifeline for this journey. This manifests as various kinds of nurturing and sustenance, perhaps practical, perhaps conceptual (the teachings), certainly as an important emotional and psychological support. We can easily begin to unconsciously expect to receive more than we give, to our own as well as others' detriment.

This may be especially true in the West in the early 21st century. Many teachings that were developed in Asia are based on a model of generosity, and these teachings and practices are still relatively recent arrivals in the Americas and Europe. As previously mentioned, in the East this system or practice is called *dāna*, the Sanskrit word for generosity. For more than 2,500 years Buddhists, Hindus, and probably adherents to even older spiritual traditions have honored spiritual teachings, teachers, and practice by contributing so that they would flourish.

That's given these traditions and peoples plenty of time to develop a strong culture of generosity. It's well understood that each individual gives what and however they are able, and the merit they generate[147] is based on their aspiration and the relative value of the contributions to the individual's circumstances, rather than quantity. When we visit temples and monasteries in Asia today, our experience is the fruit of contributions from countless numbers of community members over innumerable generations.

Westerners of course can be extremely generous; the Judeo-Christian (and other spiritual traditions') virtue of charity and traditions of philanthropy are remarkable testimonies to some of the best qualities of humankind. Dāna practice is different, however, in that it specifies that the act of giving benefits the giver far more than the receiver. It's in our own best interest to be generous. It also entails giving without expecting anything in return. As a result, dāna is also meant to be an anonymous practice.[148] If we give dāna to an Asian monk or nun, it's unlikely

---

[147] For more on the important practice of generating merit, see Reflection 5 on Karma Yoga, under the subhead *In the Land of Two Thousand Temples*.

[148] It's worth conceding that, with the increase in travel and physical distances between us, and the ongoing decrease in the use of cash, giving anonymously can be challenging.

they will express appreciation, because it's understood that we as the givers are benefiting more from the transaction than they are.

For those of us practicing generosity in the West, all this is easy to understand in theory, but more challenging to live. This story may illustrate how challenging it can be to change our mental models. A friend and I (Catherine) went to lunch together. When it came time to pay, we both wanted to treat the other. We each insisted, neither backed down, and so we agreed to play rock-paper-scissors for it. I won, upon which my friend offered, "So I have to pay." I countered, "No, I won, so I *get* to pay." He looked at me for a moment, speechless, and then with a smile asked me to stop messing with his mind and let him pay.

The profundity of dāna practice comes from leaving the contributions up to our own discretion. What price would we put on spiritual awakening? Spiritual well-being? Inner peace? A loving heart? Wisdom? And what do I contribute when (not if but when) my teacher is kind of pissing me off? Challenging my identity to its core?

If we consider spiritual welfare—perhaps along with environmental health—as one of the most precious products or services on the planet, one might imagine that true spiritual teachers would be valued highly and supported commensurately. However, in both the East and the West, there tends to be an unspoken and largely unexplored expectation that our spiritual leaders should demonstrate their virtue through remaining relatively poor.

Some of these expectations are based in historical and cultural facts: Christian Jesuits, for example, did and still do take vows of poverty, and some Buddhist lineages (particularly Theravadin) vow to have only enough food and clothing to do one's work. These can be profound and spiritually enriching practices and comprise a very powerful experience (even when only a temporary one) for those on a sincere spiritual path. But it is important to note that the idea behind undertaking poverty as a vow is to see all of life as a gift, rather than as a journey of accumulation. This practice helps us not to be fooled into thinking that wealth is effective insurance against our fears.

Unfortunately, in the capitalist system we live in, "poor" generally means "failure." These days, many feel that fame or wealth equals success, so spiritual teachers who may not be wealthy or famous may be dismissed, or taken for granted, not so unlike how we treat our mothers and the planet.

Meanwhile, due to the very fact that some spiritual teachers *are* famous, they may become commoditized. Without malintent, they may end up becoming a consumer product and thus disposable and somehow marginalized. The public may resonate with the image while losing track of the message, or more importantly, of the journey that person undertook to become who and what they are. Which is also, in fact, who and what we'd really like to be.

With the dāna system in Buddhism (or in whatever context it's being practiced), teachers give their time and energy to support, educate, and train spiritual practitioners and the community at large. Classically, texts teach us that it's impossible to repay the immeasurable value of the compassionate sharing of teachings and training. Nonetheless, spiritual practitioners try to perpetuate the health of this system by supporting the teachers in whatever ways they can.

Karma yoga and dāna are two important ways, though any heartfelt contribution benefits the giver, and our methods are limited only by our imaginations. Some other forms of support we've seen include sincere listening, sharing the teachings with others, training other students, physical therapy, massage, accommodation or nourishment, or vouchers for the same, and sharing of unique things from one's home or culture.

Recently, this system has been called sacred economics or the gift economy, and some have pointed out that motherhood is the foundation of this paradigm.[149] Since we've described how the mother-child relationship can be the basis for capitalism as well, we're hopeful that we can co-create healthy, viable

---

[149] For example, see Genevieve Vaughan (ed.), *Women and the Gift Economy: A Radically Different Worldview is Possible* (Toronto: Inanna Publications, 2007), which, notably, also looks at the economic systems of indigenous cultures.

economic systems somewhere in between. That's the beauty of the Middle Way.

THE SPIRITUAL BUFFET

In so many ways, we are fortunate to live in an era when we can access sacred teachings that, until very recently, were hidden away, little translated, and in remote mountain hermitages. Yet, due to the accessibility of so many different kinds of teachings, we may feel entitled to them, gratis, whenever convenient to us. Our consumer habits may influence us enough that we end up treating sacred teachings like consumer items, picking and choosing what we like in the moment and turning away from that which we don't.

This smorgasbord-style approach to spiritual traditions runs the risk of rendering comprehensive, highly effective spiritual paths into something of a hodgepodge. This approach probably feels good sometimes but contains just whiffs of its true potential glory for our spiritual unfoldment and associated benefits for all beings.

And the hodgepodge can make for a rather strange model for our spiritual life. For example, we may want to be spiritual, but not poor. That's okay. But being "not poor" is different from being ungenerous. If we hedge our bets by over-relying on others' spiritual resources for our own benefit, we are missing a crucial element of our spiritual path. Alternatively, we may skillfully cultivate a business and image based on our spiritual practice and sharing our spiritual foundations in this way could be a wonderful thing. However, if we're not using our business success to support those who've guided and supported our spiritual growth, then we've created a false economy, and not a sacred one. It's the unwholesome side of the mother/child dialogue all over again.

The important thing here is a generative energy exchange. What that exchange consists of in terms of content, quality, and quantity is up to each person to decide. We must each determine how we'd like to invest in our own spiritual development, pay it forward by supporting the ongoing flourishing of the Triple Gem, pay it backward to our mentors, all while looking after the requirements of daily life in the world. We feel this is why sacred economics and the gift economy have captured our attention, because a sincere dāna practice is so liberating: it is a combination of art, science, heart, and breakthrough.

Here's an example of one traditional approach. In Asia, the local communities support their spiritual organizations while going to work to do so. When I (Doug) undertook a three-month meditation retreat in Malaysia, local Chinese Buddhist women came to cook breakfast for all the meditators very early, after which they cooked for their own families, after which they went to work all day. Local families took turns sponsoring lunch for us meditators, our last meal of the day. After local women cooked and ate their evening meal at home, many returned to the temple to practice for a while.

This was how they combined their dāna with their spiritual discipline: it was insightful of them to feed two birds with one hand this way, and I felt deeply impressed by all the merit they generated. These women admired a sincere dedication to practicing meditation and found value in supporting others— including Westerners—to do so. When we Westerners are guests in Asian temples and monasteries (often at extremely financially accessible prices), it's vital that we appreciate how supported we are by the genuine commitment and support of countless generations of practitioners such as these women. In many ways, the immeasurable practice and devotion by committed communities—current and previous—are always supporting and subsidizing our own.

REACHING SPIRITUAL MATURITY

To truly mature, we know that the child must one day become a parent themselves, actually or metaphorically. In the same way, if we continue to draw on our teachers' spiritual capital indefinitely, we are choosing to remain spiritually immature. By nature, youth and youthful people enjoy the creativity of play and recreation, so these spiritual resources are most likely spent on short-term pleasures and less where they are best invested: on the longer-term needs of our planet, our spiritual communities, and the welfare of future generations.

In some parts of the world, we have between one and three generations of Peter Pans and Cinderellas, people who have chosen, consciously or unconsciously, not to mature into interdependent human beings. It's understandable; the nuclear era instilled us with the fear that everything could end tomorrow, so it makes a kind of sense to enjoy ourselves while we can. Growing planetary challenges like climate change and mass species extinction add weight to that societal mental model.

But "growing up" in the form of undertaking responsibility can also be a joyful and empowering experience. We have the power to choose to imagine and create a future where food that's good for people and the ecosystem is the norm. We ourselves can choose to balance our human population at sustainable levels given our planetary resources, and to recognize fair trade as the obvious choice to ensure that international commerce and human relationships are healthy and mutually supportive. We also know that we don't live by bread alone. It's within our power to craft a society in which artists are supported for giving expression to our joys and sorrows, thereby easing our daily burden and raising our eyes to the stars. It is well within our means to ensure that parents are honored and supported for giving and nurturing life, and, along that same theme, to care well for the planet, the ultimate life-giver and nurturer.

Our most significant accomplishment would be to craft a society where our spiritual guides—the people who help us learn to safeguard inner peace, calm, joy, and wisdom, elements of the path to freedom—are sincerely valued and appreciated. What a victory it would be for humanity to construct successful social and economic models built on the practice of *dāna*, generosity. People who live and work based on a *dāna* model are trusting the universe enough to share the teachings without charge, recognizing that natural laws, such as karma, safeguard that the universe will give back.

We're all familiar with the shortcomings of capitalism and consumerism, and it's a privilege, creative act, and responsibility for each of us to be able to create alternative economic models. A growing number people are doing beautiful things with such alternatives already, transforming dreams into robust business models and lifestyles. The more of us who join in, the faster we can create the world we dream of living in. It's a wondrous part of growing up.

REFLECTION 15
ONLY THE SHADOW KNOWS

The Part Of The Spiritual Journey We'd Like To Skip

While deeply challenging, integrating our shadow[150] may be one of the fastest ways to unfold spiritually and reduce our suffering. How so?

The shadow consists of those aspects of our being that are hidden to us. They act like cement, steadfastly holding the ego's unacknowledged fears in place, constricting our freedom. By undertaking the arduous but growth-filled process of bringing the shadow out of the closet and into the light of the conscious mind, a humongous amount of energy becomes available to us.

Metaphorically speaking, since the shadow is blocking our access to higher levels of energy, then our normal conditioned consciousness is working at a home-energy level (110–120 volts). When we clear the energy blockages constrained by the shadow elements in our being, that would take us up the power grid to the power poles and even into the generating station, as it were. We can become human energy generators.

This may seem dangerous or scary to some and keep some of us housebound, energetically speaking. Nevertheless, this energy

---

[150] We're using the term "shadow" in line with Carl Jung's work, referring to what Freud called "the unconscious."

source can power whole cities and countries. After all, the energy itself hasn't changed; its availability has been limited by resistance rooted in the shadow. Once liberated, we can then use this energy toward more wholesome pursuits, such as integrating our spiritual practice with our daily life and getting creative about ways to benefit all beings.

We heartily advocate integrating the shadow, and a lot of what we do as teachers and trainers is geared toward this intensive, transformational work. To begin, we need to understand how the shadow operates. It's comprised of the unconscious parts of our mind that hold instinctual drives and terrors out of our conscious reach. This dynamic is part of being human. Our ego senses these urges and fears as potentially destructive, bad, or even evil, precisely because they feel beyond our grasp. When we don't understand something, it's more intimidating, so little-understood fears (for example) feel more fearsome. But if we allow these "demons" to be seen, they can be understood, accepted, integrated, and transformed.[151] As a result, our degrees of freedom and energy increase dramatically.

This energy allows us to see what lies beyond (and within) the structure of the ego, and how resisting letting go is what limits our unfoldment. The ego comprises clouds; freedom is clear sky. The latter has been called awakening, Buddha nature, Christ Consciousness, and so on. Whatever its name, it is spiritual. And let's recall that the word "spiritual" means "breath," or "free-flowing energy," and by implication, non-clinging. It is liberation. The ego by itself, on the other hand, is a type of slavery.

It's important to be clear and honest here: by its very nature, shadow work is not fun or pretty. It takes courage and fortitude to see parts of our being that are not as we wish them to be, and that mess with our self-image. It takes enormous resilience and dedication to transform these parts of ourselves into something healthy and beneficial. And once we decide to meet the shadow's darkness, it inevitably moves toward greater and greater light.

---

[151] We go into more detail about this process later in this reflection.

The energies locked in the shadow elements now get released and can be directed toward supporting transfiguration through integration. This is both beautiful and exciting. Significantly, it is also the beginning of the end of suffering.

The Buddha said, "I teach suffering and the cessation of suffering."[152] Many of us may think that we aren't suffering because that word seems too big for what we are feeling. Or we look at disaster-stricken parts of the world and rightly appreciate how fortunate we are.

However, the Sanskrit word for "suffering," *dukkha*, is also translated as: uneasy, uncomfortable, unpleasant, difficult, painful, calamity, distress, woe, and restlessness. In short, dukkha refers to any kind of struggle. Discontent, restlessness, or dissatisfaction may be forms of dukkha that most of us can relate to as a daily occurrence.

So, what is the nature of our discontent? Typically, it can manifest as depression, anxiety, or worry. Ultimately, these boil down to a feeling of separation, a sense of loneliness, and sometimes just the feeling of missing something indeterminate. FOMO (fear of missing out) might be one of the more contemporary manifestations of dukkha.

BABY EGO MEETS BABY SHADOW

Let's revisit this feeling of separation, which in a physical sense begins at birth when we are born (separated) from our mother's womb. Although some form of consciousness is present even from conception, there's no self-consciousness until around two years of age.[153] With this emerging self-consciousness, ego awareness, we also become aware of other, principally in the form of mother. It's a huge shock to slowly understand that mother is other. Before this, we felt we were one being, but now we start to realize she is not part of us, and more to the point, she's not

---

[152] *Majjhima Nikaya,* 22: 37.
[153] We introduce this in Reflections 3 and 4.

under our control. That means we are separate and ultimately alone—not a feeling for the faint of heart, so naturally it is tough for a toddler to come to terms with.

Even more catastrophic to us at this tender age is the dawning that we are completely dependent upon mother (or her substitute) for our survival. In that sense, we feel incredibly vulnerable and dependent: we cannot afford to alienate her, as we may be abandoned as a result. This is, of course, unlikely (what a powerful force a mother's love is!), but the child doesn't know that at this point in their development.

This fear of abandonment causes us to begin to repress any instinctual energies of ours that seem to threaten, anger, or disturb mother,[154] and slowly these energies take up residence in our subconscious as the shadow. Parents play an important role in training their children to function well in the larger community, so the instinctual energies that get buried in the shadow are typically focused around defecation, emotional responses, sexuality, and our emerging independent will.

We could say that this is the reason the terrible twos are so terrible. We start to have independent desires and willfulness, which on a bad day can drive mother crazy. Not only are they terrible for mothers who are trying to train us—sometimes against our will—how to behave amicably in public, they are also terrible for us at this age. As two-year-olds, we scream, cry, have tantrums, and generally suffer our way through this challenging phase. We cannot afford to be abandoned (it would mean death), so we first suppress and then repress any desires we have that offend or disturb mother. Her suffering—albeit perhaps unacknowledged—has

---

[154] Or mother substitute—for example, when a child is raised by a single father or the father is the primary caregiver, he'd fulfill this role. When a child is raised by both a mother and father figure, and the former is the primary nurturer of the child, father is less influential on the child at this stage. However, he's still important because the child may observe, for example, how mother refers, or maybe defers, to father.

become ours, and it continues to move forward through the generations as a kind of psychological biogenealogy.[155]

Eventually, we have a society that is built on certain kinds of repression, and unconscious enforcement of that repression becomes collective. Naturally, this serves some important functions: it's important for community hygiene and health that we are all toilet trained. However, other forms of conditioning—let's say circumcision—may no longer serve the useful purpose it once did and may actually do more psychological harm than good.

In other words, even in pre-awareness (i.e., infancy or fetal stage), our organism can record an experience of trauma. This takes place when there's some form of aggression in our energy field that's supported (directly or indirectly) by the parents but conjoined with some kind of aversion on their part. Please note that often this aggression is well intended, or at least not mal-intended, as in the case of circumcision. To avoid the Four Deep Ego Fears,[156] we sublimate or repress the experience. As we develop an ego and learn to behave according to societal norms, repressed material amalgamates[157] to form the shadow.

Let us emphasize that much of our collective life together is positive. Nonetheless, we all have impulses and desires that our family or society deem unacceptable. As a result, these urges threaten our emotional and ego-identity survival, so we drive them out of our awareness in favor of fitting in. But the organism—or perhaps the awakening being inside each of us—cannot be fooled, and the impulses find ways to surface in our lives.

For instance, parents who came through two world wars and a depression could have grave security issues and use money as a way to try to feel more secure. By contrast, their children grew up in the 1960s or 1970s during North America's very strong

---

[155] Until someone in the family integrates the shadow. This can clear generations' worth of karma in the form of these conditioned patterns.

[156] See Reflection 3 for the Four Deep Ego Fears.

[157] As mentioned, common themes pertain to defecation, emotional responses, sexuality, and our emerging independent will.

bubble economy. The children may behave cavalierly with money because of the economic climate of their youth, but still hold shadow insecurities around survival from their parents. This is an example of what we mean by psychological biogenealogy. It could manifest by, for example, the children being oddly ungenerous, or by unconscious clinging to jobs they dislike, based on the security issues dwelling in the family shadow.

IT'S NOT MY SHADOW; IT'S YOURS

Initially, our shadow typically manifests in the guise of other people—whom we happen to find unbearable. As Sartre said, "Hell is other people." Depending on the particular characteristic, our shadow can be triggered by people we magnetize in various relationship contexts, such as a colleague, a life partner, or a series of strangers.

"How come three different girlfriends of mine have all had the same hang-up?" "I have really bad karma with bosses, they are always so authoritarian." "My significant other has some terrible habits that they refuse to quit." Do any of these sound familiar? These are all classic hallmarks of our own shadow raising its head in the guise of other. If you're cringing, don't worry; you're not alone. These kinds of experiences are universal.

The shadow can also manifest as guilt or shame. When such feelings are too intense, they can be displaced in a process referred to as hysteric conversion. Subsequently, they may appear as bodily symptoms, emotional unavailability, or mental defensiveness. They can also show up as compulsions, including addictions.

Most of our interpersonal conflicts get their energy from the shadow. The feelings of abandonment, being taken advantage of, not being appreciated, or being taken for granted all stem from our feelings of separation that are then projected onto other people. To the ego, it seems much safer to blame these feelings on other people as perpetrators, rather than looking deeply and honestly at what's going on inside ourselves, and then taking responsibility for changing it.

Most neuroses can be attributed to shadow elements. Although we can see our neuroses, they serve to hide the shadow very well. In addition, neuroses manifest through action, whereas the shadow can be glimpsed in silent urges that we often work hard to hide from others, sometimes by projecting the urges onto these other people or another external agent (such as the government or "the system"). This is why many spiritual teachers treat what society calls "mental illness" as spiritual crises: the shadow can manifest as physical, emotional, or mental issues through which it tries to come "out of the closet" and into the light of day where it can be integrated.

Sometimes, people distressed by these arisings of the shadow go to psychiatrists and pharmaceuticals. Alternatively, they might drop out of the medical system and discover a spiritual path, or they might get degrees in psychology and use it in conjunction with dharma to cope with their inner struggles. Some examples of struggles with these decisions come to mind. Buckminster Fuller considered jumping off a bridge before deciding to devote his life to the furthering of humanity. St. Francis rejected his family's wealthy mercantile way of life, running around naked, and then embraced monkhood. Eckhart Tolle was on the verge of suicide before he experienced his spiritual awakening. Nearly all awakening or awakened beings that we know, including ourselves, have similar stories.

In my (Doug's) case, I wondered whether I had gone crazy, and suicide was starting to feel like a viable option. I felt completely out of step with the world. I did psychedelics, which showed me the fragmented, deluded state of my mind, feelings, and behavior, which I realized matched the definition of schizophrenia. One day, I said to myself, "I need help." (This is a vital first step, as AA has shown.) I started reading about the spiritual path and looking for guidance from someone who was awakened. I found my teacher, and over years, he helped me to integrate the shadow. This transformed my understanding of the world: what had previously seemed crazy now made good sense, contextualizing it as a spiritual crisis and quest. I then spent many years practicing the path of awakening to integrate that alternative view with the "normal" world. This allowed me to move back inside the mainstream while still making room for the altered view that triggered my crisis. In this process of reintegration, the altered view of transcendence brings tremendous value to the status quo one, including the awareness that anyone can awaken in this lifetime. The shorthand expression for this experience is "in the world but not of it."[158]

While it's true that the brain functions on the basis of electro-chemistry, it's also true that the electrochemistry can be altered from inside the mind through methodologies like meditation. This may not occur as quickly as it can with drugs, but it does so without the need for external agents, without the very unpleasant side effects of drugs, and eventually, at will.

In the process of integrating the shadow (more on how this works to come), we meet and transcend the Four Deep Ego Fears.[159] We thereby gain access to the considerable amount of energy that was previously tied up in the energy-intensive shadow repression. It's now available to be directed toward things that bring us, and others, joy and growth: exploration, discovery, and creativity, and fostering spiritual awakening.

It sounds so straightforward, but the shadow has a profoundly elusive quality: whatever its nature, we tend to want nothing to do with it. Somehow, it's repulsive. Couldn't it just go away? Typically, we use strong emotions, cling steadfastly to attachments, consume substances, or distract ourselves with entertainment to keep it hidden. We can get violent, upset, stubborn, and addicted to shield ourselves from its messages. These strategies of hiding have their own counterproductive fallout, which over time exhaust us, wreak havoc with our relationships, stifle our energy, and generally sabotage our innate joie de vivre.

However, it's worth emphasizing again that, when we have the courage to lean into the repugnance and get to know the

---

[158] Based on 1 John 2:15-17 (NIV).
[159] See Reflection 3.

shadow, tremendous amounts of positive energy become available to us. The qualities that bothered us both in our self and others becomes integrated into our own personality in a much healthier way. We also have much greater empathy and compassion for other people's struggles with their shadow elements.

Let's take Jun as an example. Jun was a friendly, talented, intelligent, ambitious, and direct young woman. She also tended to be somewhat controlling and bossy. She couldn't understand why more people didn't warm up to her: in her mind and heart, she was gentle and sweet. That was one side of her, too—one she didn't show to many people. When people close to her suggested that she was also something of a tyrant, Jun felt unfairly attacked and thought they were projecting onto her. Weren't they the ones being tyrannical, she thought, by criticizing her? Given the dynamics, she wasn't shy about arguing her perspective, but the pain of it all—since part of her was tenderhearted—would make her weep.

Jun was (and is) part of a sangha, a community of Buddhist practitioners. Part of the role of such a community is to form a healthy container in which people can act as mirrors for one another to support each other's spiritual unfoldment as compassionately and skillfully as possible. So, Jun's sangha persisted. If she acted bossy, they suggested she have a look. They described how it felt to be on the receiving end, how she might say things another way and still get the results she desired, and so on.

Jun still didn't see it. However, eventually a large enough number of different people shared the same kind of perspective with her that she had to concede there must be *some* truth to what they were saying. Of course, she wanted to share her best qualities and be a pleasant person to be around, so she started checking in with people. She asked people whether they understood where she was coming from, and if they saw things differently, or had other ideas. Jun made efforts to share her more vulnerable feelings, be more supportive to other people, and give encouragement and empathy. She could sometimes still get bossy, but by now, it was more mixed in with other qualities.

Gradually Jun became less controlling as a default. She learned to make suggestions rather than pronouncements. She came to see how her inner taskmaster was trying to protect her tender-hearted nature. She learned how she could both be sensitive and directive. In other words, she transformed her inner tyrant into a skillful supporter, team member, and leader.

Integrating the shadow is no easy or small feat: Jun worked at it for years and is still working on it. The future prospects are promising. And everyone feels better about living, working, and relating with Jun. Including Jun.

INTEGRATING THE SHADOW: TWO APPROACHES

There are two principal paths to integrating the shadow, one deeper than the other. The more accessible route is therapy, which is close to our daily lives. Here we learn to take responsibility for our mind-states and heart-states, whatever is happening with us, what's going well, and what's going awry. With courage and self-honesty, like Jun, we gradually learn to acknowledge that our default behavior is mostly reactive and develop awareness and other skills to become more responsive.

Therapy lets us see what's been hidden in the subconscious, bring it into awareness, and start to work with it consciously. This is outstanding. The more people who do this, the better off we are as individuals and as a society. By far.

But therapy works within the framework of the ego, and the ego can't release at the core of our being through this method alone. Therapy can reveal and inform us of how the ego was built, how it functions, and how it can be better used, but the ego is unable to get past the ego itself.

In other words, we can't get there—to a state of spiritual awakening—from here, the ego. To do that, we also need the deeper path.

The deeper path's agenda entails embracing a spiritual life, including a regular meditation practice. Remember that the word "spiritual" means *pertaining to breathing, wind, or air,* and so has a feeling of natural flow. As such, the spiritual agenda is to liberate the ego from itself, to help ensure that the innate, wonder-filled flow of an integrated, spiritual being and life become free to move again.

How did the flow get blocked to begin with? The ego is like a mask we show the world. It served a useful function when we were first learning how to show up and get along in the world, but by the time we were adults, we forgot we had it on. Many people may never become aware that the ego, or persona, functions like a mask of sorts. Nonetheless, it doesn't feel comfortable. Most of us distract ourselves from this discomfort by staying busy with engagements like work, entertainment, and relationships.

For those fortunate enough to be unable to divert ourselves enough in these ways, a time of crisis inevitably comes. It may come in multitudinous guises: unbidden and unwelcome during sleepless nights, when a loved one leaves us, or when we can no longer deny that our distractions or addictions no longer work to numb the pain. Or just with a pervasive feeling of loneliness or restlessness, that life isn't turning out the way we thought it would.

Whatever it looks like, this is a crisis of meaning or purpose. We feel something like, "There's got to be something more to life than this!" or "This isn't the life I want." At this point, we acknowledge a feeling of separateness, but don't yet have a healthy reference point, framework, or methodology with which to address it.

This is the shadow calling for our attention, pressing the question, helping us see our own misery and our longing for something more, a sense of release or a tinge of wonder.

This is the beginning of the spiritual path, sometimes called the hero's journey. It's the ancient principle of alchemy: transmuting lead into gold. The hero's journey and spiritual path are about the transformation of our worst qualities into ones that we accept, integrate, develop, offer, and are eventually loved and respected for. Or from a permaculture perspective—with time and care, decaying manure and other organic matter are transformed into nutrient-rich hummus that feeds amazing new growth, delighting and nurturing us.

Our human nature is the same. The lead or manure are the energies locked up in the shadow, where they get heavy and smelly. It's only when we allow ourselves and others to see our shadow elements that they can be integrated, catalyzing the transformation into gold, creative expression, or other fecund natural processes.

A more fully awakened being—one of whose characteristics is that the shadow has been integrated—dwells in spacious non-attachment. As a result, she or he also naturally manifests the intrinsic and active human qualities of loving-kindness and compassion. They dwell unruffled and serene, clinging to naught in this world.

CATCHING THE SHADOW IN ACTION

For any of us, the absence of serenity, loving-kindness, and compassion is a flag waving to alert us that the ego is caught up in its own web of self-oriented intrigue. In other words, this is a good way to know that the shadow is being triggered.

We can catch our shadow in action any time the ego is attempting to distract from, ignore, or repress it. Instead of continuing this charade, we can use this opportunity to turn toward it. As we've described, the ego serves an important function: it plans, makes decisions, and organizes experiences and information. And when it's serving this function well, helping us explore this amazing universe we live in, many of the ego's adventures are quite wonderful. But when our vitality gets locked up, repressing the fears hiding in the shadow, these pursuits are, one way or another, doomed to limited success at best. This low ceiling holding back our success (which sometimes means failure, too) is one of the catalysts for our ability to sense that there has to be something more to life than what we currently know.

It's not just the absence of serenity, loving-kindness, and compassion that heralds the shadow: feelings of frustration, anger, or conflicting emotions might be more obvious signs. These feelings represent one of two fears: either *not* getting what we do want or getting what we *don't* want. For example, we may be afraid that we won't get the award, job or promotion, the admiration of someone we esteem, or enough love from our partner. We worry that we may get sick or be saddled with responsibilities we dread. Whatever the particulars, the results are feelings of worthlessness, or some variation thereof, which we understandably avoid. The power of these two fears can't be underestimated; they dwell in our shadow and drive our behavior.

Additionally, the shadow is likely raising its head when we feel consumed by extreme urges that are often taboo. Typically, these may be sexual, violent, or otherwise destructive, and are often covers for what are essentially power dynamics. These urges usually mirror the Four Deep Ego Fears[160] of every ego, perhaps in particular the fear of being evil or a bad person. Everyone experiences these feelings at some point, either inwardly or projected outwardly. Among other manifestations, they've provided material for an endless number of horror movies and thrillers. Such creative expressions of these energies provide a vicarious catharsis to support our subconscious efforts to relieve the tension inherent in suppressing these fears.

Acknowledging that we ourselves have such feelings can, of course, feel disturbing. It's worth noting that this is also part of our cultural conditioning; some cultures have found ways to accept the arisings as a natural part of life. The early Greeks, Romans, Hindus, and Buddhists all used forms of deity practice to incorporate and integrate the shadow elements (Hades, Kali, Maha Kala, etc.) in their psyches. Historically and today, many indigenous communities include rites of passage like vision quests or plant medicine journeys as part of their cultural mapping. Examples like the walkabout in Australia, the Sun Dance, sweat lodges, peyote in North America, or ayahuasca ceremonies in South America (etc.) are valued methodologies to help integrate

---

[160] They are the fear of abandonment, annihilation, insanity, and being evil. See more on these in Reflection 3.

and transform shadow elements of the participant and, by extension, the community.

In terms of specific cases, let's take the example of Arjun,
an Indian British man who came to his first retreat ever with
us around the age of thirty. He'd never been to therapy, nor
engaged with spiritual teachings, except for some family gatherings, more cultural than spiritual. Arjun's a very polite, proper, and
gentle-natured person, also cheerful, articulate, and perceptive.

In some of the classes we addressed the nature of the shadow.
At his first interview, he asked inquisitively, "About this shadow,
I had a dream last night where I killed my mother. Would that
dream be coming from the shadow?" He added that his relationship with his mother was fine, not marked by any particular
distress.

In response to Arjun's query, yes, his dream was from the
shadow; the dream expressed some aggressive feelings that weren't
part of his waking awareness. While he had no desire to harm
his mother, this dream allowed him to access the resentment all
children have toward their mothers. (Of course, we have loving
feelings toward our mothers, too, but those aren't in the shadow.)
Again, this stems back to our infancy, when we felt rage about
not being able to control her, that we were subject to her will,
and dependent on her for our survival.

It's not uncommon for shadow elements to surface through
dreams and then into the subconscious on the way to the conscious
mind, and Arjun's dream is a high-speed example of this process.
What was especially interesting to us was that Arjun was able to
speak so objectively about his dream, without shame or fear. We
can only surmise that something in his conditioning—perhaps
exposure to Brahma, Vishnu, and Shiva, Hinduism's creator,
preserver, and destroyer[161] deities, as three integral aspects of a

---

[161] Note, too, that Shiva is considered the destroyer and transformer of
malevolence, and that his destroying is recognized as necessary to usher in
new creation.

whole—made him comfortable with what might be considered destructive arisings.

Not all of us feel as dispassionately as Arjun when our shadow arises, and it can arise in waking life as well as dream life. People driven to accumulate vast wealth often have a shadow of feeling unsupported or unnourished; money becomes a poor substitute.

The key to integrating the shadow, however, is to just witness the sensations, emotions, or imagery surface and pass away, like a storm cloud across an otherwise vibrantly clear sky. Shadow elements are forces in the collective unconscious of humanity; it's not "me," it's not about me, it doesn't say anything about the kind of person I am. It's simply a shadow element of the psyche, coming up from the depths into the light to be released.

Since the shadow is by nature what we, our family, community, and society have tried to hide, learning to work with it is like swimming upstream from everything we've known before. It's a new skill we need to learn with support from others who have the courage to have done—or to do—the same.

Like Jun, we must initially rely on others to help us see what's been hidden in the shadow. People who have been trained to do this with compassion, wisdom, and skill are best qualified to help us lean in to this often painful and challenging process, and different traditions offer this in different forms. In Buddhism, qualified teachers have been trained to guide students in transforming the shadow, while the teachings describe its nature and means of transformation. A community of practitioners naturally has empathy and experience to offer, since they're on the same path. Hence, the Buddha (or his representative, a teacher), dharma (teachings), and sangha (community) are so highly valued as Buddhism's Triple Gem. With this triangulation of ongoing support, we eventually learn to be able to acknowledge and integrate our shadow elements ourselves.

In the light of our consciousness, the shadow elements can—both of their own accord and with our active intent—metamorphose into healthier expressions. What's more, we no longer need to expend the considerable energy required to keep these drives (and our fear of them) locked away where no one can know they exist. Freeing this energy up again makes it available for more constructive pursuits. And puts a spring back in our step and a smile on our face.

USING THE SHADOW AS A RESOURCE

Indeed, if we knew how much of our natural vitality was knotted up in our shadow, we would make haste to liberate it. To be a modern and integrated human being, to experience the full benefits of spiritual awakening, we need to integrate the shadow by accessing the deep resources of our mind.

To do this, we need to understand two things. First, we need to realize that our egos are scripts and we are actors. We are following scripts (or running software, we could say) that have been written by our family and society, and were written by their family and their society, and so on, back countless generations. The study of biogenealogy supports this, pointing out that, "Because our ancestors live within us, we can find the roots of our illness in our family history, in our family tree."[162]

Second, once we can perceive the scripts or software that we're following, we must see that, in a sense, their contents are arbitrary. They have been invented and crafted and adjusted over countless generations for us to get along and be able to live and work together reasonably well. If our family conditioning—let's say that it was "boys will be boys" but girls need to behave and be responsible—had been even a little different, we would have grown up with a different software program and would, therefore, be different people. It's within our power to choose to make those changes. In this way, our conditioned beliefs and behaviors are not reality in the sense of being beyond examination, review, and adaptation.

---

[162] Patrick Obissier, *Biogenealogy: Decoding the Psychic Roots of Illness: Freedom from the Ancestral Roots of Disease* (Rochester, Vermont: Healing Arts Press, 2003).

The scripts and programs laid down in our youth will continue to arise, as they are a part of us. However, if we can recall that they are a form of conditioning, we are on our way to freedom. Conditioning is not necessarily bad, but it is not the same thing as truth or reality; or we could say it is one kind of truth, one kind of reality, among many different kinds.

There's a useful mantra to help us create space between the conditioned arisings (thoughts, feelings, sensations) and the belief system we choose moment to moment: "This is not me; this is not mine; this is not who I am."

Note that the key here is not to reject the shadow—because what we push away has the tendency to come back again, like a boomerang—but to introduce a feeling of spaciousness between me and it. Reminding ourselves that we are not our arisings allows us to see behind the curtain of the ego to our primary refuge and source of spiritual sustenance: the spacious clear mind, emptiness, or *sunyata*.

Additionally, there are two other extremely useful practices to liberate blocks and access the energy behind shadow manifestations when they arise. The first is a technique called reframing where we take what we think is going on and look at it from diverse perspectives. It's important that we choose alternate points of view that are more open, clear, and more energized, and as a result, more compassionate to both ourselves and others. Questions that probe the nature of the block can be very liberating.

For example, let's say that Felix is very angry with Philippe because Philippe did something Felix didn't like. This situation is framed by the principle that, when someone (in this case Philippe) does something Felix doesn't like, it makes him angry. To reframe it, Felix could ask himself, for example, "What is the nature of dislike?" Or "Who or what is it that's angry?" Another one might be, "Why anger?" And so on.

Let's look at another example of how to use reframing. Even after many years of meditation and reframing practice, sometimes I (Catherine) feel some mild anxiety when I think about finishing this book. I then don't enjoy working on it, because I've framed the situation with the notion that something about writing this book feels bad.

This could be reframed by beginning with, for instance, examining what happens physically in this state of discomfort. There's a faster heart rate, feeling of flatness, muscle tension, and shallow breath. Because of these symptoms, I infer that I am feeling something called "anxious."

But that's just one possible perspective. It could be a different physiological event: these symptoms are very similar to those when making love. Does it seem too much of a reach to consider anxiety a form of lovemaking? Or better, a metaphorical lovemaking: making love to our anxiety can help us transcend it. Hopefully it will at least bring a smile to our face, which is the first step. I feel better already.

Questions such as these look behind the surface of the situation and feelings, touching upon the hurt child hidden within the shadows of the dislike and the anger. They also help bump us out of the ruts of our reactions into a more choiceful response. This approach helps us to reframe the energy of anger into the joy of investigation or the thrill of understanding. The anger falls away, the energy improves, and the new formation is interest.

Our minds are incredibly potent instruments. Using them to probe more deeply in these ways empowers us to create new neural pathways and habits of perception. Moreover, we liberate the conflicting emotions that had been tied up in our unexamined shadow.

Meditation trains us to be able to do this. When we are meditating on a cushion, we eventually have to face up to whatever is arising and take a good look at what's actually going on. It takes many hours of meditation to start to see the patterns in our arisings, and frankly, to get tired of our own mental, emotional, and sensing habits.

One common pattern that arises for many is loneliness, which links to the Deep Ego Fears of abandonment and annihilation. When we're meditating alone, we can feel isolated and disconnected from the so-called real world. We can feel that no one cares or that we are forgotten because, in a sense, we are. Life goes on. Such feelings can be intense. I (Doug) experienced intense and excruciating feelings of abandonment during a three- month solitary retreat in New Zealand. After two sleepless, agonizing days, a thought arose in my mind: "If everyone has abandoned you, just abandon yourself." Just like that, the torment let go. Never again has loneliness arisen in my life.

Unwholesome conditioned patterns are pretty tedious for everyone, most of all for ourselves. We like to say that they're like old reruns of bad sitcoms that we've already seen countless times. Do we really want to go through that same worn storyline again? Or are we ready for a new storyline, a healthier one, one that we've chosen based on loving-kindness, compassion, and wisdom? The feeling of liberating these old conditioned sto- rylines, letting them go, is like walking out into the first sunny day after a long, dark, and cold winter. Or out of bondage and into freedom. That's why it's called liberation.

In Reflection Four, we introduced another exercise for working with the shadow, *Going to the Core*, something Doug developed to help break through blocks and liberate the energy behind shadow manifestations. It's a powerful way to look behind the curtain of what seems to be reality to access something deeper. It is simple but effective—and fast. Breakthroughs for busy people![163]

Here's how it works. Whatever unwholesome arising is on the table, we look inside it, in its core, to see what is there. Whatever quality is there, we then go to the center of that quality and find out what's inside that second layer. We continue this process until we get to the core, which is always spaciousness. Spaciousness is at the center of everything.

Until we get good enough at it to do on our own, this exercise is best done with someone we trust as a facilitator. Their role is

---

[163] It's introduced under the Reflection 4's Protective Belief #2. A short reference guide with instructions for the Going to the Core exercise is available for download on planetdharma.com/pureland/learn.

to keep asking, "What's in the middle of that [quality]?" There may be a tendency to slip sideways on this exercise, and instead of going to the core, to a new, deeper level, we may name a synonym, thereby circling round on the same quality. Here the facilitator can catch this repetition and encourage us to penetrate more deeply to the center of the quality arising.

For example, let's look at the previous example of my (Catherine's) anxiety around finishing this book. In the center of that anxiety, I feel a tight stomach. In the center of the tight stomach, I feel a holding on, a clinging. In the center of that, I feel a tightness—and here I've start to circle around to the same or similar quality as before. So, I go back a step to looking in the center of the clinging, and in the core of that, there's a fear of failure. In the center of that feeling, the stomach relaxes, and there is simply a spacious unknown, which actually feels good, like relief. The anxiousness and accompanying tightness are gone.

Once more, the key to this exercise is to discern between what takes us back into the troubling feeling (shadow), and what takes us deeper into the center toward the peace and feeling of resolution that await us. If we find we get stuck circling, not progressing, it's best to go back to the last quality that had power or energy in it and start again from there. In the example, Catherine circled back to tightness, and so went back to the previous insightful word, which was clinging, and looked into the core of that again. Sometimes, it takes a number of tries to get out of the circling and penetrate toward the core, so perseverance is useful.

Note that our ego's tendency is to move back out toward the surface and get endlessly stuck in repetitive stories about the causes and conditions of our fear. Remember, these are unwholesome patterns that are within our power to change. We don't need to change the facts, just the patterns of our response or perception. Going to the core releases the locked structure of whatever pattern is being held.

Once the pattern is released, a sense of peace or relief is experienced. Then, it is often likely that some insight will arise, one that helps us continue to liberate the pattern moving forward.

In this sense, the shadow has given us a gift of insight as a result of the energy shifting. Because the pattern has been loosened, in the future it will be less and less likely to occur as a default reaction. Consciously recalling the release also helps loosen the pattern more. Once again, initially a trusted teacher, guide, or friend who possesses good insights and compassion can be very supportive mentoring us through this process.

Another side benefit of freeing ourselves from our reactive patterns is that we become much more compassionate toward others who exhibit similar patterns. Now, we have the experience and understanding to support their growing awareness and shadow integration. Reminiscent of the Hero's Journey, the monsters and demons lurking in the shadow have been transformed into our helpers.[164] As such, they assist in transforming the dysfunctional parts of our psyche into assets that can be channeled into creativity, wholesome relationships, and better physical health, manifesting primarily as flexibility and ease. Plus, the precious gift of greater skill in aiding others.

As part of this path, we gradually learn to live in the spacious, radiant, and blissful core of our being that has always been there. The volatile and turbulent world that we live and work in doesn't change, but we've changed, and how we meet the world has changed, too. We have much more empathy, patience, and kindness toward ourselves and others, knowing that at the depth of each of our beings we are, in fact, one. The unitive state becomes our refuge, and the turbulence of the world our adventure park. We've learned to dwell in the clear sky mind, play in the clouds, and—through our embodiment in form—dance in joy.

Even death loses its sting: we've come to know that while clouds are born and die, arise, and pass away, the clear sky mind remains eternal.

---

[164] In parts of the Brazilian Amazon and ayahuasca culture, this same dynamic manifests in a belief that every human is possessed by a few troublesome resident spirits. A person's resolute dedication to live a virtuous life inspires these spirits to convert themselves to a more honorable path as well, and they become that person's allies and supporters.

REFLECTION 16
ASTRODHARMA

Because We're Made from Stardust

Western astrology is a tool we've found very useful to assist with our spiritual awakening in this lifetime. We've combined it with Buddhadharma, the teachings of the Buddha, to help bridge the personal and the transcendental. Buddhadharma is all about the transcendental, but it can be challenging to get there from here. Astrology takes our extremely personal horoscope, unique to the time and place of our birth, and moves it through the transpersonal. From there, we can transition to the universal dharmic principles of the transcendental. We call this combination AstroDharma.

Why astrology? Our particular interest is in transpersonal astrology, based on a merging of astrology with Jungian psychology, both of which draw on Western mythological archetypes. Transpersonal astrology employs a mosaic of different modalities that include archetypes, roles or functions (such as nurturing, building, expanding, etc.), and spheres of life to represent different aspects of an integrated psyche. As we've described, our path includes a lot of psychology, so including transpersonal astrology occurred organically.[165]

---

[165] Catherine studied and taught transpersonal astrology in the mid-1990s in Japan. Sangha members started asking her for chart interpretations, there were requests for courses on the subject, and it unfolded from there.

Moreover, we can tend to forget that humanity is profoundly connected to the entire cosmos and vice versa. Astrology takes this link into account literally as well as metaphorically. It also provides a framework for better understanding how the cosmos might be significant in our lives.

The twelve zodiac signs and celestial bodies in the solar system each represent different archetypal energies, as well as the four elements of fire, earth, air, and water. Additional features include the ascendant and the moon's nodes, and the spheres of life are represented by the twelve houses in an astrology chart.[166]

Our location and time of birth distills these various factors into a snapshot that is unique to each of us, our natal horoscope, what some call a "soul map" for this lifetime. A skilled student of astrology can use the horoscope to perceive strengths and challenges, conditioning, biogenealogical patterns, potential, and so on.

One certainly doesn't need to know about or even believe in astrology to be aware of these things. However, astrology is one tool to become more aware of them and work with them with ever-increasing understanding and skill. It's also an interpretative model or map to decipher the influences that surround us.

Let's back up a bit. In Europe, up until the seventeenth-century, the science of astronomy and the interpretive art of astrology were one and the same. Under the umbrella of *Astronomia*, one of the original seven Liberal Arts, great astronomers like Copernicus, Kepler, and Galileo provided astrological counsel as well as astronomical discoveries as part of their service to their patrons.

During the seventeenth-century Age of Reason and subsequent Enlightenment, empiric methods gained favor. While the resulting split between matter and spirit or mechanistic and integrated approaches had many unfortunate side effects, it was also an important stage in human consciousness. Scientific method allowed us to free ourselves from certain kinds of superstition.

---

[166] Like anything, astrology is a vast study. More resources on AstroDharma are available on planetdharma.com.

It also resulted in the defamation of many philosophies, understandings, and spiritual practices that could not be explained through scientific methods. Among many others, astrological interpretation became suspect, a state from which it is still struggling to recover. The ancient art of alchemy and modern chemistry followed a similar relational path to astrology and astronomy, with chemistry gaining favor and alchemy falling into use on the outer fringes of mainstream.

One of the many wonderful things about science is that it provides insight into how many aspects of our physical universe function, and—to some extent—empowers us to take advantage of these functions for new applications. How can birds and airplanes fly? Why do the sun, moon, and stars appear to move across the sky? Why does my heart beat faster when I'm nervous? How can I speak to someone on the other side of the planet in real time?

The strength of spiritual philosophies and practices is that they allow us to understand what we may *not* be able to perceive with our senses, including our inner cosmos. Why do I respond the way I do? How can I learn to respond in ways that I feel better about, for example, with greater wisdom and compassion? Spiritual philosophies and practices also help us understand some things that science can't yet explain.

When we draw on both science and spirit, we enjoy a tremendous freedom to explore—this universe we live in and this extraordinary opportunity we call life.

ASTROLOGY AND DHARMA?

Vajrayana Buddhism is the branch of Buddhist philosophy that took root in the Himalayan kingdoms of Tibet, Bhutan, Sikkim, Ladakh, and Nepal in the seventh to eighth centuries, later extending to places like Taiwan, China, and Japan.

Buddhism has always integrated local belief systems. Even the orthodox Theravadin school of Buddhism in Myanmar incorporates local nature spirits, called *nats*, into their belief system and practices. When Buddhism went from India to Tibet, it incorporated elements of Bon, the native animistic religion. Some of Bon is still a part of what we know as Tibetan Buddhism today.

Nowadays, Buddhism is cross-pollinating with the likes of neuroscience (What happens in our brains when we meditate? Why does it feel good?), organizational learning, and business management. "The success of our actions as change-makers does not depend on *what* we do or *how* we do it, but on the *inner place from which we operate*,"[167] comments Otto Scharmer in his book, *Leading from the Emerging Future*. While this book is categorized as economic theory, it resonates deeply with—and clearly draws upon—Buddhist philosophy.

In a similar way, it's been natural for us to start exploring how astrology might be a mutually enriching tool for our dharmic explorations. Because our focus is on spiritual awakening in this lifetime, our interest in astrology is directed toward that end as well. In particular, our experience has shown astrology to be an effective tool for understanding our particular conditioned patterns and, more to the point, gaining the freedom to be able to transcend them when appropriate. As mentioned, we call the confluence of Buddhist philosophy (dharma) and astrology AstroDharma.

So how can AstroDharma be helpful? We begin with our natal charts, the horoscope showing the position of astral bodies at the time, date, and place of our birth.

Once we've looked at a number of horoscopes, some universal truths begin to emerge. While each one of us has a very unique makeup, approach to life, and journey to undertake in this lifetime, nonetheless, we are all working with variations of the same energies, the same twelve zodiacal signs, same planets, and same archetypes. While the music each of us makes may be strikingly different, it's all comprised of the same collection of notes arranged in different ways.

---

[167] Otto Scharmer & Katrin Kaufer, *Leading from the Emerging Future: From Ego-System to Eco-System Economies*, (San Francisco: Berrett-Koehler Publishers, 2013), 13.

This points to a fundamental truth, one of the three marks (characteristics) of existence in Buddhist philosophy, *anicca*: everything is always changing and is, therefore, impermanent.[168] A pattern spotted in an astrological chart will manifest one way when we're children, in a different way when we're teenagers, and differently again as adults. How we manifest the same energies is constantly in flux. This also means we have the power to craft how we express these dynamics.

And while AstroDharma helps us to transcend challenges we encounter in life or in our own personalities, it also reveals the second characteristic of existence: *dukkha*, which refers to the fact that all formations are in struggle. All of our natal charts reveal intense challenges each of us must face, contradictory energies that we must learn to harmonize in some way. While working with these challenges with awareness helps, there's no escape from this struggle, not through spiritual practice, nor even through spiritual awakening.

We can, however, better understand the nature of struggle, and thereby become wiser, more compassionate, and more skillful. This alleviates suffering for others and ourselves. We don't have to struggle so much or so hard. We don't have to struggle about struggling.

Lastly, with AstroDharma, we discover the third characteristic of existence, that as Doug likes to say, "It's not personal even when it's personal." There's no inherent thing we can call a self, since we're each really a collection of patterns or energies (zodiac signs, planets, etc.) put together in unique ways and constantly changing. In a sense, we are like compost heaps—when we add something new, the whole chemistry changes over time. It takes a good sense of humor to appreciate that metaphor.

---

[168] The three marks of existence are: impermanence (anicca), struggle or suffering (dukkha), and lack of an inherent self (anattā).

AstroDharma Basics

The most important place to start with AstroDharma is to get a copy of your own natal horoscope; for this you'll need your date, time and location of birth, plus some astrology software to plug this data into.[169] The next step is to familiarize yourself with the location of your sun, moon, and Ascendant, by sign and house. If we only know or remember a little bit about our chart, these three are the most fundamental and helpful elements to know. These are the great shapers of how each of us uniquely experiences life.

The sun, moon, and Ascendant are each in particular zodiac signs. The sun and moon are also located in an astrological house (the Ascendant always marks the border between the 12th and first houses). These are the three different layers or modalities of an astrology chart: planets and other celestial markers (such as the Ascendant and the moon's nodes, which we'll talk about shortly) tell us *what* is happening in our chart: our sun is our essence, the moon is our nurturing nature, and the Ascendant is how we view the world. The zodiac sign tells us *how* it is happening: it's happening in a peaceful Libran way or a Leonine flamboyant way. Last, the houses tell us *where* in our life (or the world) this energy is expressed: in relationship, beneath the surface of things, in our sense of values, career, etc.

For example, given that our astrology chart shows our journey in this lifetime, a soul map, let's call the sun the hero of our journey. The sun's location by sign and house tells us what our heroism is like, and in what parts of our life it's going to manifest. As mentioned, the zodiac sign shows *how* these energies appear—an Aries sun will show up boldly, a Cancer sun sensitively, a Capricorn sun builds their life's work diligently, and so on. And again, the twelve houses in a horoscope tell us in which arena of life the sun's energy will be drawn to shine: for example, a third-house sun orients toward communication, a fifth-house

---

[169] There are free ones on the Internet. We recommend www.astro.com.

sun is vitalized by creative acts, a ninth-house sun radiates toward travel and higher learning, and so on.[170]

Given that spiritual awakening is about en*light*enment, part of our spiritual path is about learning how to let our light shine. The light illuminates our own path in times of darkness, and acts as a beacon and a source of radiance for others as well. Understanding more about our sun's placement in our natal astrological chart helps us learn how to let our light shine brightly, as it's meant to do.

The moon represents our feeling nature, our nurturing abilities, and those kinds of relationships—how we nurture and feel toward others and toward ourselves. It also represents our body and our mother, our two earliest relationships, originally one.

If there's one thing that every single one of us was born to do, it's to care for one another. Imagine the world we could be living in if we were all skilled at this important role. And to be good at taking care of others, we first must be good at taking care of ourselves. What makes each of us feel nurtured is different, sometimes strikingly so. For example, I (Catherine) have moon in Sagittarius, a sign that is about exploration. I feel cared for when I am exploring. My relationship with my partner, Doug, has been built on inner exploration through meditation, exploration of philosophy and various world views, as well as extensive world travel.

For a different kind of person, whose moon was in a different configuration, this might not make them feel nurtured at all. This is especially important if, for example, this person is your significant other, and you are trying to care for each other in ways that the other person doesn't necessarily experience as supportive. For example, Doug's sun sign is Cancer, which is associated with the moon. He likes to care and be cared for in Cancerian

---

[170] Like any ancient study, there's a lot to keep track of in astrology. Our assistant extraordinaire created a brilliant two-page reference guide to help people out, available for download at www.planetdharma.com/pureland/learn. I wish I'd had it when I was first learning!

ways: through taking care of the body and home, with massage, physical affection, and attention to personal care like good rest, relaxation, and nourishment. So we need to pay attention to the fact that our ways of caring and feeling cared for are different, and adapt care-fully.

The key, as always, is self-knowledge. Ironically, it's only when we truly know ourselves that we can appreciate that every person is different, and that every difference is not only valid but to be celebrated. Our astrological charts can be valuable resources for understanding ourselves, others, and the choreography of this dance together.

Our birth time and location determine our Ascendant, which shows the zodiac sign that was rising on the earth's horizon at the moment of our birth. It's the filter through which we see and experience life. If Taurus is the Ascendant, for instance, then we see life and the world through Taurus-colored glasses, so to speak, making us deliberate, methodical, and strongly oriented toward the senses. By contrast, a Scorpio Ascendant would experience life with sensitivity around power dynamics and things that are hidden or unsaid. Buddhist philosophy (and other world wisdom traditions) helps us understand that we are creating our own reality moment-by-moment. Examining and learning more about our Ascendant's configuration helps us understand the perspective that we default to using, its challenges and opportunities. As a result, we have greater awareness about the choices available to us.

This trio of the sun, moon, and Ascendant provide a sound foundation to better understand our orientation toward life. Much of this, as mentioned, comes down to conditioned patterns we inherited in our youth. AstroDharma helps us learn how to make our unconscious patterns conscious, transform them into healthier expressions, and, ultimately transcend them: we don't need to rely on patterns. AstroDharma helps clarify how we *are* manifesting, and how we *could* be, to feel that we're best fulfilling our own unique purpose for being on the planet at this particular time.

After we're familiar with this fundamental trio, the inner planets—Mercury, Venus, Mars and Jupiter—flesh out some more details about our persona and how we show up in the world and in relationships. Depending on where they're located (for example, if they were right next to our sun, moon, or Ascendant), they may exert a stronger influence. These are fruitful to explore as we become more comfortable with the overall astrological paradigm.

THE LORD OF KARMA

Saturn is the father or teacher archetype, and carries the energy of authority and the functions of structure, discipline, and foundational strength. Earlier in our life we may receive wisdom and support from an external Saturnian agent (i.e., our father or father figure). At times, we also experience this energy or its representative as restricting our personal freedom, perhaps as a stern or punishing figure. As life goes on, we continue to project the authority archetype and feeling of constraint onto external agents, most commonly a parent, partner, boss, the government, or "the system."

Psychologically, the shadow of Saturn is the tyrant. However, for someone or something to be tyrannical in our lives, we must give them the ability to do so. We maintain a victim role (or stay) in the relationship or job, or remain passive in our political or social systems, thereby allowing the situation we claim to abhor to continue. When there's a tyrant in our lives, it's the shadow of our own Saturn: we're not manifesting our own healthy authority. When we do, oppression has no traction. Rather than being held in a confined position, we can flow around it like water flows around stone.

Responsibility is one of the qualities in Saturn's domain. Taking active responsibility for our reality by stepping into our own authority is the key to integrating a healthy Saturnian function. We can't fix another person or an institution, but we *can* be the change we'd like to see in the world. That makes a difference.

In this sense, with a healthy Saturn, we own our current situation, and we address it as it is by being the person we feel we need to be. Karma—the fruit of our actions or of our community's or society's actions—shows up in our life no matter what. As individuals, we can either blame it on someone or something else or we can take responsibility for it ourselves. This is why Saturn's also called The Lord of Karma.

A person who takes true responsibility for herself is remarkably rare.[171] They distinguish themselves with their natural inner authority. Based on an internal source, a kind of personal mastery, it's an authority that feels reliable and supportive rather than oppressive. Its domain doesn't need to be large, but it is solid. This personal accountability doesn't waver according to what other people do or don't do, and it is both reassuring and inspiring to others. This is authority in a healthy sense.

THE OUTER PLANETS

Saturn's known as the gateway or gatekeeper to the outer planets. When we've integrated our own authority, then we gain access to the ability to work consciously with the energies of Uranus, Neptune, and Pluto.

Why is this particularly significant? The outer planetary bodies move much more slowly through the zodiac signs and thus influence entire generations around the world for decades at a time. They affect us collectively, happening to society at large and the whole planet. For example, linked to the ancient Roman and Greek gods of the sky and underworld, respectively, Uranus's energy manifests as "transformation through revolution," while Pluto's energy can be described as "transformation through destruction." Everyone born from 1963–1968 had Uranus and Pluto conjunct (next to each other) in their astrological charts. Meanwhile, the whole planet experienced these powerful forces of transformation through revolution and destruction through that important, tumultuous era of the civil rights movement, Vietnam War, and summer of love.

---

[171] Our teachings and practices focus on trying to support the emergence of an ever-greater number of such beings.

In 2008, Pluto entered Capricorn, the zodiac sign representing material stability, status, and the structures that support those. The 2008 financial crises on Wall Street and numerous other countries represent the transformation (through destructive energies) of the traditional frameworks supporting the materially and status-oriented financial markets as represented by Capricorn.

When Saturn is not integrated, we experience the outer planetary bodies' influence as happening to us from external circumstances. With an integrated Saturn, we're more able to work with these energies consciously, so that we can take advantage of their transformative potential.

Here's how this works. Since they influence entire generations at once, Neptune, Uranus, and Pluto are considered collective or transpersonal planets. They offer opportunities for transformation on a collective scale.

Let's look at the upside of Pluto in Capricorn, for example, or of crises in general: they wake us up to the fact that we need better alternatives. Capricorn is about building structures, and Pluto's destructive forces make room for new creation and transformation. So, while Pluto's been in Capricorn (which it will be until 2024) we've also seen the emergence of the growing social finance movement, which focuses on leveraging money and investment as a force for social and environmental good.[172]

As indicated by the Roman deities or archetypes they represent, Uranus is linked to the Roman sky god, whose behavior was erratic and radical. As mentioned, this planet offers us the potential for transformation through revolution. Neptune relates to the ocean god and offers transformation through watery dissolution. And again, with its links to the Roman god of the underworld and its relationship with death, Pluto offers us the potential for transformation through destruction.

---

[172] See Joel Solomon, *The Clean Money Revolution: Reinventing Power, Purpose, and Capitalism* (New Society Publishers, 2017).

What do these three planetary energies have in common? For one, they are quite terrifying.

Few of us are going to volunteer to be transformed through revolution, dissolution, or destruction, which are, by their very nature, processes that remain out of our control. To us as individuals, they may manifest as a shocking revelation, deep disillusionment, or an unexpected disruption that shakes our life to its foundation. Though we might see the value of this process to revitalize an external institution, or to wake up someone else we've perceived as needing a new approach to *their* life, if given a choice, we are likely to reject the visitation of such a phenomenon to our own lives.

If we have managed to integrate our Saturnian energy—that is, realizing that we are creating our own reality in each moment and living accordingly—then we can see with hindsight how we personally set ourselves up for the cataclysm, and what gifts the calamity is bringing us.

Gifts? What gifts? There are indeed people who successfully transform apparent catastrophe into something profoundly meaningful and beneficial for themselves and many others. These are inevitably the people we most admire, whose praises are sung for posterity. Witness the likes of Wangari Maathai, Nelson Mandela, Rigoberta Menchú, José Mujica, and Gandhi. Their personal journeys distill the struggles and victories of entire nations, peoples, and eras, showing us the transpersonal or collective nature of these energies.

Meanwhile, the triumph of their inner fortitude and natural authority over remarkable tyranny—the positive and shadow sides of Saturn—demonstrate the transcendental power of the human spirit that can draw on the transformational resources offered by these planetary energies.

Again, we see why Saturn is referred to as The Lord of Karma. When we take responsibility for ourselves, the results of our choices and actions, we are choosing our karma and how to work with it, rather than merely coping with what happens to us.

The results have the potential to inspire all of humankind.

FROM KARMA TO DHARMA

From an AstroDharma or transformative point of view, the South Node-North Node axis comprises another very intriguing feature in natal horoscopes.

We could say that our South Node represents what we are born into: it often describes our environment when we were growing up. For example, my (Catherine's) South Node is in Libra, and out of a family of six, four are Librans. I grew up bathed in Libra energy: my family conditioning as I experienced it emphasized being well-mannered, considerate, and harmonious. And with a South Node in the 6th House, the house of service, I grew up enjoying doing things for other people.

On the surface, anyway.

That's the nature of the South Node. Like anything in life, every sign and celestial body has its upsides and downsides. Because it represents our family conditioning, we are overly familiar with the energies of our South Node sign and house. We take their virtues for granted and their less optimal qualities become our normal. In Buddhist philosophy, there's a saying that, with too great a dose, the medicine becomes a poison.

Let's take a 6th-House Libra South Node, for example. The 6th House encompasses the areas of our vocation, our calling: where do we feel called to be of service? There is a strong mind-body connection related to our calling and fulfilling it (or not). When we're fulfilling it well, we feel our best, physically and otherwise. Among other things, Libra excels at harmonious relationships.

Someone with a 6th House Libra South Node, then, may be conditioned by their upbringing to automatically do things for other people and have a pleasant demeanor about it. But the nature of the South Node, as we explained, is for otherwise positive qualities to become somewhat worn and stale. So, while Libra demands maintaining a good appearance on the surface of things, below that—likely beneath the person's awareness, certainly mine—the South Node chafes and resentment may simmer.

Over time, the veneer-like quality of the good manners and pleasantness become more apparent, and this disparity with what's really going on inside becomes a tension that's uncomfortable for everyone. One response to this discontent is ongoing suffering. Part of the challenge of the South Node is that change feels beyond our reach, almost incomprehensible. Isn't what we grew up experiencing just how the world and life are?

The other option is an irresistible drive to a spiritual quest, the Hero's Journey. This is the North Node calling us to fulfill our spiritual journey, our path to integration.

One of AstroDharma's strengths is that it represents very graphically that there are many other ways to experience the world and life. It also highlights how we have the freedom to make different choices. For our major spiritual transformation in this lifetime, our optimal choice is the North Node, located in the exact opposite position (by sign and house) as the South Node. The nodes represent a journey of spiritual transformation for us to make in this lifetime. The South Node is a starting point (karma), and the North Node is our desired destination (our dharma or spiritual destiny).

Initially, the North Node seems so foreign to our nature that it feels as though there must be some mistake. For someone rooted in harmonious Libra ("Is everyone okay with how things are going?"), embodying the independent, trailblazing, and leadership qualities of Aries ("This is what I'm doing no matter what.") may feel not only unappealing, but also preposterous.

It's important to point out that, to properly integrate the North Node, the opposite of our conditioned South Node nature, we must also integrate a broad range of other intermediating energies along the way. Metaphorically speaking, to undertake a journey from the Yukon to Patagonia, we also need to traverse and thereby somewhat familiarize ourselves with everything that lies from here to there.

This journey may take decades, a lifetime, or numerous lifetimes. Learning to skillfully manifest the polar opposite of how we were conditioned since infancy is a major accomplishment. To emphasize that point even further, one school of thought holds that the South Node represents karma carried over from previous lives, back again, front and center, to be further resolved in this lifetime.

After we've begun to get comfortable in our North Node, life becomes a much richer experience. The qualities that we are able to embrace in others and ourselves take on a different order of magnitude. We've explored the human experience in all of its diversity, its joys, and its challenges, so we are more patient with others' shortcomings, recognizing them as familiar signposts on the transformative journey we're all on. We also become more adept at drawing on the diverse range of experiences available to all of us—sunlight, kindness, humor, dance, music, science and math, joy, beauty, problems over here becoming solutions over there, etc.—as valuable resources, for ourselves and others.

Buddhadharma tends to be all about getting over our self or appreciating that there is really no such thing. This can be very challenging for our egos, particularly in our contemporary, individualistically-oriented culture. We first awaken spiritually—the milestone known as Path, Stream Entry, or *sotāpanna*—at the moment we recognize there is no such thing as an inherent, permanent self—a me. In our ego-aggrandizing culture, this notion can take time to get used to, and a bit more to actually perceive.

This is why we love AstroDharma. It provides an array of tools to help us better understand the self, to free ourselves from the prison of clinging to it, thinking it's a fixed thing we are stuck with. AstroDharma helps us to understand the uniqueness and wonder of self and other, and most of all, to transcend this sense of self and other, to meet in a divine experience of union.

REFLECTION 17
MONEY, SEX, AND POWER

The Path to Self-Sovereignty

Some of the material in this reflection might be considered controversial, especially in the current climate of discussions around sexual misconduct, scandal, and abuse of power within spiritual teachings. We raise it here to open up constructive discussions and investigation that lead to deeper understanding and personal empowerment. As with any topic, we feel that a diversity of perspectives and approaches are valuable and necessary, so we offer some that seem under-represented in the current dialogue.

Our central point is that the ego's main defenses center around money (security), sex (identity), and power (control). These drives are not just primitive but also limiting. Compassion, non-clinging awareness, and clarity are the remedies to transcend the ego-bound tyranny of these three ego defenses. However, they need to be addressed and integrated skillfully for our unfoldment, as we'll explore in this reflection.

The cultural conditioning of men and women is clearly different. To generalize, in the past, men have been raised to act to get what they want, while women have been raised to accommodate to be secure. But times have changed, particularly in regard to women's empowerment. Women now understand that they, too, can act to get what they want. Men are in varying degrees of response and reaction to this paradigm and not always skillfully. Having said that, there's an imbalance inherent to assigning blame to men for seeking out what they want even as we encourage women do the same. Money, sex, and power (a.k.a. control) are central to our all lives; these spheres can be a battlefield, but they can also be exciting explorations. How we experience them is up to each of us and our own choices.

We recognize and advocate the importance of raising our children to step into responsibility for their own decisions. Girls, in particular, need to be trained to become women (and boys to become men) by owning their choices, their yeses, nos, and maybes, their declines, consents, and in betweens. Boys need to be trained to become men (and girls to women) to understand that they aren't necessarily entitled to whatever they want. We address these issues here largely through the lens of the student/ teacher relationship because this is where we spend our time, but we feel that much of what we write here could be applied to society at large.

Much of the spiritual path consists of deconstructing our views and personality to see how they're built. It's a challenging process, but the emerging awareness gives us the flexibility and freedom to choose to grow the optimal components, ones based in loving-kindness, compassion, and wisdom.

As we progress along our spiritual journey, our explorations ultimately leave no stones unturned, including around the sensitive themes of the lower three chakras: survival (resources/ money), sexuality (identity and belonging), and power (control or independence). The fruits of this are courage, resilience, holistic health, and tremendous empathy, all essential for being of service to ourselves, others, and the planet.

To this end, practicing ruthless self-honesty is fundamental. We must spelunk our way through the unconscious, bringing it to the light of consciousness to foster our own, and encourage and support others', developmental maturity. This enlightening process cultivates ever more blissful states and wondrous clarity.

Money, sex, and power are juicy areas of exploration for all of us, fraught as they can be with conditioned emotional baggage and ego insecurities, and often with hidden unconscious elements. For this reason, it's incumbent upon all of us who seek transformational change, greater awareness, and spiritual awakening to investigate these foundational realms of human experience with valor, intellectual rigor, and emotional integrity.

The nature of the ego is to seek self-interested versions of security and control in an attempt to be comfortable. To experience spiritual awakening, we must transcend the ego, and this can be uncomfortable. Part of this process entails learning to relinquish our instinctual desire to control everything around us. In so doing, the realization dawns that the only true security we can have is inner peace.

How do we get there from here? By practicing giving up control and irrational drives to security, which are ultimately unattainable in the external world. When we do this by our own free will, we are less and less disturbed (and finally equanimous) when the universe inevitably presents us with situations where we don't have control, or that don't feel secure. Practice makes perfect, as the saying goes.

While spontaneity is an important quality of life, please note that we are not promoting chaos or recklessness. In terms of money, sex, and power, we recognize the value of balanced budgets, good planning and execution (including family planning), wholesome relationships, healthy boundaries, and so on. In fact, these are some of the skills we train people in through our programs. It's important to get our ducks in a row, and then it's good to let them waddle, swim, and fly. Because that's what healthy ducks do. Or conversely, as the Muslim proverb says, "Trust in Allah, and tie up your camel."

Given that money, sex, and power are central to our daily lives (in that we wouldn't be here without them, and they touch us in some way every day), this reflection explores some alternative views of these delicate subjects.

To begin, some readers may be wondering why spiritual teachers and Buddhist practitioners would address these topics at all. In fact, numerous schools of spiritual thought address these issues of money, sex, and power by not addressing them, that is, by practicing renunciation. This is a powerfully revelatory approach. Theravadin Buddhist monks and nuns, for example, take vows to abstain from many things that some people simply think of as fun, such as partaking of intoxicants, sexual pleasures, or even just food outside of mealtimes. By removing these experiences from our lives, we have far fewer opportunities to become attached to or overindulge in them.

However, Mahayana Buddhists, and some Vajrayana Buddhists in particular, claim that using the energy in desire to help us transcend the pitfalls of desire—namely clinging—is a faster and more integrated method. This approach doesn't deny any aspects of life, but instead embraces them.

This is how we've been taught and trained, how we teach and train others, and what most of this reflection is about. Please note we don't claim to speak for everyone, nor do we suggest that this path is for everyone. However, we believe our views reflect one true and valid approach, and that it's not being adequately or well represented in the West today. But first, let's look at context, in the form of societal values and human needs.

MASLOW'S HIERARCHY OF NEEDS

We're born into a landscape that's been painted by the colors and shapes of our society's values and ethics. As part of that, we are also born into some very specific needs that motivate us. As psychologist Abraham Maslow pointed out in 1943, these needs have a hierarchy, which he depicted as a pyramid or triangle (see image).

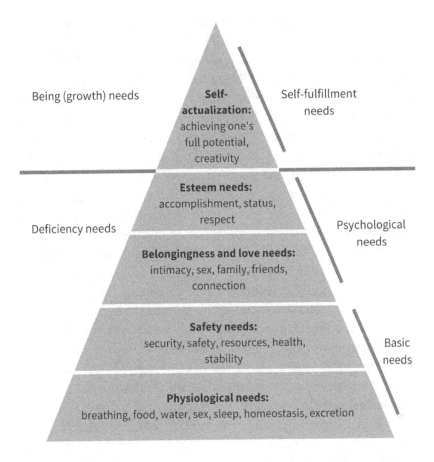

The needs start at the bottom, each one forming the foundation for the needs above it for a healthy body, mind, and psyche to develop. Each of us must meet the bottommost need before we can move to the next one in a balanced way, and so on.

Maslow points out that our most fundamental needs are physiological: to thrive we must first survive, so he considered breathing, food, water, sleep, clothing, shelter, and sex as central to this need. Although these needs are biological, the way we typically take care of them in developed countries is by earning money and purchasing these things or experiences, or the means to them (e.g. access to safe drinking water). In this fundamental way, anyone or anything that interferes with our access to money is perceived as a threat to our survival.

Money is just one kind of resource that we draw on for our natural instinct to flourish. Resources also speak to Maslow's second need: safety and security. The more or better-quality resources we have, the safer we feel, and in some cases, are. For example, a more expensive car may have more safety features than a less expensive one. Most wisdom traditions, however, teach that the quest for security in the material world is an elusive one; since nothing endures, nothing can be relied on. Without years of spiritual practice under our belts contemplating impermanence (and sometimes even with it), our sense of the ephemeral nature of everything in life can lead us to apprehension and worry. When we feel this need is in jeopardy, we can get very anxious.

Once the need for security is generally met, the third need in Maslow's hierarchy is a sense of love and belonging. Our friends, family, and other intimate (including sexual) relationships form the structure for this category. Who we're friends with, who we favor or don't, who we accept or feel accepted by, who we're intimate with, who we marry, who we resonate with, who we admire, all form a mosaic of our identity.

Again, everything is impermanent, so when our relationships end or we lose family, we often feel devastated. In a sense, we may feel we don't know who we are anymore, and that causes great uneasiness, at least until such a time as we can regroup.

The fourth need, according to Maslow, is esteem. This speaks to our sense of personal dignity and mastery. There's self-esteem, and there's the desire of esteem from others. Our abilities, accomplishments, and recognition of them shape our place in our group and community. Cultivating this self-worth from the inside out is not something that comes naturally in a consumerist society. For this reason, loss of a job or a failure in our career can cause havoc in our psyches, often making us feel powerless or ineffectual.

Maslow's first two needs—physiological well-being and security— are considered basic to survival. The next two—belonging and esteem—are psychological. All four are what he called deficiency needs, meaning that we feel them most keenly when they are not met. Once they're met, fully or perhaps even partly, they don't motivate us as much.

Finally we come to Maslow's last and highest need, which he called self-actualization. It refers to a sense that there has to be something more to life than just satisfying the previous needs, and the drive to find out what that something is. In contrast to the first four needs, the more we self-actualize, the more motivated we become to keep self-actualizing. This is the deep longing we each have to be a part of something greater, and as such, we could call it a spiritual need.

Together, the first four needs define our lives and ourselves, forming the matrix of our belonging to the tribe. The fifth need, self-actualization, involves moving into the world of spirit: what does it mean to actualize oneself? What is this "self?" Once we start asking these questions, we've moved beyond conventional religion: going to church, temple, or mosque once a week probably won't answer these questions—even though the people who founded religions were the ones who asked these deeper questions. Jesus did it, as did the Buddha, and so have countless others down through the ages through to today.

Paradoxically, because we only know who we are in relation to others, *self*-actualization requires *others* to come to fruition. Awakening arises the moment we truly realize that self and other are fundamentally the same. The self is but an instrument, a lens through which to perceive that which is greater: the unitive experience that can include a sense of self but transcends it. Every mystic experiences this when they can let go of self-referencing, even if only temporarily.

RELIGION, SPIRITUAL TEACHERS, MONEY, AND DOILIES

What do we mean when we write about moving beyond conventional religion? The main difference between religion and spirituality is the central focus. Religion helps us attend well to

Maslow's first four needs, whereas spirituality defines them as starting points for the fifth, for self-actualization.

As we've mentioned before, religion forms one part of society's value structure; government, law, media, etc. As such, religion changes as society does, albeit more slowly. For example, as society gradually accepts a more fluid gender spectrum, so do many religions.

We're raised with the values of our culture, which for some of us include religion. These values are embodied primarily by our parents and their behavior, and as children we're judged and course-corrected by how well we keep these values. As previously noted, these social and religious values serve the important functions of helping us all get along so that we can work and play well together. They form one way to stay connected with our families, tribes, and communities. They may also constrain our exploration of self-actualization—with, for example, guidelines about gender and sexuality, interracial relationships, the rights of other species, the definition of morality or the morality of war—when they don't resonate with our own experience.

In this way, spiritual values sometimes step beyond societal and religious morals and ethics. This isn't done out of a sense of entitlement or licentiousness, but out of exploration. When explored with the intention of self-actualization, spiritual practitioners draw on various experiences to examine how the nature of ego conditioning and identity can be shaken when the four lower needs are disrupted. This shakeup is certain to happen in every one of our lives from time to time—major illness, accidents, etc.—so being spiritually resilient entails being able to maintain a heart of loving-kindness, compassion, and wisdom even when, for example, we feel insecure or disrespected. If our primary relationship ends abruptly or we suffer a career failure, are we still manifesting a radiant state of consciousness?

We'll find out when upheaval inevitably comes, and in the meantime, we can prepare by practicing, testing these waters, so that when crises arise, we have a better chance of living through them with grace. It's a service to ourselves and to everyone involved. Vibrant spiritual teachings include this preparation as part of the path. This is why Buddhism places such emphasis on impermanence: we know that this (whatever "this" is: a relationship, a job, a way of life, our life itself, etc.) will end. Are we ready?

Let's share one example of what this practice might look like in a student-teacher dialogue about the topics of money and control (power). In the late 1970s, I (Doug) was traveling and studying with my teacher, Namgyal Rinpoche, in Italy. I was newish to the path. I had about US$300 to my name and was planning to use those funds do another retreat with Rinpoche in Greece after we finished the course he was leading in Italy.

Rinpoche was an aficionado of traditional culture, arts, and crafts, and one day, while traveling through town, he stopped to admire some handmade lace in a shop window. Being a young man from Saskatchewan, I had no interest in lace and was keen to move on. But Rinpoche lingered, asking me which items I liked. They all looked the same to me, but I indicated a particular doily. "But this doily here is much nicer than that one," he commented. *Whatever!* I thought. Later, I learned to appreciate how he used this technique to teach us to recognize the quality that comes from a combination of applied awareness, training, and experience: art.

Later that day, Rinpoche told me, "Go spend all your money on doilies from that shop." I could hardly believe my ears; spend all my money on doilies! I begrudgingly went and bought $250 worth of the lacey things. When I returned, Rinpoche inspected them. "How much did you spend?" he asked, and when I told him, he furthered, "and how much did you have?" When I told him $300, he replied, "I told you to spend *all* your money." Then he added "And you got the ones *you* liked, not the ones *I* liked!"

Later that day, he gave them all away to various female students in class saying they were chosen by him especially for them. They were deeply touched at his thoughtfulness, generosity, and good taste. As he was handing them out, he would occasionally look my way with a broad smile. I never told anyone, and I don't think he would have cared less if I did. He was teaching me non-clinging awareness and trust in the universe and giving these women nice gifts at the same time.

How did I manage with $50 to my name? For the rest of the year, Rinpoche supported me financially as well as spiritually. Was he taking advantage of me? Hardly. My feeling is that he rightly intuited that I might run away if my buttons got pushed. (Sound familiar?) I could still have left, but the lack of funds kept me from fleeing on a moment's notice. I'd have to think it over, and fortunately, that gave me time to perceive that I was trying to escape from having my buttons pushed. Which was precisely the reason I had come to study with him to begin with: to get over myself.

It was a tremendous teaching on letting go. I let go of the money I had and my definition of security. I let go of need to control and my preferences (doilies?). I let go into a trust in the teacher and in my own unfoldment, in the spiritual path itself.

Through this and other experiences, with time, I learned not to get upset when I didn't get my way, or even when I got the opposite of my own way. I learned to consider that if I lost the feeling of control over my situation, or if I lost all my money, everything might work out fine anyway.

This is not a how-to guide for spiritual teaching or teacher-student relationships. Times were very different then. It was easy to find work and make money when we needed it, and as a young man, I didn't have any responsibilities. I had shown up asking to be taught and trained, and that's what my teacher, skillfully, generously, and compassionately (and with humor too) shared with me. This is an example of how a teacher used money and power (power which I'd given him) to help me learn how the ego tries to hang onto a narrow definition of what we want or need, and how we can benefit and grow by giving that up.

This is a kind of freedom. A valuable one.

THE ROCKY PART OF THE ROAD

Typically, a committed spiritual path requires a guide (variously known as a guru, teacher, mentor, or coach). For the aspirant, working with a teacher can occasionally present rocky surfaces on the path.

While it's funny in retrospect, at the time, spending nearly all my money on lace doilies felt like an extreme trial. And not just because of the money but also because of the apparent deceit of telling the women he'd chosen them himself. Trust is a big issue. What I learned is that real trust is not just in an individual, but in the process as well.

Did Rinpoche get me to spend most of my money on lace doilies? Yes. Was it frivolous? Since he gave them to students who really appreciated the gift, it seems not. Was it abusive? I never felt so; I felt it was a valuable teaching. What's more, in turn, he supported me in the period that followed. For him, it was never about money—or doilies.

It's easy to see how some people may think that I was exploited or that the money was wasted. That's okay. It's in each person's power to choose or decline to (for example) spend their money on doilies when a mentor suggests it. Another's choices may be different than mine, and we can learn from each of our experiences. However we do it, what's essential is that we recognize that learning to let go of attachments and control is part of the path of spiritual awakening. If we perpetually make choices that keep the ego in self-protected control, we are limiting our own growth. Spiritual unfoldment requires courage and experimentation, in whatever way that manifests for you.

When an aspirant enters into an apprenticeship with a true spiritual teacher of any flavor, then money, sex, and power will be some of the issues that need to be worked through. They are central to our lives and to our neuroses, so *true* spiritual unfoldment depends on us transforming *any* and ultimately *all* of our neuroses into healthier qualities.

What this looks like depends on the tradition, so we must each choose a path that is suitable for us. This is different from quitting one teaching and starting another each time our buttons get pressed. We have to stay with a practice long enough to get to where the pressing of those buttons doesn't upset us anymore.

We get to the pleasant point where we think, smiling, "What buttons?" We'll recall them as things that *used* to perturb us, and now allow us to share our insights about the nature of such suffering—and becoming free of it—with others.

Mahayana Buddhist traditions use these button-pressing experiences as fuel for the fire of spiritual awakening, and as such, the ethical boundaries of the practice become much more interpretive. Let's take one of the most illustrious examples of this. In Rinzai Zen, for instance, the famous fifteenth-century abbot (and illegitimate emperor's son) Ikkyū distinguished himself with his compassionate non-clinging awareness. He wielded clarity of mind to criticize contemporaries who curried renown and patronage over enlightenment. Ikkyū also garnered attention for abandoning his overly politicized monastery in favor of the raw integrity he found in the company of prostitutes and *sake* drinkers, publicly shunned by his peer monks. He documented it all in his celebrated poetry:

> *The autumn breeze of a single night of love is better than a hundred thousand years of sterile sitting meditation.*[173]

He's still admired as a great awakened master today.

Over decades, we've noticed that a bad teacher can't harm a good student. To be explicit, this statement doesn't cover sociopaths or psychopaths, and it's up to each of us to practice our discernment and ensure we don't find ourselves unwittingly heeding the counsel of such individuals or of charlatans. And a good student is a sincere, committed one, not a dilettante who's unprepared to apply themselves to a real spiritual path, which is a challenging endeavor. The maxim refers more to the phenomenon of a musically gifted youth first learning to play the piano from their amateur older sister, then their local elementary school's music teacher, before finding their way to, say, Julliard.

---

[173] From translator John Stevens' *Wild Ways: Zen Poems Of Ikkyū* (Buffalo: White Pine Press, 2003).

While each serves an important supportive role on the musician's journey, a teacher can only lead us where they've been themselves. And not every aspiring music or spiritual student has the motivation, determination, and fortitude to become a master.

And this is how it should be. Like any other, the spiritual ecosystem thrives on diversity. Not every tree in the forest will be a sacred Ceiba,[174] and besides, the forest relies on scarcely-visible mycelium. We can make our peace with our spiritual choices and make the most of them to keep our practice alive, however we choose to do that. In the realm of spiritual ambition we may feel tempted to blame our teachers for our spiritual life not turning out as we'd hoped. We can upcycle these human feelings by taking responsibility for our choices and using them better clarify our own aspirations.

CHAKRAS MEET MASLOW

As many readers may be familiar with, Indian or Hindu philosophy holds that there are seven *chakras* or energy centers in our bodies (the Buddhists typically use five). These chakras are not physical, like organs, but rather energy vortexes located along the central axis of our bodies.

Each one pertains to a different function. The root chakra (located a few centimeters up from the perineum, inside the body) is associated with survival and safety. As such it corresponds to Maslow's first two basic needs—physiological survival and security.

The second chakra is located above the pubic bone and known as the sacral or sexual center. It relates to sexuality, as well as emotions and creativity. Depending on the system, the third chakra is sometimes located in the solar plexus and sometimes in the *hara* (four fingers' width below the belly button). It pertains to our social self and our sense of identity and will—in other words, to

---

[174] The sacred Tree of Life in Mayan cosmology, connecting this world with the heaven and underworld.

our power. This chakra corresponds to Maslow's psychological needs, the feelings of belonging and esteem.

In short, these three chakras are about survival, identity, and independence or control. In modern terms, our measures for these three chakras are money, sex, and power. When we feel we have lost control over these central life forces, we may feel mistreated. The fundamental cause may be not taking good care of ourselves—a formidable life skill to develop—but we may also project this feeling of being mistreated onto an external agent, perhaps onto another person, an organization, or life in general. We're using the word "mistreated" here to include feelings of being taken advantage of, disrespected, or otherwise wronged.

In Buddhist terms, when combined with ego-clinging, these three chakras are also associated with what are called the three poisons or passions: namely, greed, hatred, and delusion. However there's good news: when liberated from clinging through spiritual practice, these three poisons are transformed into generosity, loving-kindness, and wisdom. The difference between the two versions of these sets of energies determines whether we lead a life full of misery, or one overflowing with love and joy. Obviously, the difference between clinging and non-clinging is immense, and that's why the entirety of the spiritual life hinges on this transformation.

The truth is that we never actually have control (third chakra—power) over these aspects of our life. We may have the impression that we do, but eventually, life reveals that this is an illusion. A painful break-up, the death of a dear one, or a failure in our work are as much out of our control—probably much more so—as a spiritual mentor's well-intended attempts to teach us that we don't have control. Naturally, none of these are welcome experiences. It can be frightening to face up to the fact that our lives are as ephemeral as gossamer.

We are all born having access to the lower three chakras; we could call it our base model. We can learn to choose and develop the higher four chakras as an act of will. What gives us this will?

We are all born with a drive to fill Maslow's first four needs and to balance the seven chakras. However, the programming or conditioning from society's imperative to maintain the status quo to ensure survival and safety may overpower our higher or ultimate need for self-actualization or transcendence. For whatever reason—we could call it karma—some of us cannot fit in, and such people are pulled or pushed away from the mainstream. Many indigenous societies were familiar with this phenomenon and sent these people to a shaman where they could be educated and trained in this important role.

In mainstream Western culture, no such established rite of passage exists. Still, such beings exist, with this longing for something greater, or an inability to fit into the status quo. Some may get lost in addiction, mental health crises, or crime, while others are drawn to a spiritual life. Some of us experience several of these options. The key determining factor between behavior resulting from emotional pain or deep discomfort with oneself, versus embarking on a journey of spiritual transformation is *choice*. While historically the shaman's apprentice had few or no alternatives (there was nowhere else to go), today prescriptions and recreational drugs are easy to come by. As a result, lost souls abound. The spiritual life must be chosen, and part of that choice entails being trained.

This spiritual training allows us to spend time in the higher chakras, to choose to live and act from them, rather than from the lower three chakras. The fourth chakra is the heart, associated with our ability to feel compassion and love. Each of us has many reasons to feel hurt and abused by life, but the spiritual journey is about learning to forgive and move on.

The fifth chakra, in the throat, is about communication. We may have received extensive educations, but few of us are taught how to communicate accurately and honestly what we are feeling. Most of our arguments (and relationship splits) arise from unskillful or out-of-sync communication.

The sixth chakra is located between the eyes and represents intuition, inspiration, and insight. It involves raising questions from the depth of our being. Being driven mostly by consumption and entertainment, society's status quo doesn't tend to inquire very deeply. We can see this in, for example, the stock market, self-described as being driven by greed and fear.[175] We can investigate how to use greed and fear to make money, or we can question how to live in the truly flourishing state that lies beyond greed and fear.

Lastly, the seventh chakra at the crown of our head pertains to wisdom. Wisdom is a human birthright, but as mentioned, it must be developed. If we look at the decisions we're making as a society or species about climate change, resource consumption, overpopulation, and the global economic system, we'd clearly benefit from choosing to cultivate greater wisdom, both individually and collectively.

Wisdom is rare only because of the dedicated and somewhat onerous journey that we engage in for the kundalini (or energy) to make its way from the lower chakras up the spine to this uppermost chakra. To do so, we must transcend the negative side of the lower three chakras (greed, hatred, and delusion), and instead embrace loving-kindness, skillful communication, rigorous analytic thought, and insight. Then, we've qualified to enter the pearly gates of wisdom.

These higher four chakras are all part of what Maslow's refers to as self-actualization. The ego and persona live in the first three chakras and Maslow's four foundational needs. The spiritual life is embodied in the four higher chakras and Maslow's fifth need. Accessing and balancing these chakras and expanding on our self-actualization is the spiritual path that every valid spiritual tradition embodies and through which every valid spiritual teacher trains their students. By "valid" we mean sincerely dedicated to the experience of spiritual awakening for the benefit of all beings.

---

[175] Again, see for instance CNN Money's Fear and Greed Index. Fortunately, healthier paradigms are emerging as explained in, for example, Joel Solomon's *The Clean Money Revolution: Reinventing Power, Purpose, and Capitalism* (Gabriola Island, New Society Publishers, 2017).

SEX (OR NOT), POWER, AND THE SPIRITUAL PATH

When I (Catherine) met Doug, I'd been celibate for two and a half years. In my mid-20s, I realized that, while my partners had all been fine people, our relationships were not what I wanted them to be. To be fair, they were probably not what my partners wanted, either. I knew that at least fifty percent of the responsibility for that was mine. If I had any complaints about my former partners, I had to recognize that I'd chosen to be with them, so that responsibility was mine, too.

Several years before that, I'd gotten involved with someone who had a lot more apparent power than I did. We got along well, and he was kind, generous, supportive, and interesting. He was also wealthy, well-connected, older, my boss, my landlord, the sponsor for my immigration visa, and interested. Getting into a more intimate relationship seemed like it might be a very bad idea, but I was lonely, confused, and flattered, and I liked and admired him, so we did.

It was short and marked by a stressful ending, without skill on either of our parts. Among other things, after we broke up, I felt unsafe (and naturally unwelcome) in the house he owned. It was extremely uncomfortable to work together, and I had to find a new visa sponsor, not an easy task. It was a terrible situation.

I had seen the potential for this happening and gotten involved anyway. He wasn't acting from a good place, and I knew I wasn't either. I felt my judgment had been poor, and the consequences had come home to roost. Now, I felt even more lonely and more vulnerable. I share this story so that readers know that I'm familiar with what happens when relationships between people of what's been called "an imbalance of power" go awry.

Another poorly-ending relationship later, I took stock. I realized I'd been a serial monogamist, I felt somewhat incompetent in relating skills, and I'd been in relationships too deeply to see what my own issues were.

At age 27, I decided to be celibate for a spell to sort out my views and habits around relationships and sex. Choosing to be celibate was one of the smartest things I've ever done. (Happily, another was getting together with Doug.) Without the distractions of sex, partners, and associated hormones, my attention was freed up to see my unconscious mental models and behaviors more clearly.

One revelation was how much I wanted a significant other to distract me from discomfort with myself. I didn't feel okay in my own skin; it wasn't that fun to be me. Clearly, though, it would be impossible to have a healthy relationship with someone else if I didn't have one with myself. One good thing about being intentionally celibate is that you have the time, space, and energy to sort through this kind of life-changing stuff.

By the time I met Doug as a teacher of spiritual awakening two and a half years later, I was far from done but had made progress. I wanted to make my spiritual practice the center of my life, so when the position of Doug's attendant became available, I jumped at it. He told me that women traditionally didn't fulfill this role because serving a man was too similar to their conditioning. A woman serving a male teacher, the historic view held, would only cement the conditioning. I argued that this was sexist and strengthened my resolve. Besides, serving men was not a major part of my conditioning. I'd argued for gender equality in our home as a ten-year-old, singing *I Am Woman* ("hear me roar . . .") on the piano. He made an exception.

I wasn't looking for a relationship because I'd gotten comfortable, even content, being by myself. Celibacy had helped me make this invaluable transformation. Nonetheless, Doug and I lived together, worked together, enjoyed one another's company, and had a common spiritual vision. Prior experience notwithstanding, a romantic relationship felt natural. On the one hand, it seemed like a good idea: how optimal to integrate spiritual practice with one's life, work, and primary relationship!

On the other hand, it seemed like a familiar bad idea. What if it turned out painfully? I had to ask myself piercing questions and use all the clarity I could muster to come up with honest answers. Was I was hoping to get something out of the relationship? Special treatment? Status? Some control over my teacher? Or was he just using me? Was he a testosterone-driven man sharing a spiritual view of sex as a higher teaching as bait in an ego trap, one requiring a woman with less apparent power devoted to a male with more apparent power? What would happen to my spiritual practice if the relationship didn't work out?

We had a lot of frank discussions and ran through what we'd like to do, together or separately, in case of numerous what-if scenarios. Addressing these fears together strengthened our relationship, and my relationship with myself. We both committed to making our and others' spiritual unfoldment the main purpose of our relationship. As a touchstone, that commitment has served us well over the last twenty years.

Usually, when we hear about teachers and students sleeping together, it's under distressing circumstances and often in the context of what teachers and students should not have done nor do (have sex). With all respect to other people's experiences and sincere wishes for healthy resolutions of what are surely very challenging feelings and circumstances, we feel it's important to add to the ongoing conversation that when a teacher and student have sex together, it isn't always bad. In fact, sometimes it's good.

If we consider who we know and what we've heard, it seems there are not a small number of students who've had sex with their teacher and felt it was a positive experience (and vice versa). Sex is usually somewhat private, and also something that can give rise to an unwholesome curiosity, jealousy, or judgement from others, depending on the situation. People tend to be discreet about these kinds of things, understandably and perhaps wisely so. It's possible that people who've chosen to be discreet may be wiser than we are, choosing to discuss the topic. It's our hope, however, that addressing it is compassionate.

Practicing discretion is different from hiding something or feeling ashamed. Unfortunately, since more challenging sexual situations attract so much negative attention, our views about sexuality as part of a spiritual path can become very imbalanced. It also seems that some of the challenges arising may be about cultural misunderstandings based in very different attitudes toward sexuality from Asian and Western perspectives. Sometimes we wonder whether Buddhism in the West is more influenced by Judeo-Christian conditioning—such as views about original sin and feelings of guilt related to sexuality, which are prominent in the West but not in Asia—rather than the other way around.

Please take note: we are not advocating sex between teachers and students. We're also not discouraging it. Like nearly any other relationship, it's not necessarily designed from the outset to be long-term. We encourage healthy sexual expression (which, importantly, can include celibacy) as part of a full and meaningful life. How that manifests is up to the individuals involved.

We're also not trivializing the pain that people have suffered through inappropriate relationships. What we are doing is promoting the notion of self-sovereignty. We are each sovereigns of ourselves. We are each in charge of our own choices. We have the power to say yes or no or let me think about it. We have the power to leave or stay. And we have that responsibility.

As we've remarked, whether or not we are having sex and regardless of with whom, sexuality or sexual energy need to be addressed and healthfully integrated as part of our ongoing spiritual unfoldment. Otherwise, we run the very real risk of being unconsciously driven by this energy. In the case of sex that is not based in awareness, loving-kindness, and compassion, this can result in self-harm and offense to others. In the case of unconscious repression, we risk losing our vitality and joy.

Sometimes we make choices that seemed good at the time but turn out to be not so good. Sometimes they are painful in the short term but help us become wiser and kinder in the longer term.[176] As long as we use them to learn, to understand ourselves and human nature, and to make healthier decisions in the future, we believe there's no such thing as a bad choice. In fact, much of

---

[176] This is true of the relationship that I described earlier, for example. Years later, we became friends again, and over time, the value of our friendship and what I've learned from it far outweigh the distress.

our learning and most of our growth has come from what we may have previously considered bad choices or poor decisions. That's how we move into a better place; by making better decisions and learning from our missteps.

The teacher's job isn't to make the right decisions for us, but to encourage us to learn from whatever decision we make. In that sense they lead us over the cliff of our own agenda.

A STUDY OF POWER

It's worth repeating that the nature of the ego is to desire power. That is, every ego-oriented being feels vulnerable, and so to protect ourselves, we try to be in control of ourselves and the situations we find ourselves in. To try to acquire and maintain this power, every one of us uses just two techniques: manipulation and control.[177] With varying degrees of awareness and skill, we are always using one, the other, or both, as we try to get what we want, or avoid what we don't want. In this sense we are all alike.

Perceptions of power are extremely subjective and very conditioned. The bravado that makes an American feel invigorated and self-assured seems childish in the Japanese context. The humility that Japanese cultivate as a virtue appears unconfident to North Americans. Where or with whom power lies depends on our conditioned beliefs. Money and influence may be the most potent forms of perceived power, alternatively it may be spiritual realization and wisdom, or perhaps beauty, intelligence, youth, or talent. Or something else, depending on our conditioning and life choices.

We maintain that, in the truest sense, there is no inherent power difference between people. The world we've co-created features what we call relative power dynamics that include systemic injustices like government legislation, institutionalized racism, threats of physical violence, etc. But in an absolute sense, someone who lives in their power as a human being—like Malala

---

[177] More on this in Reflection 9.

Yousafzai—can change world history for the better. We move closer to living in our power, our self-sovereignty, as we develop greater awareness about how. Often, when we feel someone has power over us, it's because we've tacitly or explicitly gone along with this dynamic. And we don't have to. There are risks to changing the dynamic, but there are risks to staying in it too, so the choice is ours.

For our communal well-being, we advocate that all of us, youth and adults alike, be educated about how to exercise our self-sovereignty. As in the case of the doilies or in romantic or sexual relationships, we may choose to enter into situations where the outcome is uncertain. Or we may choose not to. It behooves us all to cultivate and help others develop skillful discernment, so that we make these choices with our eyes wide open, knowing that the responsibility for the choice is ours.

Power dynamics are certain to come up in any teacher-student relationship, particularly one that's about transcendence. The purpose of spiritual training is to get us past our ego, that is, being self-centered. The ego doesn't enjoy attempts to be transcended, because its nature is to stay in control. As an experienced mentor tries to help an aspirant on this path, the latter's ego usually feels threatened; attempting self-preservation, the ego may project outward this desire for power, confusing training for what it self-servingly perceives as the teacher's ego-oriented control trip.

Skilled teachers are familiar with this dynamic and know how to work with such energies adroitly, so that spiritual aspirants can continue being victorious over their own egos. One reason we place so much emphasis on the teacher-student relationship is that there is a chain of verification: we know who has taught, trained, and otherwise supported each teacher. It's also a chain of responsibility for a teacher to do everything they can to ensure that the teachings and people who share them stay healthy and vibrant moving forward.

As aspirants, it's up to each of us to check the credentials of teachers we study or train with. It's a good idea to ask some of our deepest questions up front and early when meeting a teacher.

This is not to challenge them for the sake of challenging them, but to learn early on whether we feel there's a basis for trust to undertake this important journey together. This has nothing to do with what they look or sound like or how many students they have. Appearances can be deceiving, and fame is no measure of realization.

The journey to awakening is a bus ride with many potential stops on the way. When we meet a boundary we feel we can't cross, we're often tempted to simply get off the bus. Most teachers struggle with this, too, for example, by simply not teaching or otherwise interacting about sexuality, money, and power on the spiritual path because these are such sensitive topics. For each of us, the places we won't go define the edges of our clinging and attachment.

For a fully awakened being, there's no clinging, no attachment, and no place that's out of bounds. This is why some consider the Vajrayana path the fastest and most powerful—and perhaps most challenging—way to achieve enlightenment, possible within this very lifetime: *everything* in life is fuel for our spiritual unfoldment.

As we evolve as a species, spiritual awakening does too. As our developmental maturity grows, the boundaries of our self-imposed limitations around our ego-bound identity extend out in front of us, gradually becoming less and less about status quo standards. Since topics around money, sex, and power tend to be some of our touchier ones, these boundaries in particular call us to explore. Then, we can learn how to embody loving-kindness and compassion more fully, and wisdom more deeply, in these parts of our lives as well.

THE HERO'S JOURNEY

Fundamentally, we are optimists, or more accurately, realistic optimists. That is, we feel there is a rich and unfolding wonder in store for humanity—but first, we have some serious problems to resolve. Most of us know what these are, and we repeat some of them here: diminishing energy resources, the over-exploitation of nature, corporate influence on global politics, disruption of local economies by the global economy, dehumanization of the international work force, growing inequality in the distribution of wealth, social injustice, climate change, overpopulation, and so on. These are external issues. There are also internal issues, such as loneliness, ambivalence, fear, rage, discouragement, and feelings of helplessness. All of these create worry and anxiety that lead to depression and giving up.

These difficulties all stem from two fundamental and erroneous views. The first view is that happiness lies reliably in an object (whether a physical, emotional, or mental one). As a result, we seek to acquire and accumulate as many objects as possible as though we can furnish our lives with happiness that we've acquired piece by piece, project by project, or accomplishment by accomplishment. This desire to collect—even something positive like our notion of happiness—is the wolf of greed dressed up in sheep's clothing. As modern people, we need to take great care that consumerism doesn't devour what's best about being human: our drive to spiritual awakening, and to cherish and take care of one another and all of life.

The second view at the root of all our troubles is the illusory idea of a permanent, inherent self. We craft an identity for ourselves through our objects (or the lack of them), so the need for or lack of objects will determine how we see ourselves. This includes the phenomenon of seeing ourselves as another object. The self is the high-level object that holds all of the other objects.

In this context, the only way to be a bigger and better me is to have lots of objects, which means more greed. This approach is doomed to certain failure for one reason: there is no inherent self and there are no inherent objects. Quantum physics is recently demonstrating what wisdom traditions have known for millennia: things that appear real (including me) are mostly space. The life of identifying with objects and seeking happiness exclusively in those objects was, is, and will always be a wasteland. This wasteland is devoid of meaning, good feeling, and nourishment.

Seeking welfare in objects is a false refuge. False refuge is rooted in greed and delusions that color our choices, opinions, and values. By its nature, the ego can never feel secure, and so it drives us to try to accumulate in hopes of attaining security, meanwhile substituting quantity for quality. Our modern civilization worships acquisition and individuality to the point that some studies have shown that UK schoolchildren perceive that fame for its own sake equals success.[178] Other studies, more hopefully, show that greater numbers of people are realizing that success is more about happiness.[179] So then, how do we grow happiness?

The answer is very simple: seeking refuge in the absence of inherent objects creates reliable happiness. Another word for this absence is emptiness or spaciousness, and it is conjoined with

---

[178] Hood, *The Self Illusion*, p 257.

[179] Jacqlyn Smith, *This is How Americans Define Success*, Oct. 3, 2014, http://www.businessinsider.com/how-americans-now-define-success-2014-10.

equanimity and peacefulness. Objects can come and go, and we still feel good. This is the Pureland! Coming from this place, we can still engage in the relative world of these objects and enjoy them, but we don't expect happiness from them. As such, this mind-state remains forever radiant, clear, and bright.

From this experience of spaciousness, many metaphors to describe it have graced our poetry, paintings, dance, and sciences. As the Diamond Sutra so beautifully describes:

> Thus shall ye think of all this fleeting world:
> A star at dawn, a bubble in the stream;
> A flash of lightning in a summer cloud,
> A flickering lamp, a phantom and a dream.[180]

This passage illustrates the heart of these teachings so clearly: the impermanent appearances of objects can enrich our lives, but their ability to do so quickly degrades if we try to cling to them.

FOUR WAYS TO BE GENERATIVE

We dwell in the Pureland whenever we take refuge in the clear, blissful, and radiant state of being that has been called spiritual awakening. From this state, generosity or *dāna* is a natural result. From this space, we feel effortless inspiration to work toward a more delightful relationship and healthy engagement with the world. In our case, it manifests in a desire to support the quadruple bottom line (spiritual, financial, social, and environmental sustainability), and we use our retreat center, Clear Sky, as one vehicle to do so.

The four bottom lines refer to measuring whether we're in a state of deficiency, sufficiency, or surplus in these four fundamental

---

[180] A.F. Price, *The Diamond Sutra and the Sutra of Hui Neng* (Boulder: Shambhala Publications, 1969), verse 32, p 53. This particular verse is from Dr. Kenneth Saunder's translation in *Lotuses of the Mahayana* (Wisdom of the East Series).

parts of our existence and the systems that support them. Ironically, the more we're driven to unconscious consumption or accumulation, the greater our inner feelings of insecurity and scarcity. What's more, while some of us continue to accumulate more, others survive on far less. In 2015, 71 percent of people in the world lived on less than US$10 a day,[181] while in 2013, 10.7 percent of the global population (more than 721 million people) lived on less than US$1.90 a day.[182]

The good news is that the latter figure is down from 35 percent in 1990.[183] It's one of the great challenges of our times to continue to work together creatively and compassionately to create a more equitable and sustainable world.

As described, we emphasize the spiritual bottom line as our first consideration to keep the spiritual horse in front of the material cart. If our spiritual aspiration fades or goes awry, then the other three bottom lines can easily get warped by the ego's drive for an ever bigger and better self-identity through false refuges.

As Goethe articulated so well,[184] the past meaningfully informs the present. And just as with any good movie, our lives must keep moving forward or we lose interest. For it to be engaging, it must keep progressing. Our best forward momentum as a species, and as a collective of species, is to heed the call to embrace the best of what lies within us: our incredible ability to innovate to resolve challenges, to discover both on and off planet, and to empathically work together to develop skills, methods, and technologies that enrich all our lives. We've found the quadruple bottom line helps us stay on track in generative ways. Human beings are not

[181] Tami Luhby, *71% of the world's population lives on less than $10 a day,* CNN Money, July 8, 2015, http://money.cnn.com/2015/07/08/news/economy/global-low-income/index.html.

[182] "Poverty: Overview," World Bank, last updated April 11, 2018, http://www.worldbank.org/en/topic/poverty/overview.

[183] Ibid.

[184] As quoted earlier, Goethe said, "A person who does not know the last 3,000 years wanders in the darkness of ignorance, unable to make sense of the reality around him."

meant to live scrambling to survive and fit in. Our birthright is to live a life that is rich in the true sense: explorative and caring toward other people and all of life.

With notable exceptions,[185] in most of the world and for most of human history, the outer material world has dominated most of our attention to the detriment of our inner exploration. The New Age Movement and growing interest in mindfulness and other spiritual matters could bode well for our future as a kind of communal spiritual bottom line. We'd be wise to ensure that our spiritual search remains unsatisfied by superficial results and instead grows ever deeper and stronger.

FROM THE WASTELAND TO THE PURELAND

This malaise of the human spirit that clings to superficial quests for happiness rooted in greed, anger, and confusion is what T.S. Eliot called "The Waste Land." We recall it here:

> *I have heard the key*
> *Turn in the door once and turn once only*
> *We think of the key, each in his prison*
> *Thinking of the key, each confirms a prison*[186]

The key here represents our freedom of choice, but since choices are conditioned and thus habitual, we risk keeping ourselves locked in prisons of our own making. On the spiritual journey, the hero or heroine is the spiritual psychonaut who perceives the key for what it is and uses it to step out of the prison of ignorance. They choose instead to courageously undergo the trials and tribulations along the path of wisdom, the path to the Pureland.

In Buddhism, the completion of this journey is marked by the moment of spiritual awakening called The Great Healing. The

---

[185] For example, saints, Tibetan culture designed to support the ongoing spiritual awakening of many beings, shamans in various cultures, etc.

[186] T.S. Eliot, "The Waste Land," lines 412–414.

awakening leads us forward to a future of discovery and exploration that we dream into being moment to moment. When we are at our visionary and altruistic best, whatever we undertake—science fiction, film, science, activism, poetry, environmentalism, etc.—can shape a current mythology, sparking the imagination with feelings of awe and wonder for what comes next, stimulating the next engaged participant. But while spiritual awakening pays respect to this kind of imagined future of humanity, its fundamental aim is grander: its objective is transcendence.

To meet this objective, awakening entails a shift of view. Compassion and insight are both the causal factors and results. "Awakening" is a gerund in that, when we are practicing compassion and insight in our life, we are in the process of awakening. Wisdom is the result: "awakened" is also a state of being. There are milestones in the process when we get awakened enough, or awakened in particular ways, so that there is no backsliding back to unawakened states. Still, it can't be explained with words; it must be experienced to understand. To get there from here, for this change of orientation to take place, we must somewhat remodel our identities by stretching our comfort zone to open up this sense of me to wider horizons. For those who hear the call, the path to the Pureland awaits.

What then? The universe is a highly ordered place and awakening is no different. The work of the human being is to perceive and understand patterns and that is what the discipline of the spiritual quest is about. However, patterns are not always easily seen and often require special equipment. For instance, in the material world we have studies like chemistry and physics with instruments like microscopes and particle accelerators to help us see underlying patterns. In the spiritual realm, we have something even more powerful: our mind's vast ability to observe itself.

For those who can't escape the suffering inherent in our lives—it's the Buddha's first Ennobling Truth,[187] after all—through

---

[187] As noted in Reflection 4, the second Ennobling Truth is that this struggle has a cause: craving. Thirdly, the struggle has an end. Fourthly, the end of struggle lies in the Eightfold Ennobling Path.

distraction by possessions, relationships, career, family, entertainment, or drugs, the spiritual life is the only option left. It's the room at the end of the hall, after we've tried all the other rooms. Somewhere in our lives, we are all touched by suffering, by trauma. Some live with it through therapy, others through diversion, and others through medication. Alas, short-term fixes tend to make things worse over time, but a quick, accessible feeling of temporary release can be tempting.

Not all who undertake the journey complete it; some go on scenic detours and others get stuck in the middle. But those who complete the path return to the world reborn. This does not mean just accepting Christ (or the Goddess, Buddha, the Great Spirit, etc.) into our life; it also means becoming Christ-*like*. It was after Jesus returned from his hero's journey that he was called Christ. He urged those who listened to his word to make haste and look to their own liberation, as did the Buddha. As we quoted in Reflection 2:

> The Dhamma of the Blessed One is perfectly expounded; to be seen here and now; not delayed in time; inviting one to come and see; onward leading (to Nibbāna); to be known by the wise, *each for himself.*[188]

This is the process of turning a myth into a lived reality. It's the hero's journey.

The hero's journey is both myth and allegory. It's also a metaphor for the spiritual search. Unlike myths and allegories, however, the spiritual search also has a determinable basis in fact. People we know have walked this journey and can describe it to us in language that matches the experiences of countless other spiritual seekers. However, like a mother's love, it's extremely difficult to quantify. Committed spiritual practitioners also struggle to find ways to calibrate meaning and measurement to match the profundity of the experience itself.

---

[188] "Homage to the Dhamma," Narada Thera and Bhikkhu Kassapa, *Mirror of the Dhamma* (Kandy: Buddhist Publication Society, 2003), 7. (Italics ours.)

Nonetheless, we continue to try. Contemporary science allows us to measure and track the brain waves of meditators and monitor their chemistry to see how they differ from non-meditators. It also allows us to measure how a mother's levels of oxytocin rise when she holds her child. But for the seeker, the experience itself means far more than brain waves, just as a mother's love for her child means more than body chemistry.

To understand the depth of a seeker's experience, we would do well to turn to the meditative traditions of the East, specifically Buddhism, and their highly evolved maps of consciousness. They have been studying this for millennia. While the West has been studying the material world and the mechanics of the mind externally through science and art, the East has been studying the mind directly, internally, through self-observation. This is a potently valid art and science of its own.

While the West was developing aqueducts, clocks, eyeglasses, and printing presses, the East was making equal breakthroughs in its experiential study of consciousness. Science today may report on the chemistry, neural firings, and regions of the brain and body that are affected by anger, for example, but they can't tell us much about how we *feel* when we experience it, or more importantly, how to transform it into loving-kindness. Eastern meditative traditions do. They help us to learn the subtle nuances of our patterns of action and reaction. We learn what is certain to come before and sure to follow. More importantly, we learn how to release unwholesome patterns and how to cultivate healthier ones.

HEEDING THE CALL

Crisis usually precipitates the commencement of the journey for every heroine, shaman, or seeker. This crisis is driven by the individual's struggle with the split between society's professed values and its observed actions; between the drive for survival and the need for wisdom and understanding.

She sets out on her quest to resolve the existential crisis she calls her life. At the outset, she feels like anything but a hero. Yet, her trek through the labyrinths of the mind are going to make her one—just as it did for Buddha, Jesus, and countless others who have braved the sometimes turbulent seas of the mind.

As we've described, it's imperative to let the seeker go through their experience, however distressing it may seem. Along the way, they may appear to have tipped over and be sinking, even drowning in the waters of their unconscious nature. But as the mythic tales of heroes relate—from Gilgamesh to Buddha to Christ—there is life down there in the dark depths, and it is this life that sustains us all. We must not interrupt their journey but actively help them on their way.

In one way or another, the seeker requires training. Ultimately, it is training oneself to see what we have not or do not see. This seeing requires active—sometimes revolutionary, in terms of the ego's patterns—participation in the search. Most training, if not all, requires someone with keener sight to mentor the student in cultivating this emerging vision. Those with such sight are called trainers. Remember, the Buddha was called a trainer,[189] not just a teacher.

Alas, the ego, by its nature, resists going beyond itself. A pseudo sense of independence and fear of being controlled or abused resists training, even as we sense it is our route to freedom. As the Dalai Lama said, "Whether our action is wholesome or unwholesome depends on whether that action or deed arises from a disciplined or undisciplined state of mind. It is thought that a disciplined mind leads to happiness and an undisciplined mind leads to suffering. In fact, it is said that *bringing about discipline within one's mind is the essence of the Buddha's teaching.*"[190] In

---

[189] The Buddha was renowned as a trainer: the Recollection of the Buddha prayer calls him "the unsurpassed trainer of people fit for training." In the Pali language (spoken by the Buddha): *Anuttaro purisadammasarathi.*

[190] The Dalai Lama XIV, *The Art Of Happiness,* (New York: Riverhead Books, Penguin Group, 1998). (Italics ours.)

this context, discipline means learning rather than punishment. Training here means skill development, not subservience.

While escaping the wasteland to journey to the Pureland entails hearing the call to awakening, we must also respond to the call. This means leaving the familiar and routine behind, perhaps even separating from family and society, at least for a time. To the person heeding the call, this can feel distressing. We may feel lonely, like we don't fit in, split off from the so-called normal world. We may worry that we're neurotic or beginning to succumb to mental illness.

This is where training becomes so important. An experienced trainer helps remind the student to stay oriented to our wholesome aspiration: spiritual awakening, to benefit all beings. Training also consists of learning how to stay in a clear, radiant state of consciousness come what may. Disturbing experiences still arise. But without a spiritual realignment, anxiety, depression, mental illness, and other stressful feelings can arrive unannounced and unsought. For the increasingly conscious hero or heroine, the ongoing, active search for clarity and understanding, and the aspiration to benefit others, make positive outcomes far easier and far more likely. Spiritual training entails learning how to transform these negative arisings into clarity, nonattachment, and compassion.

The fundamental difference is in the aspiration and virtue of the journeyer. Consequently, spiritual practices focus keenly on generating merit through wholesome activity, for example, by practicing dāna (generosity) daily in physical, emotional, and intellectual ways. Additionally, the spiritual path cultivates the ability to maintain a good state in unpleasant circumstances: we need to practice now for some future time when the going may get *really* tough.

Meanwhile, our status quo ego orientation involves pushing unpleasant phenomena away with fear or disgust, or hanging on to pleasant ones with greed. If unabated, these tendencies can result in physical, emotional, or mental illness.[191] It's something all of us humans do, to varying degrees, and we must be trained and train our own minds to learn how *not* to orient this way. To this end, the spiritual quest is rooted in an attempt to understand the nature of experiences, to perceive the radiant emptiness that lies behind all phenomena.

It takes time to learn how to do this, and even more time to remember to do this. This is why it's a called a spiritual path, a journey of a lifetime or lifetimes. When the seeker has completed their journey, experienced the transcendental, he returns to the ordinary world. He brings the gift of his experience to help awaken his community from their unconscious slumber in the wasteland. This is what makes him a hero. He uses and integrates his experience of dream-like symbols—a star at dawn, a flash of lightning in a summer cloud—to stimulate the society and its forms to new discovery.

The heroine, the seeker of liberation or awakening, follows a fairly common path with others of her kind. Once more, the basic message is "Wake up! The universe is love. Go forth, explore, and share. You are free."

THE JOURNEY CONTINUES

We feel that the main path to spiritual awakening for contemporary Westerners lies with Karma Yoga, the path of awakening through action or service. Meditation is an essential support, as is training, to speed up, round out, and integrate the awakening. Historically—at least in the Buddhist world—meditation has been the main path. Our sense is that this worked well when life was slower, and we

---

[191] The recurring point here is that, from the point of view of awakening, all unawakened beings are—in some degree—mentally unwell. The "illness" is taking the ego as an identity. This can become more or less pathological for all sorts of reasons, potentially including the body's chemistry and DNA. This is karma, and each of us has to work out our own karma. The teacher's job is to orient the being wholesomely to the nature of the struggle, to train them in remedial practice, and to help transform the shadow, to such extent that undertaking this path requires rare courage and fortitude.

lived closer to nature. Meditation integrates very naturally with subsistence agriculture but less so with technology and multitasking.

Through this path of action, Karma Yoga is designed to bring mindfulness and awareness to everything we do. The way we practice it, it's also a reflection on the balance between individual exploration, team building, and community development. These could be considered modern manifestations of the three pillars of Buddhism, called the Triple Gem: the Buddha, Dharma, and Sangha. The Buddha is the representative of the awakening mind, the dharma are the teachings that help us become more awake, and the sangha is our community of trainers and fellow seekers.

Together, adepts, trainers, and communities of practitioners dismantle unwholesome conditioned patterns so that we can rebuild them with more wholesome ones. This is an essential part of the healing we all long for. Meanwhile, we emphasize the sense of exploration and discovery that are at the heart of liberation. We use study and practice to catalyze actual first-hand experience, the embodiment of spiritual awakening. This requires consistent and applied effort. Lastly, we aspire to use our lives and work to demonstrate the value of these practices and experience, to share a sense of why transcendence is worth the investment of our lives and life force.

In closing, we thank our teacher, Venerable Namgyal Rinpoche, and all our other trainers, without whom we'd be sorry messes, ignorant of the beauty and glory of the spiritual life.

May whatever benefits these words may inspire be for the welfare of our planet and all its inhabitants.

As we say at the close of all our classes, meetings, and meditations:

May these wholesome and powerful activities
eliminate ignorance and negativity,
while producing happiness and illumination
for the uplifting of the world.

The End
or
A Beginning

ACKNOWLEDGEMENTS

How does one begin to acknowledge the formation of our thinking, feelings, and sensibilities that all came together to write this book? First, we'd like to appreciate the contributions of our biogenealogy, our mothers and fathers, their parents, and back to all our ancestors. They've all contributed traits and patterns down through the ages to arrive in this embodiment here and now. Neither we nor these teachings would be here without you.

There are so many people and other beings—our teachers, friends, pets, and encounters in nature or meditation—who have shaped us. There have been many other seekers who planted a thought or introduced us to a book that inexorably led to insights in this book. Our heartfelt thanks to all of you.

Many books we've read and courses we've attended have influenced our thinking and orientation. We acknowledge the invaluable wisdom shared by the creators of these works.

We'd also like to recognize all of those people whom we didn't particularly like, and vice versa. These are the people who tell us what our friends can't or don't want to see. Thank you for being the sand in our oyster; any pearls in these teachings are a co-creation with you.

We'd like to thank our many teachers in Buddhist, Western mystery, ayahuasca, metaphysical, and other traditions. Specifically, we pay homage to our root guru, the late Venerable Namgyal Rinpoche. He was an eclectic and intrepid explorer of East and West and translated ancient teachings into terms that the Western ego could relate to and in so many phenomenal ways. Thanks as vast as the skies to you, sir!

We express our sincere gratitude to our spiritual community, including our peers, students, and other people who have attended our courses and retreats. Your presence has helped shape our thoughts, perceptions, and actions, adding much wealth to our offerings. We feel honored to live according to the ancient tradition of dāna and recognize that our work is only possible thanks to your and many other beings' vibrant dāna practice. May your generosity be returned a thousandfold. It is our prayer that eventually the whole world can live by spontaneous generosity. Let's continue to always give before we've received.

Numerous beings have directly contributed to this book. Thanks to our editor, Erin Robinsong, who has been a pleasure to work with. Curt Dowdy, Christina Souza Ma, Segovia Smith, and the rest of the team at Interplicity have helped us to explore the strange new world of book launches with creativity, smarts, curiosity, and humor. Chris O'Byrne and Debbie O'Byrne at JETLAUNCH felt like true members of our team. We've felt deeply touched by the generous support and sense of community from all the people who agreed to endorse this book and by the cheering on from the sidelines by other supporters.

We'd like to thank one another for persevering through the unique experience—part mud-wrestling match, part lovemaking—of writing a book together.

To the teams at Planet Dharma and Clear Sky, we remain inspired by your commitment to the path of awakening through action. May all the merit you accumulate benefit beings as countless as stars in the sky.

We thank all of Creation for showing up as it is so that each of us can add something to the mix in our own particular way. When stirred up, we co-create such a truly messy and truly beautiful thing called life.

BIBLIOGRAPHY

Argyris, Chris and Schon, Donald. *Organizational Learning: A Theory of Action Perspective*. Boston: Addison-Wesley, 1978.

Barks, Coleman and Moyne, John. *Like This. The Essential Rumi*. New York: Harper Collins, 2010.

Benjamin, George. "How Stravinsky's Rite of Spring has shaped 100 years of music." *The Guardian* online, May 20, 2013. https://www.theguardian.com/music/2013/may/29/stravinsky-rite-of-spring.

Buchanan, Leigh. "The New York Bakery That Hires Everyone, No Questions Asked." *Inc. Magazine,* Sept. 21, 2015. https://www.inc.com/leigh-buchanan/greyston-bakery-hires-everyone-no-questions-asked.html.

Bhadantacariya Buddhaghosa, *The Path of Purification*. Boulder: Shambhala Publications, 1956.

Brooks, Arthur C. "The Real Victims of Victimhood." *New York Times*, Dec. 26, 2015. https://www.nytimes.com/2015/12/27/opinion/sunday/the-real-victims-of-victimhood.html.

Buddhaghosa. *Visuddhimagga*. Kandy, Sri Lanka: Buddhist Publication Society, 2010), http://www.accesstoinsight.org/lib/authors/nanamoli/PathofPurification2011.pdf.

Campbell, B., & Manning, J. (2014). Microaggression and moral cultures. *Comparative sociology, 13*, 692–726.

Campbell, Joseph. *Myths To Live By*. New York: Bantam Books, 1972.

Campbell, Joseph. *The Hero with a Thousand Faces*. Princeton: Princeton University Press, 1973.

Chamie, Joseph. *The Rise of One-Person Households,* Interpress Service News Agency, Feb. 22, 2017, http://www.ipsnews.net/2017/02/the-rise-of-one-person-households/.

Chamorro-Premuzic, Tomas and Sanger, Michael. "How to Boost Your (and Others') Emotional Intelligence." *Harvard Business Review* Jan. 9, 2017. https://hbr.org/2017/01/how-to-boost-your-and-others-emotional-intelligence.

Chapman, Gary. *The Five Love Languages: How to Express Heartfelt Commitment to Your Mate*. Chicago: Northfield Publishing, 2000.

Chisholm, Kenneth. *The Queen of Versailles*, documentary film, directed by Lauren Greenfield, released by Evergreen Pictures, 2012.

CNN Money. *Fear and Greed Index. Accessed June 22, 2018.* http://money.cnn.com/data/fear-and-greed/.

Dalai Lama XIV. *The Art Of Happiness*. New York: Riverhead Books, Penguin Group, 1998.

Duhigg, Charles. *The Power of Habit: Why We Do What We Do in Life and Business*. New York: Random House, 2012.

Eisenstein, Charles. *Sacred Economics: Money, Gift and Society in the Age of Transition*. Berkeley: North Atlantic Books, 2011.

Eliot, T.S. "The Waste Land." *The Waste Land and Other Writings*. New York: Random House, 2002.

Engelhart, Matthew and Engelhart, Terces. *Sacred Commerce: Business as a Path of Awakening*. Berkeley: North Atlantic Books, 2011.

Elsinger, Jesse. "Why Only One Top Banker Went to Jail for the Financial Crisis." *The New York Times Magazine*, April 30, 2014. https://www.nytimes.com/2014/05/04/magazine/only-one-top-banker-jail-financial-crisis.html.

BIBLIOGRAPHY

Gascoigne, Bamber. "History of Capitalism." *History World*. Accessed June 22, 2018. http://www.historyworld.net/wrldhis/PlainTextHistories. asp?historyid=aa49.

Ghent, Emmanuel M.D., "Masochism, Submission and Surrender: Masochism As a Perversion of Surrender." *W.A.W. Institute,* 1990. www.wawhite.org/uploads/PDF/E1f_9%20Ghent_E_Masochism.pdf.

Gladwell, Malcolm. *Outliers: The Story of Success*. New York: Little, Brown and Company, 2008.

Greenfield, Kent. "If Corporations Are People, They Should Act Like It." *The Atlantic*, Feb 1, 2015. https://www.theatlantic.com/ politics/archive/2015/02/if-corporations-are-people-they-should-act-like-it/385034/.

Grof, Stanislav and Christina Grof, *Spiritual Emergency: When Personal Transformation Becomes a Crisis*. New York: St. Martin's Press, 1989.

Hirschler, Ben. "World's eight richest as wealthy as half humanity, Oxfam tells Davos." *Reuters*, Jan. 15, 2017. https://www.reuters.com/ article/us-davos-meeting-inequality/worlds-eight-richest-as-wealthy-as-half-humanity-oxfam-tells-davos-idUSKBN150009.

Hood, Bruce. *The Self Illusion: How the Social Brain Creates Identity*. Oxford: Oxford University Press, 2013.

Irwin, Neil. "This is a complete list of Wall Street CEOS prosecuted for their role in the financial crisis." *The Washington Post, Sept. 12, 2013*. https://www.washingtonpost.com/news/wonk/wp/2013/09/12/ this-is-a-complete-list-of-wall-street-ceos-prosecuted-for-their-role-in-the-financial-crisis/?noredirect=on&utm_term=.73b0fdbf9486.

Jeter, Clay, dir. "Dan Barber," *Chef's Table*, Season 1, Episode 2, 12 Feb. 2015. Produced by Netflix and Boardwalk Pictures.

Jung, Carl. *Aion: Researches into the Phenomenology of the Self*. Collected Works of C.G. Jung Vol. 9 Part 2, 1952.

Kahneman, Daniel. *Thinking, Fast and Slow*. New York: Farrar, Straus and Giroux, 2011.

Ledgerwood, Alison. "Getting stuck in the negatives (and how to get unstuck)." Filmed June 22, 2013 at TedxUCDavis, Davis, CA, Video, 9:59. https://www.youtube.com/watch?v=7XFLTDQ4JMk.

Lencioni, Patrick. *The Five Dysfunctions of a Team.* San Francisco: Josey-Bass, 2002.

Lovell, James A. "Houston, We've Had a Problem." *Apollo Expeditions to the Moon.* Chapter 13.4. Accessed 30 Oct. 2017. https://www.hq.nasa.gov/pao/History/SP-350/ch-13-4.html.

Lowen, Alexander. *Bioenergetics: The Revolutionary Therapy That Uses The Language Of The Body To Heal The Problems Of The Mind.* London: Penguin Books, 1976.

Luhby, Tami. "71% of the world's population lives on less than $10 a day." *CNN Money,* July 8, 2015. http://money.cnn.com/2015/07/08/news/economy/global-low-income/index.html.

Luhby, Tami. "The 62 richest people have as much as half the world." *CNN Money,* Jan. 18, 2016. http://money.cnn.com/2016/01/17/news/economy/oxfam-wealth/index.html.

Lund University. *"Do viruses make us smarter?"* Jan 12, 2015. https://phys.org/news/2015-01-viruses-smarter.html.

Mahathera, Ven. Narada. *Buddha and His Teachings.* Somerville: Wisdom Publications, 1988.

Matthew 13:45-46, *The Holy Bible, New King James Version.* New York: Harper Collins, 1982.

Miller, Sara G. "1 in 6 Americans Takes a Psychiatric Drug: Antidepressants were most common, followed by anxiety relievers and antipsychotics." *Scientific American.* Dec. 13, 2016. https://www.scientificamerican.com/article/1-in-6-americans-takes-a-psychiatric-drug/.

Morell, Virginia. "Monkeys master a key sign of self-awareness: recognizing their reflections," *Science Magazine,* Feb. 13, 2017. http://www.sciencemag.org/news/2017/02/monkeys-master-key-sign-self-awareness-recognizing-their-reflection.

Netflix, *Chef's Table*, Season 1, Episode 2, *Dan Barber*, Produced by Netflix and Boardwalk Pictures, aired Feb. 12, 2015. https://www.netflix.com/title/80007945.

Obissier, Patrick. *Biogenealogy: Decoding the Psychic Roots of Illness: Freedom from the Ancestral Roots of Disease*. Rochester, Vermont: Healing Arts Press, 2003.

Online Etymology Dictionary. "Relationship" and "Spirit." Accessed June 16, 2018. http://www.etymonline.com/index.php?term=relationship.

Palazzolo, Rose. *Studies: Love Is Good for Your Heart*, ABCnews.com, May 21, 2017. http://abcnews.go.com/Health/story?id=117439&page=1.

Price, A.F. Price, *The Diamond Sutra and the Sutra of Hui Neng*. Boulder: Shambhala Publications, 1969.

Queen of Versailles. Directed by Lauren Greenfield. 2012. Los Angeles, CA: Evergreen Pictures, 2016. *Amazon*. Web.

Reich, Wilhelm. *The Function of The Orgasm: Sex-Economic Problems of Biological Energy*. New York: Farrar, Strauss and Giroux, 1973.

Renzetti, Elizabeth. "Life of Solitude: A loneliness crisis is looming." *Globe and Mail*, Nov. 23, 2013 and updated March 25, 2017. https://www.theglobeandmail.com/life/life-of-solitude-a-loneliness-crisis-is-looming/article15573187/.

Rinpoche, The Venerable Namgyal, *Right Livelihood*. Kinmount, ON: Bodhi Publishing, 2008.

Rinzai Obaku Zen. "Head Temples." Accessed April 2, 2018,

Rogers, Everett M. *Diffusion of Innovations*. New York: Free Press, 2003.

Rubin, C.M. "The Global Search for Learning: What Meta-Learning?" *Huffington Post*. Dec 12, 2016. https://www.huffingtonpost.com/c-m-rubin/the-global-search-for-edu_b_13343564.html.

Salzberg, Sharon, "Sit," last modified Jul. 28, 2014, reprinted from *O Magazine*, Nov. 1, 2002. https://www.sharonsalzberg.com/sit/.

Scharmer, Otto and Kaufer, Katrin. *Leading from the Emerging Future: From Ego-System to Eco-System Economies*. San Francisco: Berrett-Koehler Publishers, 2013.

Schnarch, David. *Passionate Marriage*. New York: W. W. Norton & Company, 2009.

Schumacher, E.F. *Small is Beautiful: Economics as if People Mattered*. New York: Harper Perennial, 2010.

Senge, Peter M. *The Fifth Discipline: The Art and Practice of the Learning Organization*. New York: Doubleday/Currency, 1990.

Senge, Peter, Smith, Bryan, Kruschwitze, Nina, Laur, Joe and Schley, Sarah. *The Necessary Revolution*. New York: Doubleday, 2008.

Simons, Daniel. *The Monkey Business Illusion*, published Apr. 8, 2010. https://www.youtube.com/watch?v=MFBrCM_WYXw.

Smith, Jacqlyn. "This is How Americans Define Success." *Business Insider*, Oct. 3, 2014. http://www.businessinsider.com/how-americans-now-define-success-2014-10.

Sokol, Kathy Arlyn. "Zen at War." *Kyoto Journal,* April 13, 2011. https://kyotojournal.org/the-journal/conversations/zen-at-war-2/

Solomon, Joel. *The Clean Money Revolution: Reinventing Power, Purpose and Capitalism*. Gabriola Island: New Society Publishers, 2017.

Stanford University. *Two Stanford professors win prestigious Kavli Prizes*. June 2, 2016. https://news.stanford.edu/2016/06/02/two-stanford-professors-win-prestigious-kavli-prizes/.

Stevens, John, translator. *Wild Ways: Zen Poems Of Ikkyū*. Buffalo: White Pine Press, 2003.

Thera, Narada and Bhikkhu Kassapa. *The Mirror of the Dhamma*. "Salutation to the Buddha" and "Homage to the Dhamma." Kandy, Sri Lanka: Buddhist Publication Society, 1963.

Tolle, Eckhart. *A New Earth*. London: Penguin Publishing Group, 2008.

Totenberg, Nina. "When Did Companies Become People? Excavating the Legal Evolution." *NPR,* July 28, 2014. https://www.npr.org/2014/07/28/335288388/when-did-companies-become-people-excavating-the-legal-evolution.

United Nations Department of Economic and Social Affairs, Population Division. "World Urbanization Prospects: The 2009 Revision." Accessed 24 Oct. 2017. http://www.un.org/en/development/desa/population/publications/urbanization/urban-rural.shtml.

University of North Carolina at Chapel Hill, Department of Statistics and Operations Research. "Subprime mortgage crisis." Accessed July 1, 2018. http://www.stat.unc.edu/faculty/cji/fys/2012/Subprime%20mortgage%20crisis.pdf.

Urban, Hugh, "Rajneesh, the Guru Who Loved His Rolls Royces." *The Wire,* May 12, 2016. https://thewire.in/books/rajneesh-the-guru-who-loved-his-rolls-royces.

Vaughan, Genevieve (ed.). *Women and the Gift Economy: A Radically Different Worldview is Possible.* Toronto: Inanna Publications, 2007.

Walker, Barbara G. *Women's Encyclopedia of Myths and Secrets.* San Francisco: Harper & Row, 1994.

Whitaker, Robert. *Anatomy of an Epidemic: Magic Bullets, Psychiatric Drugs, and the Astonishing Rise of Mental Illness in America.* New York: Broadway Books, 2011.

Wilber, Ken. *Integral Spirituality.* Boston: Shambhala Publications, 2006.

World Bank. "Poverty: Overview." Accessed April 11, 2018. http://www.worldbank.org/en/topic/poverty/overview.

EXPERIENCE MORE OF THE *PURELAND*

For a comprehensive package of free resources designed to give you more of a taste of the Pureland, please visit our website.

Here you'll also find our retreats, online courses, a minicourse, blogs, videos, exercises and other supports to your ongoing spiritual unfoldment.

To ensure you get the most out of the journey from the *Wasteland to Pureland*, access bonuses at this link:

www.planetdharma.com/pureland-paperback

ALSO BY DOUG DUNCAN:

Dharma If You Dare
http://www.planetdharma.com/pureland-dare

Doug Duncan studied with the Ven. Namgyal Rinpoche from 1974 until the latter's passing in 2003. Doug received lay ordination from Namgyal Rinpoche in 1978 and is a lineage holder in that teaching. He also received teachings from the 16th Karmapa, Kalu Rinpoche, Sakya Trizin Rinpoche, and other Tibetan Rinpoches, as well as from the Ven. Sayadaw U Thila Wunta, and from a Master of the Western Mystery School. In addition, Doug has undertaken numerous three-month solitary meditation retreats.

Doug has been leading retreats, teaching, and training in universal practices of spiritual unfoldment since 1985, helping many students in numerous countries liberate themselves from suffering. His teaching also draws on contemporary psychology and science.

Growing up in Saskatchewan was a pretty "flat" experience, so Doug caught the travel bug early. As a small child, he wandered such that the local police often had to bring him home. This desire to see the world and understand it more fully has led him ever since.

Catherine Pawasarat began her spiritual practices in earnest in her early 20s, to transform personal suffering and international environmental and social justice challenges. She worked as an advocacy photojournalist and studied traditional Japanese arts in Kyoto for 20 years, culminating in her landmark work on the 1,100-year-old Gion Festival.

She became a student of metaphysics, Western spiritual traditions, and the ayahuasca sacraments in the 1990s, and has trained daily with Acariya Doug Duncan since 1998 in an intensive spiritual apprenticeship that is rare in the modern West. She received lay ordination from Namgyal Rinpoche in 2003.

With Doug she is co-founder of Clear Sky Retreat Center in the BC Rockies and Planet Dharma, and a lineage holder for these teachings. As such she's advocated sustainability, social business, and social enterprise as natural counterparts to spiritual practice and vice versa. Since the early 2000s, Catherine has provided dharma training and taught the path of awakening to hundreds of students.

Having lived overseas for many years and traveled extensively, Doug and Catherine draw on intercultural and trans-cultural experience to share their understandings of liberation as a truly planetary vehicle.

*May we awaken speedily and fully
For the benefit of all beings.*

CPSIA information can be obtained
at www.ICGtesting.com
Printed in the USA
BVHW04s1006270918
528474BV00034B/64/P

9 780998 588636